A PROCESSION OF SAINTS

A PROCESSION OF SAINTS

by JAMES BRODRICK, S.J.

LONGMANS, GREEN AND CO.

NEW YORK

1949

LONGMANS, GREEN AND CO., INC.

55 FIFTH AVENUE, NEW YORK 3

BRODRICK

A PROCESSION OF SAINTS

FIRST EDITION

Printed in the United States of America

VAN REES PRESS • NEW YORK

DE LICENTIA SVPERIORVM ORDINIS

NIHIL OBSTAT: EDVARDVS CAN. MAHONEY, S.T.D.
CENSOR DEPVTATVS

IMPRIMATVR: E. MORROGH BERNARD
VICARIVS GENERALIS

WESTMONASTERII: DIE IV OCTOBRIS MCMXLVII

To

My brethren, hosts and very good friends

THE STAFF OF AMERICA

THE Saints briefly commemorated in this book have the ad-
vatage, so to call it, of being relatively unfamiliar in America.
That surely must be so, or else some town or village in the
seven thousand square miles of the Diocese of Rochester, New
York State, would have found room for a church in honour of
St. John Fisher, Bishop of the original Rochester. Sanctity
renders men dateless, and Fisher, with three others listed here,
St. Anselm, St. Hugh of Lincoln and St. Thomas Becket, have
more than an antiquarian interest for our times in that they
lived, suffered and died to keep the lamps of at least two of
the Four Freedoms burning. They were the counterparts in
their totalitarian ages of such heroic men as Archbishop
Stepinac and Cardinal Mindszenty in our totalitarian age, and
it was for them and their kind that one so little of a sacristy
poet as Siegfried Sassoon openly confessed his enthusiasm

> God's martyrdoms are good,
> And Saints are trumps, no matter what they did.
> Therefore I celebrate Sebastian's blood
> And glory with Lorenzo on his grid.

This is not a book of grave or, one hopes, arid erudition,
though it entailed much hard and dreary work in old tomes
that were decidedly arid. Against the numerous notes and references, the reader, if he prefers his dish without such garnish-
ings, has the easy remedy of skipping them. The absence of
women saints from the procession is due, as God best knows,
to no lack of such holy persons, but solely to a woeful lack of
evidence. One woman, not yet even beatified, has been included
because she represents in her single person the love, sacrifice
and heroism of millions of wives, mothers and nuns. Besides,
her glory, which vies with that of the great Teresa, is a heritage
from colonial days in North America.

CONTENTS

SAINT AELRED

Abbot of Rievaulx

AELRED, the "dulcedo monachorum", as a poet of his time called him, the St. Bernard of England, the Saxon troubadour of friendship in Jesus, well deserves to lead off this little cavalcade of saints, if only because he was himself so great a one for delving into holy lives and conserving their fragrance. How did the author of the *Wandering Scholars* come to omit Aelred's portrait from her fascinating gallery? If he never wandered much except once to Rome and Citeaux, and a few times to Scotland, he loved his classics as dearly as any Italian Fortunatus or Irish Sedulius, and Christianized Cicero in a little golden dialogue *De Spirituali Amicitia,* which begins: "Here we are, you and I, and I hope that Christ makes a third between us." Aelred had the ambiguous distinction of being the son and grandson of two eminent and combative priests named Eilaf, who did something to atone for the irregularity of their lives by restoring with much love and labour St. Wilfrid's priory in Hexham, after Danes and Normans had ravaged it. As Eilaf is a peculiarly Danish name, perhaps our Saint had a few drops of the ravager's blood in his veins. Five out of Hexham's twelve bishops had been canonized, and their bones were the glory of the little high-perched ancient Northumbrian town on the Halgut, the holy stream, which makes a humble contribution to the Tyne twenty miles west of Newcastle. There Aelred was born in the year 1110, when Henry I, the Beauclerc, and his Good Queen Maud ruled England, while Maud's brother Alexander, a man "amiable and humble enough with the monks and clergy but to the rest of his subjects a terror",[1] did the same for Scotland. Alexander's

[1] So Aelred himself in his *Genealogia Regum Anglorum* which he wrote for the edification of Henry, Duke of Normandy, a little later Henry II of England. Migne, *Patrologia Latina,* vol. 195, col. 756. To save footnotes, references to this primary source will be given in brackets in the text as *P.L.,* followed by the numbers of the volume and column.

brother David, who succeeded him in 1124 and reigned for
nineteen exciting years, is central in St. Aelred's story as being,
in his own words, the man he "loved best in the whole world".
David had much to do, not always peaceably, with Northumbria and often visited Hexham to worship at the shrines of
the saints. He was quickly attracted by the little son of the
parish priest, and took Aelred into his suite as page and companion for his own son Prince Henry. Another boy in that
happy garden of youth also destined to be an abbot and to be
canonized was the charming Waltheof, great-grandson of
the giant Dane Siward, Earl of Northumbria, who fought the
Normans and lamented at the end of his gory days that he had
not been killed decently in one of his countless battles but left
"to die in bed like a cow".[1] Aelred's schooling with those small
inheritors of the earth was extremely casual, but it gave him
immense satisfaction. "I used to thrill with the joy of their
company," he said, "and my whole soul went out to them in
affection and love, till I felt that there was nothing on earth
sweeter or pleasanter or more of a gain than to love and to be
loved" (*P.L.,* 195, 659).

But if Aelred loved Henry, "tam dulcis, tam amabilis, tam
affabilis," he absolutely worshipped Henry's father, and David
as both prince and king returned him the compliment. He
made the Anglian youth, while still only in his teens, his
seneschal, high office described by Aelred as knighthood of
the pots and pans, and would have put a jewelled mitre on his
fair head if the same head had not conceived a grander dream.
It was a case of David and Jonathan all over again, with the
dignities reversed, and, indeed, Scotland's David bore a curious
resemblance in sin and repentance to the David of Israel.
One day he is unmistakably the son of St. Margaret, and the
next as plainly the child of the fierce marauding Malcolm of
the Big Head who is alleged to have transported Birnam Wood
to Dunsinane. But Aelred's pen was as selective as a sun-dial

[1] Waltheof's mother, Matilda, married as her second husband King
David of Scotland, so the boy was that monarch's stepson.

and numbered only his friend's serene and shining hours. "With my own eyes I saw him", he writes, "take his foot from the stirrup and return to the palace with a poor suppliant who had run up at the last moment, there sweetly and patiently to listen to his story, all thought of hunting for that day forgotten. . . . He was just the same to everyone who appealed to him, priest or soldier, rich or poor, his own liegeman or a stranger, merchant or rustic, dealing with them so humbly and appropriately that each went away believing his own case to be the King's only concern" (*P.L.*, 195, 714).

David himself told Aelred a beautiful story about his sister Matilda, the Good Queen Maud of England and mother of the other Matilda who fought Stephen and was anything but a saint. "When as a lad", he said, "I was serving at the English Court, the Queen summoned me to her apartments one evening. And what do you think I found, but the whole room full of lepers and the Queen standing in the midst of them! At sight of me she put aside her mantle and taking a towel and basin began to wash and wipe the feet of those lepers, gathering each foot into her hands as she finished and kissing it with the greatest devotion. 'O, my Lady,' I cried to her, 'what are you doing? If the King knew this, never again would he kiss a mouth tainted by the feet of lepers.' She smiled and said: 'I like even better the lips of the Eternal King. Come, dearest brother, I brought you here so that you might learn this service. Take a basin now and do exactly as you see me doing.' At that I trembled with horror and told her it was utterly beyond me. You see, I did not yet know the Lord nor was His spirit revealed to me. When she persisted, alas I just took to my heels and rejoined my companions" (*P.L.*, 195, 736).

When Aelred was twenty-three, King David sent him on a mission to the great and holy Archbishop Thurstan of York, the indomitable old Becket of the North who five years later roused the county parish by parish to meet and overthrow the same peerless David, on foray bent, at the Battle of the Standard. Aelred himself, as we shall see, was to be the

Homer of that famous fight in which the saints took so prominent a part. Both men guessed that they would not meet again, and many years later, after David's death, Aelred was still affected by the memory of their good-bye: "O my sweet lord and friend, I shall never forget the kiss you gave me that day we parted and the tears you shed. You are enshrined in my heart of hearts, to be remembered lovingly each morning, when the Son is immolated to the Father for all men's salvation." Even more touching was his cry from the cloister when he heard that David was dead: "O sweet soul, where hast thou gone away and stolen from sight? Our eyes seek thee and find thee not. Our ears strain to catch thy pleasant humble voice, the voice of thy confession and consolation, *et ecce! silentium.* Where is that sweet face which showed itself so gentle to the poor, so humble to the servants of God, and so merry and loving to thy own servants. And where are those eyes full of tenderness and graciousness whose smile made happy men happier and whose tears were mingled with the tears of those who wept? As for me, I shall never cease to weep, remembering my sweet lord and friend." [1]

The year before Aelred's visit to York, a great thing had happened in the county. A band of Cistercians, thirteen strong, sent by St. Bernard himself under the leadership of his friend and scribe William, an Englishman,[2] came to found the first English daughter-house of Clairvaux on land given them

[1] Cited from a Latin Cottonian manuscript by Raine, *The Priory of Hexham,* Surtees Society, vol. i (1864), p. 16. In the Chronical of Prior John of Hexham published in this volume there is an excellent account of Archbishop Thurstan's activities, austerities and charities. But the humourless and obtuse Canon Raine, as bad an editor as he was bigoted a Protestant, professed himself shocked by the great prelate's last act on earth. He joined the Cluniac community at Pontefract shortly before his end and as he lay dying caused the monks to chant the Office for the Dead in his cell, himself taking the whole nine *Lectiones!* (L.c., pp. 128–31).
[2] Canonized locally if not in Rome, for his shrine has been discovered and on it may plainly be read the words, SCS WILLMUS Abbas (Peers, in *The Archaeological Journal,* vol. 86, 1929, pp. 20–8).

by Walter Espec, lord of Helmsley, in the lovely secluded
Rye Vale, from which their monastery took its famous name
of Rievaulx. There was not much of Rievaulx's future grandeur
to be seen when Aelred wandered there in 1133, perhaps a few
mean huts and thirteen white-robed men digging and hewing
as if their lives depended on it, which they did.[1] According to
William of Newbury, who lived only a few miles away, it was
"at that time a place of horror and vast loneliness". But the
visitor had not come seeking any beauty except the beauty of
holiness, "which consists in a tender and eager affection towards
our Lord and Saviour", and before his first day at Rievaulx was
over he knew that here, with those silent, smiling, friendly
navvies of God, lay the clue to his long-frustrated quest. Of
course, he would have us believe that he was the prodigal son
coming home, with the stench of the pigsty still in his rags,
but all the saints conspire to tell that story because they have
glimpsed the perfections of God. No Christian ever born had
a more tender and eager affection for our Lord and Saviour
than Bernard of Clairvaux, but in the judgement of the
Cistercians themselves his English son, Aelred of Rievaulx, ran
him very close. *Bernardo prope par, Aelredus noster*—such was
the Order's verdict ages ago and such it remains.[2]

The dates of his quiet history are soon given. The Battle of
the Standard, fought in 1138 almost at the monks' back door,

[1] They began in the direst poverty, with land and little else, and could
not start to build their church until ten years later. The ground was so
awkward that they had to hew terraces out of the hillside and erect their
"house exceeding magnifical unto the Lord" facing north and south
instead of east and west (*The Chartulary of Rievaulx*, Surtees Society,
1887, pp. lix–lxv).

[2] Abbot le Bail of Notre Dame de Scourmont, Chimay, Belgium, in
Viller's *Dictionnaire de Spiritualité*, t. i (1937), coll. 225–34. The late
Watkin Williams, St. Bernard's great Anglican lover and biographer,
lamented that his hero was so little known as to be associated in the public mind almost exclusively with a breed of life-saving dogs. Aelred has
not even the hair of a dog, never mind the fact that the canine St. Ber-
nards were not named after the Abbot of Clairvaux, to keep him in
popular remembrance. Rievaulx is now a national monument, but Aelred,
who largely created it, is forgotten.

must have caused as much excitement to Aelred and his brethren as is compatible with the Rule of St. Benedict, strictly interpreted. Two years later, he was sent to Rome by Abbot William on the Order's business. Then, in 1141, we find him master of novices at Rievaulx, and the following year he is appointed, by William, abbot of the new monastery at Revesby in Lincolnshire, Rievaulx's third offspring in a bare ten years.[1] Abbot William died in 1145 and was succeeded by Maurice, another monk of Clairvaux, who could not manage the swarming and often difficult community. Within a few months he recalled Aelred and thankfully resigned the heavy charge of abbot into his capable young hands. Abbot our Saint remained until his death twenty years later.

From the *Vita Aelredi* of his disciple Walter Daniel,[2] we gain some idea of the extraordinary influence wielded by this one man, for we hear of no less than seventeen abbeys and monasteries in England and Scotland which bloomed before God under his gardening. Like St. Bernard, who seemed in the eyes of contemporaries to have come to Yorkshire in Aelred's sandals, he possessed a very genius for friendship, and like Bernard, too, nearly all his books were written to order, the order of his friends. Thus, his first and largest work, the *Mirror of Charity,* which occupies 115 columns of Migne, was written at the genial provocation of his friend Gervase, Abbot of Louth Park in Lincolnshire, a *filiale* of Fountains. Gervase addresses him in the following strain: "I asked your Fraternity,

---

[1] The two predecessors were Wardon, Bedfordshire, and the second Melrose, about thirty-seven miles south of Edinburgh, which had King David for its founder and his stepson St. Waltheof for its first abbot. According to the chronicler, Jocelyn of Furness, Waltheof consulted only two advisers when deciding about his Cistercian vocation, his Angel Guardian and his friend from childhood, Aelred. The same Jocelyn, who knew Aelred, has a little rhyme about him in his charming life of Waltheof. He says that he was *Facetus, facundus, Socialis et jucundus, Liberalis et discretus*—a splendid string of adjectives for any abbot's or superior's crown (*Acta Sanctorum, Augusti* t. i, p. 257).

[2] Published in part with a fine commentary by Professor Powicke, Manchester, 1922.

I even ordered you, nay, I adjured you in the name of God to write me a few pages... And what happens? You wail that your shoulders are too weak for such a yoke. Now, granted that my demand is burdensome, is difficult, is impossible, I do not grant that that is any excuse. I persist in my opinion. I repeat my orders.... You tell me that you are almost illiterate, and came, not from the schools, but from the kitchen, into the desert, where amid rocks and mountains you live like a rustic, sweating with axe and hammer for your daily bread... I am delighted to hear it, because I do not desire to read what you learned in any school except the school of the Holy Spirit... And as for that hammer you mentioned, I think it might be well employed hewing from the rock of your native sagacity such good things as must often occur to you while you rest under the shade of the trees in the heat of noon." Gervase concludes his semi-serious effusion as follows: "To spare your blushes, let this letter of ours be prefixed to your work, so that whatever may displease a reader in the *Speculum Charitatis,* for such is the title we impose upon it, may be attributed, not to you who brought it forth, but to us who made you. *Vale in Christo, dilecte frater"* (*P.L.,* 195, 501–4).

The influence of St. Augustine is strong in the *Speculum* and leads Aelred, with many a groan, to espouse that Saint's theory on the damnation of unbaptized infants, now held by no Catholic theologian. Apart from that blot, the book is a beautiful and satisfying treatise on Christian perfection, full, as are all Aelred's works, of tender and eager affection towards our Lord and Saviour, and characterized by his own special doctrine of the Sabbath of the Soul, by which he means the repose in God of mystical contemplation. Like St. Bernard and St. Augustine, his two great inspirers, he had the habit of soliloquy and expresses himself often in the most moving first-person prayers. Other friends, the monks Ivo, Walter and Gratian, who are his interlocutors in the dialogue, prevailed upon him to write the perfectly charming little work, *De Spirituali Amicitia,* which by itself is sufficient explanation why he was so widely and deeply loved.[1] Ivo is delightful. "You won't easily persuade me of that", he says when Aelred argues that friendship rightly understood is nothing else than wisdom, "cum in amicitia et aeternitas vigeat, et veritas luceat, et charitas dulcescat." *Ivo:* "Oh, what next? Would you have me say of friendship what the friend of Jesus, John, says of charity?" *Aelred:* "I admit that it is not usual nor warranted by the Scriptures, but still I do not hesitate to voice my own opinion, *Qui manet in AMICITIA in Deo manet, et Deus in eo.*" Then the supper-bell rings down the curtain on the first part, and afterwards Walter and Gratian take up the hunt in the remaining two (*P.L.,* 195, 661–702).

From first to last, the mysteries of the life of Jesus are the favourite themes of Aelred's voice and pen. His sermons deal almost exclusively with them, and he devotes to them the whole of his little burning *Tractatus de Jesu Duodenni* and a large part of his *De Vita eremitica,* written for his sister who became an anchoress, like Julian of Norwich. The *Tractatus,* full of Bernardine echoes, is one of the sweetest flowers of the Middle Ages. He pictures the soul, his own loving soul, lost in the delights of contemplation, to whom comes charity in the guise of our Lady with a reproach on her lips, *Fili, quid fecisti nobis sic?* "Suddenly, at that dear voice, we remember in the midst of our Jerusalem that such a one is ill and sad and looking for our paternal consolation, that another is labouring under temptation and needs our support,...that a third is the victim of *acedia* and runs hither and thither, seeking someone to consult and to encourage him..." (*P.L.,* 184, 849–79). That exquisite little piece also was composed to please a friend. The work written for his hermit sister is so full of Anselmian unction that to this day one finds no less than eighteen chapters of it included in the *Meditationes* attributed to the great Benedictine Doctor of the Church who

[1] This work has been translated into English (with introduction and notes) by Fr. Hugh Talbot, O. Cist., under the title *Christian Friendship* (The Catholic Book Club, Foyle's).

died Archbishop of Canterbury the year before Aelred was born. But they are Aelred's unquestionably,[1] and one has to implore his help to resist the insidious temptation to quote from this most touching anthology of the love of Jesus. He tells us what sort of a recluse he was himself in his counsels to his sister: "Open your heart in one wide gesture of love to embrace the whole world, thinking of all the good people in it that you may congratulate them, and of all the bad that you may weep for them. You will call to mind the misery of the poor, the moans of the orphans, the loneliness of the widows, the desolation of those who grieve, the necessities of pilgrims, the perils of men on the sea, the vows of virgins, the temptations of monks, the anxieties of bishops, the hardships of soldiers. To all of these you will fling wide the portals of your heart, to them you will consecrate your tears, for them you will pour out your prayers" (*P.L.*, 32, 1465).

But best of all as a revelation of this dear Saint's spirit is the *Oratio Pastoralis* which he wrote to keep his own abbatial self in mind of his duty.[2] He begins with an appeal to the Good Shepherd: "O bone pastor Jhesu, pastor bone, pastor clemens, pastor pie, ad te clamat miser et miserabilis quidam pastor, ... anxius pro se, anxius pro ovibus tuis." This is followed by an act of contrition for all his sins, and of gratitude that they are not many more, because, as he says, echoing St. Augustine, "non minus debitor tibi sum etiam et pro illis malis quaecumque non feci". Next, he examines his conscience of an abbot and is appalled at what he finds: "Such is the one, sweet Lord, whom Thou hast placed over Thy family, bidding him be careful for

---

[1] As Dom André Wilmart has learnedly proved in the *Revue Bénédictine*, 1924, pp. 60-1.

[2] It was published for the first time by Dom André Wilmart in the *Revue Bénédictine*, 1925, pp. 267–271, from a manuscript in the library of Jesus College, Cambridge. Perhaps a Jesuit may be forgiven for feeling a little pleasure that it was one of his own tribe, Father Richard Gibbons, who first saw Aelred's works in general into print: *Divi Aelredi Rhievallensis Opera Omnia ope et studio R. Gibboni, S.J., ex vetustis MSS. nunc primum in lucem producta*. Douay, 1616, 1631. This was several years before the first Cistercian edition.

them who has so little care for himself.... O wretched man, what have I done and presumed and consented to? ... Why, O fountain of mercy, didst Thou commit these Thy so dear ones to the care of such a one as I? ... See my wounds, Lord ... Look on me, look on me, *dulcis Domine,* for I hope that in Thy pity Thou wilt look as a kind physician to heal, or a solicitous master to correct or an indulgent father to pardon." Then he prays for his huge family of choir monks and lay brothers, said to have numbered more than six hundred: "Thou knowest my heart, Lord, and that whatsoever Thou hast given to me Thy servant I desire to lay out wholly on them and to consume it all in their service ... My senses and my speech, my leisure and my labour, my acts and my thoughts, my good fortune and bad, my health and sickness, my life and death, all my stock in the world, may it be used up in their interest for whom Thou didst not disdain Thyself to be consumed ... Grant to me, Lord, by Thy ineffable grace to bear their infirmities with patient, tender, helpful compassion. May I learn by the teaching of Thy Spirit to console the sorrowful, to strengthen the faint-hearted, to put the fallen on their feet, to quieten the restless, to cherish the sick, conforming myself to each one's character and capacity ... And since through the weakness of my flesh, or the cowardice and evil of my heart, my labours, vigils and frugality do little, nay nothing, to edify them, I beg Thee to grant that my humility, my charity, my patience and my pity may supply in their place. May my words and teaching edify them, and may my prayers be always their support ... Thou knowest, sweet Lord, how much I love them and how my heart goes out to them in tenderest affection, ... that I yearn rather to help them in charity than to rule them, that I would humbly be under their feet if only affectionately in their hearts. Grant unto me, then, O Lord my God, that Thy eyes may be opened upon them day and night. Tenderly expand Thy wings to protect them. Extend Thy holy right hand to bless them. Pour into their hearts Thy Holy Spirit who may stand by them while they pray to refresh them with devout compunction, to stimulate them with hope, to make them humble with fear, and to inflame them with charity ... May He, the kind Consoler, succour them in temptation and help their weakness in all the troubles and tribulations of this life. ..."

Though it does not appear so clearly in those few passages, there are no less than 59 Scriptural quotations or allusions in the 186 Latin lines of the *Oratio*, for Aelred's thoughts were completely dyed in the language of revelation. Indeed, it would seem that he must have known his Bible by heart. Among what may be called his historical works are devoutly written lives of St. Edward the Confessor, occupying fifty columns in Migne, of St. Ninian and of St. Margaret of Scotland. It was at his instance and with his aid that Prior Reginald drew up his account of the miracles of St. Cuthbert, and when the Austin canons of Hexham wanted the Legend of their own saints committed to parchment, to Aelred they turned. He must have found the writing of *De miraculis Hagulstaldensis Ecclesiae* a labour of love,[1] for he reckoned the feast day of the Hexham saints as his own birthday—*Haec est nativitas mea. ...* Easily the most interesting and vivid of his secular writings is his account of the Battle of the Standard, from which modern historians have drawn with both hands and scanty acknowledgement. It cannot have been an easy story for him to tell because half of his heart was in each of the rival camps, one

---

[1] A cynic might say, too much love and too little labour, but Aelred, though very credulous, nearly always gives the stories of miracles a practical twist which is both disarming and refreshing. He obviously enjoyed telling the story of the youth who was condemned to death for theft and saved at the very last moment by St. Wilfrid. As the executioner swung his axe this hero cried out, "Adjuva nunc, Wilfride, quia si modo nolueris paulo post non poteris", a sally which rendered the headsman helpless with laughter and gave time for two men, "equis velocissimis vecti", to arrive and effect a rescue (Raine, *The Priory of Hexham*, i, 173–203). Reginald's book about St. Cuthbert, to which Aelred contributed, is a fearful hotchpotch of imaginary miracles. One excellent story witnessed by Aelred is about a bull offered at a shrine of St. Cuthbert in 1164 but it illustrates rather the power of the bull than of the Saint.

half with King David, the beloved aggressor, and the other with the English captain, Walter Espec, that "great giant of a man with a huge black beard and a voice like a trumpet", who had founded Rievaulx and retired to die there as a monk in Aelred's arms. What he does in effect is to blame the horrible Picts for David's defeat, while at the same time glorying in the victory of Walter. In Homeric fashion, he puts a thundering denunciation of the Picts on Walter's lips, and having thus satisfied his patriotism turns to praise the vanquished friends of his youth, David and Henry (*P.L.,* 195, 701–12). He had taught that friendship, true friendship in Christ, is unalterable, and if David had burned Rievaulx over his head he would still have loved him.

In times like our own it is heartening to remember that the stormy and passionate period of Aelred's existence was one of the greatest ages of Catholic revival, when 115 monasteries sprang from the soil in the space of nineteen years to transform both the physical and spiritual face of England. Of all that marvellous renaissance the Abbot of Rievaulx, ever, like the Church herself, ailing in the body, was the soul and inspiration. "During the four years before he died," wrote a chronicler of the time, "he became so emaciated from fasting that he was only skin and bone." We are given a glimpse of him crouched on the floor with his head between his knees, rocking to and fro in the agony of the stone. "A hacking cough and other infirmities so weakened him that often after saying Mass he would stumble back to his cell and lie collapsed on his pallet, unable to speak or move for an hour" (*P.L.,* 195, 202–4). And yet he was the choir-master of the "singing masons building roofs of gold", who loved best in all the dictionary the two words *dulcis* and *jucundus*. Men called him, as they did St. Bernard, the honey-tongued and the honey-souled who, like the bees, distilled an elixir *dulcedine dulcius ipsa*. They said that nobody could read him once without wanting to read him again, which is absolutely true, as anybody can find by trying (*P.L.,* 195, 207–8; and particularly, 184, 216–8). Aelred died on 12 January, 1166, in his fifty-seventh year, a poor age for a Cistercian.[1]

[1] Walter Daniel's life of Aelred shows the usual mediaeval proclivity for miracle-stories. Unusual, however, and refreshing is the fact that two priests or bishops, "duo praelati", entirely refused to credit the marvels, even when Daniel proclaimed that he had himself witnessed them. This made him indignant, so he requested his friend Maurice to tell the sceptics the following story, which he hoped might confound them. Once, he was alone with the sick and suffering Aelred in his cell where a fire had been lighted for the invalid's comfort. Suddenly, a giant monk, temporarily deranged, it seems by toothache, rushed in, seized the frail Abbot in his powerful arms, and threw him on the fire. Walter pluckily grappled with the intruder and held him by the beard while he shouted for assistance. In their anger, the other monks might easily have killed the assailant had not Aelred, picking himself out of the fire, come to his rescue. Here, commented Walter, surpassing himself, was a charity "greater than many miracles", such as might persuade even the two prelates that Aelred was a man likely to possess, preternatural powers. It is a fair enough presumptive argument, but *a posse ad esse non valet illatio* (Powicke, *Ailred of Rievaulx*, p. 81).

Bishop of Lindisfarne

VICTRIX *causa deis placuit, sed victa Catoni.* Lost causes
have inspired some of the world's best poetry, from
Homer onwards, and it is part, at least, of the appeal of
St. Colman that his life is largely the story of a lost cause. The
name, once very common in Ireland,[1] seems to be derived
from the Latin *columba,* for it means the same thing, a dove.
It fitted our Saint, who was the most peaceable of men, to
perfection. He comes into history, like the King of Salem, out
of the blue, without father, without mother, without genealogy.
All that is known of him for certain is written in three chapters

[1] The *Annals of the Four Masters* mention eight Saints Colman for the
seventh century alone, not including, though he belongs to that period,
the delightful hermit of Arranmore and founder of the monastery of
Kilmacduagh who tamed a mouse to be his alarm-clock and a gnat
(*culex*) to act as his bookmarker: "Mus enim ita viro Dei famulabatur,
ut ultra statas . . . horas eum non permitteret dormire, sed quando natura
vigiliis, orationibus, aliisque austeritatibus fatigata, somnum ampliorem
quam viri Dei rigida vota praefixerat, lassis artubus postularet, nunc
vestes rodendo, nunc auriculus mordendo, eum ab omni quiete revocaret.
Gratum erat viro Dei ejusmodi obsequium. . . . Sed et culicis obsequia
vix minus miranda. Quando enim vir Dei piae lectioni vacabat, culici
super ejus codicem cursitanti mandabat ut lineam ad quam ipse, alio
avocatus vel aliter occupandus, sistebat, observaret usque dum reversus
ipse inchoatam denuo continuaret lectionem; quod et culex infallibiliter
faciebat" (Colgan, *Acta Sanctorum Hiberniae*, Louvain, 1645, t. i, sub die
III Februarii, p. 244). Miracles attributed to saints by uninspired hagiographers often make the dreariest reading, but that one of the gnat is
distinctly original, and its inventor, who was not the immensely learned
Franciscan John Colgan, deserves a salute, especially as his hero occurs
in this month of February. Father Colgan, however, defends the authen-
ticity of the story, and there is, in fact, no particular reason why it should
not have been true. Four Jesuit professors of Louvain paid Colgan himself a very touching tribute, printed at the beginning of his folio: "We
have observed", they wrote, "his tireless diligence in exploring the li-
braries here and elsewhere. His labours for the saints of Ireland knew no
limit, and he slaved away at the task almost to the ruin of his health.
May the saints whom he has made known to the world be his glory."
The Jesuits swallowed the gnat, mouse and other miscellaneous fauna
of the great tome without the slightest demur.

14

of the English St. Bede, who highly disapproved of his views but loved and venerated his character. One of Colman's many services to England is that he illuminates Bede's own extremely lovable character. Bede could not quite make Colman out, a thing that has happened a few times subsequently in the relations of Englishmen and Irishmen. It irritated him that so good a man should have been so obstinate in his loyalty to the traditions of Iona. He spoke a few bitter words about those traditions, even calling them heresy and schism, which was utterly unfair, but then went on in his grand generous way to pay the defeated Irishman and his monks one of the loveliest tributes ever laid at the feet of sanctity.

Bede takes for granted that Colman had come from over the water to Iona, perhaps as a little boy. Monasticism at that period liked to catch its postulants young, but in Ireland the custom was commoner than elsewhere owing to the native institution of fosterage.[1] Anyhow, Colman learned to love every rock and bush and bird and beast of his Iona, over which still brooded as a living cherished memory the great spirit of St. Columba. Columba died in 597, within a few months of the landing of St. Augustine in Kent. Twenty years later, Iona extended its hospitality to two pagan lads who were to become famous in Christian history, Oswald and Oswy, sons of the last unbaptized king of Northumbria. Sixteen years they remained with the monks or under their protection, and on them too the magical island laid its spell. During that time, their father's supplanter, King Edwin, was shepherded gently into the Church by the infinitely patient St. Paulinus, after the council so vividly described by Bede when a nameless thane preached the little homily of the sparrow, comparing human existence to its flight through a lighted hall warm with a soft fire, "from winter to winter". The King's conversion led to the establishment of Roman Paulinus, a tall, thin, great-hearted man, as first bishop of Roman York. Bede pictures him for us on circuit with his royal proselyte, "doing nothing else from

[1] Ryan, *Irish Monasticism*, London, 1931, pp. 207-16.

morning to evening" but preach to the humble folk of the hills
and dales the salvation of Jesus. We are not told how a monk
from the Coelian Hill made himself understood by the un-
lettered peasantry of Northumbria, and very likely they did
not understand much, but were happy to follow the lead of
their good King who had given them drinking-fountains and
public baths, and achieved such peace and order that, as Bede
puts it, "a weake woman might have walked with her new
borne babe over all the yland even from sea to sea, without
anie damage or danger".[1] But this idyllic state of affairs did
not long endure. In 633 the nominal British Christian Cadwallon, King of North Wales, putting race before religion,
joined forces with the formidable heathen Penda to defeat and
slay Edwin at the battle of Heathfield. Then was there "a verie
greavouse persecution in the church and a fowle murder of the
Northumberlandes", carried out by the recreant Cadwallon,
a man "more feerce and barbarouse then was any heathen
or paynim".[2]

For a year, Bede's "annus exosus", the slaughter and
destruction continued, with only one bright and gallant name
to relieve the darkness, that of the good Roman, James the
Deacon, a man "cunning in song and music", who, fearless
of the murdering Cadwallon, stayed at his post when Bishop
Paulinus fled. By some sad oversight of the martyrologists,
this humble apostle, who "toke manie preys out of the divels
teathe" and ought to be England's patron saint of plain chant,
has never been canonized.[3] His half-forgotten name is not

[1] *The History of the Church of Englande.* Translated by Thomas
Stapleton. Antwerp, 1565. Newly published, Oxford, 1930, p. 147. Stapleton's translation of Bede, the first to be made since the time of King
Alfred, was dedicated to Queen Elizabeth in hopes of influencing her
against the reformers.

[2] Bede has nothing good to say about Cadwallon, but he rather admired Penda, who, he tells us, persecuted only "such as bearing the name
of Christians, lived not according to the faithe they professed...men
wretched and worthely to be spited..."

[3] Bede's account of James is in Book ii, chapter 20; Stapleton's translation, p. 159. "He saw the overthrow of the earthly power which upheld

irrelevant in this place, for he was the forerunner of the
masterful Wilfrid, and stood beside him that day thirty years
later when he argued poor St. Colman out of England. To
brave Roman James there came rescue from Irish Iona, where,
sad to tell, they did not sing the Gregorian way, nor shave
their polls aright, nor, worst of all, keep Easter on the proper
Sunday. Towards the end of the year 634 the royal refugee
Oswald, then grown to man's estate, issued from his retreat
among the Scots, gathered an English troop around him, and
on some high ground behind the Roman Wall seven miles or
so north of Hexham gave battle to Cadwallon and his host of
bloodthirsty Britons. The night before this famous fight which
so thrilled the patriotic heart of Bede, Oswald, asleep fully
armed in his tent, had a vision of St. Columba, that most Irish
of Irishmen. The Saint, who seemed to be standing in the midst
of the camp with his shining robe spread in protection over all
save a little portion of the English army, bade Oswald give
battle at once, for the Lord would be with him.[1] The great
victory that followed brought Iona to England. No sooner was
Oswald established in his father's wooden palace at lonely
wind-swept Bamburgh, that village of wonderful memories,
than he appealed to his Irish friends for help in the evangeliza-
tion of Northumbria, and God sent him Aidan, "a man of
marvailous mekenesse, godlinesse, and modestie: and one that
had a zele in Gods quarrell, although not in every point according to knouledg, for he was wont to kepe Easter sunday

the Church; he saw violence, death, and apostasy on every side; he heard
the reasons which satisfied his ecclesiastical chief that it was his duty to
depart; he knew that Paulinus and his company were going to a land
where they would find safety and honour, yet he would not leave God's
people in their day of trial, nor cease from the work to which his Lord
had called him" (Hunt, *A History of the English Church . . . to the Norman Conquest,* London, 1899, pp. 70-1).

[1] Bede does not give the story of the vision, but it is told by his contemporary, St. Adamnan, in his Life of St. Columba. Adamnan heard it
from his predecessor as abbot of Iona, Failbhe, who had it from Oswald's
own lips (*Acta Sanctorum,* Junii t. ii, p. 199. A further reference will be
found on p. 97 *infra,* note 2).

from the fourtenth day after the chaunge of the mone, until the twentith, according to the custom of his country, whereof we have divers times made mencion." [1]

Indeed yes, dear Bede often mentions it. That blessed Paschal question which gave so many headaches to the ancient Popes and Fathers obsessed his gentle English soul. He described the Irish as "gentem innoxiam et nationi Anglorum semper amicissimam," [2] but when it came to a matter of epacts and lunar cycles he had no patience with the friendly race at all. However, the controversy remained in abeyance during Aidan's golden age at Lindisfarne, that Holy Island off the storm-beaten Northumbrian coast which he fashioned into a second Iona, and from which he and his successors, Saints Finan and Colman, led out the men they had trained, English and Irish, to carry the Gospel from the Firth of Forth to the Wash and the Bristol Channel. St. Cedd, one of Aidan's Northumbrian scholars at Lindisfarne who spoke Irish fluently, first bearded in his Mercian den the fierce old Penda, slayer of five kings, including the peerless St. Oswald,[3] and then penetrated to London to become bishop of the East Saxons. Meantime, his more famous brother St. Chad, another of Aidan's scholars who had done part of his training in Ireland, laboured in the North until in old age made bishop of Lichfield, where he died of the Plague in 672, calling his dread disease in Franciscan fashion "that lovable guest who hath been wont of late to visit

---

[1] Bede, iii, 3; in Stapleton's reprinted translation, pp. 166-7.

[2] *Historia ecclesiastica,* iv, 26. Stapleton's translation has a smile in it: "Harmelesse seely people, which had ever been great frindes to the English nation."

[3] Oswald was defeated and killed by Penda in 641, at a place probably to be identified with Oswestry, meaning Oswald's tree. His brother Oswy, who was with him at Iona, succeeded and for the following thirty years held the Northumbrian sceptre in his capable Christian hands. It is an interesting fact that all Penda's children became excellent Christians and some of them were even venerated as saints. St. Finan himself baptized Peada, Penda's son and heir, shortly before the terrible old champion of Woden fell to Oswy's sword at the battle of the Winwaed near Leeds in A.D. 654.

our brotherhood". None of those humble men with their odd tonsures and narrow Celtic outlook had St. Wilfrid's privilege of travel in Italy, but "in Columba, Aidan, Colman and their disciples we seem to see something of that absolute indifference to wealth, that kinship with Nature and her children, that almost passionate love for Poverty and the Poor which, six centuries later, was to shed a halo round the head of Francis of Assisi." [1] The masterful statesman saints, the Wilfrids and Theodores, are necessary, but one's heart goes out to those others and their kin, such as the dear old contemporary Deeside farmer, St. Nathalan, who prayed as he ploughed and held that of all the work of the world "the cultivation of the soil comes nearest to heavenly contemplation".[2]

When St. Colman succeeded St. Finan as bishop of Lindisfarne, meaning bishop of all Northumbria, in A.D. 661, the bright day of the Island missionaries was nearly done, though St. Cuthbert had not yet added the lustre of his glorious name to the monastery's annals. That same year the Paschal controversy, which was a question rather of mathematics and astronomy than of religion, came to a head, and the monks of Ripon, an offshoot of Aidan's Old Melrose on the Tweed, including Cuthbert himself and his abbot St. Eata, described by Bede as "the gentlest soul in the world", were expelled from their home by King Oswy's son Alhfrith because they would not abandon the traditional Irish way of computing the incidence of Easter Sunday. In their place Alhfrith installed his friend and mentor, the great Wilfrid, who, though also an "old boy" of Lindisfarne, had been to Rome and

[1] Hodgkin (T.), *The History of England from the Earliest Times to the Norman Conquest,* London, 1906, p. 155. This volume is by the same genial and delightful scholar, Quaker and banker by profession, who wrote the great work, *Italy and Her Invaders.*

[2] "Cum inter cunctas hominum exercitationes agriculturam rusticam supernae contemplationi propius accedere didicerat, suis propriis manibus, quamquam ex nobili familia fuerat, colendi agros artem exercuit" (*Breviarium Aberdonense,* pars hiemalis, London, 1854, Januarii folio xxv, verso). St. Nathalan died A.D. 678, two years after St. Colman.

come home more Roman than the Romans themselves. Only, with his new-born enthusiasm for the coronal tonsure and the Paschal table of Dionysius Exiguus,[1] he does not appear to have acquired much of the tolerant, adaptable, understanding mind of the Roman Church. Handsome and charming as well as holy, Wilfrid could also be uncommonly ruthless. He declared a sort of tonsorial and astronomical war against the children of St. Colman, and found, to Colman's grief, a sturdy ally in the Irish monk Ronan, who also had travelled and seen the world. Besides, Ronan had the deadly argument in his quiver that the southern half of his and Colman's native land had been keeping the Dionysian Easter for more than a generation.[2] But Wilfrid's best advocate was King

[1] The great sixth-century monk to whom we owe our A.D. and B.C. This Christian method of reckoning the years from the birth of our Lord instead of from the birth of Rome was a direct outcome of the Paschal imbroglio, and appears for the first time in Denis's Easter table, which was adopted by the Roman Church and eventually by the whole of Western Christendom. Denis himself was a few years too late in his establishment of the Christian year 1, with the paradoxical result that we have to date the first Christmas from 7–4 B.C.

[2] The southern Irish had been converted to the Roman usage at the time of St. Aidan's mission to Northumbria by the exhortation of Pope Honorius I of clouded memory, to whom England owed her St. Birinus, and by the good reasoning of their own immensely learned St. Cummian. But Iona and its dependent monasteries in the north of Ireland held to the tradition of St. Patrick, St. Columba and St. Columbanus for another seventy years. St. Columbanus, ardent "Papalist" though he was, showed himself fierce in defence of the old customs. Looked at calmly, the obstinacy of such men is seen to be only another instance of their conservative regard for Rome. A writer in the *Church Times*, 25 March, 1927, put the matter in a nutshell: "They had not invented their own system; it was simply the system in vogue when their churches were first organized. It was the old Roman method; to give it up was to cast a slur upon their origin. Rome itself and the rest of the Western Church had given up the old method, and adopted not one but several revised systems of calculating the Kalendar. But the Celts were isolated, and their conservatism really made them more Roman than the Romans. Their obstinacy was perhaps misplaced, but it was due to loyalty and not to sectarianism." A fine discussion of the whole question is to be found in MacNaught's *The Celtic Church and the See of Peter*, Oxford, 1927, pp. 68–93.

Oswy's Queen, Eanfled, who had been bred in the Roman tradition by her friend and saviour, St. Paulinus. Oswy himself, who spoke Irish like a native, remained true to Iona in this matter of the moon, a circumstance that did not make for concord in the House of Northumbria. As the year 665 approached the need for some settlement became obvious, for otherwise the King would then be joyfully celebrating his Celtic Easter while the Queen was still only at her Roman Palm Sunday.

The Frankish bishop named Agilbert, who had succeeded St. Birinus at Dorchester after a period of study in Ireland, appears to have suggested, while on a visit to Northumbria in 664, that a conference of the main parties concerned might be the best way to obtain a solution of the Paschal problem. King Oswy and his son from their opposed standpoints readily agreed, and so came about the famous meeting of kings, bishops, priests and nuns known to us, by the unintended beneficence of the Danes who destroyed, rebuilt and renamed the original and unpronounceable Streanaeshalch of Bede, as the Synod of Whitby, though synod it neither was nor pretended to be. At Whitby, on a cliff fronting the sea, stood the great double-monastery of monks and nuns ruled with the poise and suavity of a Benedict or Bernard by the spiritual child of Lindisfarne, high-born St. Hilda, "whome all that knewe her were wont to call mother for her notable grace and godlinesse". At Hilda's monastery and under her inspiration English poetry was born with the herdsman Caedmon, and there also, in 664, English and Irish sanctity crossed swords in a debate which has been described as "one of the great turning-points in the history of the race".[1] What a scene it must have made on that fateful Lenten day,[2] with the King

[1] Hodgkin (R. H.), *A History of the Anglo-Saxons*, Oxford, 1939, vol. i, p. 295.
[2] Bede, who showed such concern about the chronology of Easter, provokingly omits to say at what time of the year the synod took place, but most likely it was during Lent (Bright, *Early English Church History*, 2nd ed., Oxford, 1888, p. 202).

presiding in all his barbaric splendour and Hilda praying for the success of her dear Irish Colman, and Cedd, up north on a visit to his Irish monastery of Lastingham, whispering encouragement; while opposed to them were the smiling Queen and her ladies, James the Deacon, a venerable figure from the past, Agilbert, the roaming Frank whose atrocious accent had led so curiously to the creation of the great see of Winchester,[1] Bishop Tuda from Southern Ireland come to strike an early symbolic blow against the "Black North", and, cynosure of every eye, the young Abbot of Ripon, pugnacious, kind-hearted Wilfrid, who would give a beggar the shirt off his back and fight an archbishop through every ecclesiastical court in Christendom.

King Oswy opened the proceedings with a little exhortation on the need for unity of practice among those who were serving the same God and seeking the same kingdom in Heaven. Let them, then, diligently investigate which was the true rule for determining the date of Easter and all adhere to that. Next, the King bade Colman state his case, which he did "like a brave man", says Wilfrid's enthusiastic disciple and biographer, Eddi.[2] His few words reveal the *pietas* and leal-love which were the basis of his gentle unassuming character: "The Easter rule I follow I received from my forefathers who sent me here as bishop. It is known that all our fathers, men dear to God, kept the same rule. Nor is it something to be despised and

---

[1] Agilbert, whom it is very difficult to like, had already abandoned his see of Dorchester and subsequently returned to Gaul in a huff, because Ceawlin, King of Wessex, grew tired of his foreign tongue and set up a proper English-speaking bishop at Winchester. While in Northumbria, St. Colman's territory, this Agilbert, such a stickler for Roman usages, ordained St. Wilfrid to the priesthood without the slightest reference to Lindisfarne. However, it must be remembered that Colman was not a diocesan bishop, but rather a monastic official.

[2] Raine, *The Historians of the Church of York* (R.S. 1879), vol. i, p. 14. Eddi spent forty years in Wilfrid's service and was a terrible partisan. A fine text and translation of his life of Wilfrid was published by Mr. Colgrave at Cambridge in 1927.

reprobated, for we read that the Blessed Evangelist John, whom our Lord loved specially, observed it, together with all the churches under his care." When Colman had done, Oswy called upon Bishop Agilbert to voice his opinion, but that worthy, conscious of his small English, begged that his disciple Wilfrid might have the honour instead, so the King beckoned to Wilfrid and the fireworks began.

Wilfrid was undoubtedly well primed and stated a powerful, apocryphal and unanswerable case. "The Easter which we observe", said he, "is that which I myself have seen celebrated at Rome, where the Blessed Apostles Peter and Paul lived, preached, suffered and are buried. When I visited Gaul and Italy for purposes of study or prayer, I observed, wherever I travelled, this same custom in use. Similarly, I have learned that it is the practice of the Church in Africa, Asia, Egypt, Greece, and, indeed, the world over, save only among my friends opposite and their pig-headed accomplices, the Picts [1] and the Britons, peoples of two bits of islands in the furthermost ocean, who with stupid determination range themselves in battle against the whole world." At any rate, the coat-trailing this time was not on the Irish side! Colman mildly deprecated the thunder with the words: "It is strange that you should call us foolish for following the rule of the Apostle who reclined on the Lord's breast." The good Bishop was certainly on very shaky ground in claiming St. John, but not more so than Wilfrid when he retorted by claiming St. Peter, for if the Apostles and primitive Christians celebrated Easter as a special annual festival at all, which is doubtful, they would have kept it, to judge by the evidence of St. Polycarp in Eusebius, in Quartodeciman fashion, on the day of the Jewish Pasch, whether a Sunday or not, an idea equally abhorrent to the two disputants at Whitby. Both men were plainly out of their depth, moonstruck in different ways, and small

[1] Stapleton usually translates the word *Picti* by the delightful name, Redshankes.

blame to them, considering the mathematics involved.[1] The modern historians most carefully side-step those mathematics when they touch on Whitby, and we can do no better than follow their prudent, if cowardly, example.

After appealing to the authority of the third-century St. Anatolius, who was a mathematician and wrote a treatise on arithmetic, St. Colman himself discreetly fell back upon Iona, asking: "Is it to be thought that our moste Reverend Father Columba and his successours, vertuous and godly men who after the same maner kept their Easter, either beleved or lived contrary to holy Scripture, especially their holynesse being such that God hath confirmed it with miracles? Truly as I doubt not but they were holy men, so I wil not feare to folow allwaies their life, maners, and trade of discipline."[2]

This brought Wilfrid to his feet with glittering eye and curling lip. "In good sothe, quoth he, it is well knowen that Anatholius was a right holy man, very well lerned, and worthy of much praise. But what is that to you, who vary also from his decrees and doctrine? For Anatholius in his Easter... accompted the usuall compasse of xix yeres, whiche you either utterly are ignorant of, or if ye know it, yet though it be through all Christendom observed, yet sett light by it.[3] ... As touching your father Columba and those which folowed him, whose holy steppes ye pretend to folow, as the which

[1] Wilfrid's bland assumption, as also that of Bede's beloved abbot at Jarrow, St. Ceolfrid, in his letter to the King of the Picts (Bede, v, 22), that there had been uniformity of usage in West and East from the time of St. Peter is magnificently anachronistic. He had only to read St. Augustine's twenty-third Letter to learn that in A.D. 387 Gaul kept Easter on 21 March, Italy on 18 April, and Egypt on 25 April.

[2] Stapleton's *Bede,* p. 234. The entire story is in Bede, v, 25.

[3] The Anatolian canon which both men had in mind has long been recognized as spurious, but so far as it went it supported Colman's position rather than Wilfrid's. The great Petavius says that Wilfrid ascribed to Anatolius "an opinion of which he never so much as dreamed". The British and Celtic Churches used a cycle of eighty-four years, that being the time in which the sun and moon would have completed their round of changes and started the process all over again.

have ben confirmed by miracles, to this I may answer that in the daye of judgment whereas *many shall saie unto Christ that they have prophecyed, cast out divells and wrought miracles in his name, our Lord wil answer that he knoweth them not.* But God forbidd that I should so judge of your fathers, for it is our duty of such as we knowe not, to deme the best. Therefore I deme not but they were men of God, and acceptable in his sight, as the whiche loved God, though in rude simplicite, yet with a godly intention.... But nowe, Sir, you and your companions, if hearing the decrees of the Apostolike see, or rather of the universall church, and that also confirmed in holy write,[1] you follow not the same, you offend and sinne herein undoubtedly. For though your fathers were holy men, could yet those few of one so smal corner of the uttermost ilond of the earth prejudicat the whole church of Christ dispersed throughout the universall worlde? And if your father Columba (yea and our father, if he were the true servaunt of Christe) were holye and mightye in miracles, yet can he not by any meanes be preferred to the moste blessed prince of the Apostles, to whom our Lord sayed, *Thou arte Peter ... and to thee I will geve the kayes of the kingdome of heaven."*

So we see that not only English poetry, but English rhetoric also, with its splendid crops of New Zealanders sketching the ruins of St. Paul's, was born at Whitby. The fun of the story is that Colman's routed Easter was none other than the *vetus supputatio Romana,* the Popes' own Paschal cycle of eighty-four years, which they cherished as coming down to them from St. Peter, while Wilfrid's vaunted "Catholic" Easter was a foreign Alexandrian invention repudiated by Rome for the best part of three centuries. As the echoes of Matthew xvi died away in the hushed assembly, the King addressed St. Colman: "Were these thinges in dede spoken to Peter of our Lord? To whom the bishop answered, yea. Can you

---

[1] There were no decrees of the Apostolic See, or the universal Church, except that Easter must be kept on a Sunday, and "holy write", of course, has nothing whatever to say on the subject.

then (saieth the kinge) give evidence of so speciall authoritie geven to your father Columba? The bishop answering, No, ... the kinge concluded and saied: Then I will not gainsaie such a porter as this is, but as farre as I knowe and am able, I will covet in all pointes to obey his ordinaunces, lest perhaps when I come to the dores of the kingdome of heaven I finde none to open unto me, having his displeasure which is so clerely proved to beare the kayes thereof." St. Wilfrid's biographer, Eddi, supplies a detail omitted by Bede, that Oswy was smiling when he put his questions to St. Colman,[1] which seems to indicate that he had already made up his mind to abandon the cause of Iona. It was a lost cause anyhow, and the stars in their courses, not to mention the moon, had rendered the King's decision inevitable as well as desirable.

But Colman was not convinced, and, indeed, Wilfrid had done very little by either matter or manner to win him over. He bowed in his uncomplaining way to the storm, resigned his bishopric, to which Wilfrid, aged thirty, very soon succeeded, and said good-bye for ever to Lindisfarne. With him, besides his Irish sympathizers, and surely this was a great tribute of love, went no less than thirty English monks who preferred to die in distant exile rather than be parted from their Abbot (Bede, iv, 4). And not only his monks were attached to him, "for this bishop Colman", says Bede, "was derely loved of kinge Oswiu for his rare wisedome and vertu." He made a parting request to the King "which touchingly indicates the generosity and tenderness of his nature",[2] namely that he would appoint to rule in his stead at Holy Island the meek man of peace, St. Eata. Then, with some relics of St. Aidan for solace and remembrance, he led his devoted band first to Iona and afterwards to Inishbofin, an Iona in the Atlantic off the wild coast of Mayo, within sight of the Irish Sinai, Croagh Patrick, where they at once established another Lindisfarne, and set to work to make the desolate

[1] "Tunc Oswy rex subridens ..." (Eddi, cap. x, in Raine, *u.s.,* p. 15).
[2] Bright, *Early English Church History,* p. 209.

island bloom. But in summer-time the lure of their native shores became too strong for the Irish monks, and they sailed away, as we may hope with apostolic intentions, leaving the English brethren to gather in the harvest unaided. When they returned in the winter, expecting to share the fruits of the other men's toil, they met with the chilliest reception, which greatly distressed the pacific heart of St. Colman. He decided that the workers of his little world should have a monastery of their own, and set them up independently on a property which he purchased in County Mayo. That parcel of Irish earth can claim to be for ever England, as the new foundation was recruited exclusively from England, and in Bede's time, more than fifty years later, had "a notable company of vertuous monkes, living after the example of the worthy olde fathers".

The thought of the worthy old fathers haunted Bede, for all his joy at the victory of the Roman Easter. England had gained much, he felt, but also lost something very precious with the departure of St. Colman. There had passed away a glory from the earth. And so he wrote his epitaph on Lindisfarne: "How sparefull personnes Colman and his predecessours were, and how greatly they absteined from all pleasures, even the place where he bare rule did witnesse. In the whiche at their departure few houses were found beside the church; that is to saye, those houses only without the which civill conversation could no wise be maintained. They had no money but cattaill. For if they tooke anye mony of riche men, by and by they gave it to poore people.... If by chaunce it fortuned that anye of the nobilite or of the worshipfull refreshed themselves in the monasteries, they contented themselves with the religious mens simple fare and poore pittens ... For then those lerned men and rulers of the churche sought not to pamper the panche, but to save the soule, not to please the worlde, butt to serve God. Whereof it came then to passe that even the habite of religious men was at that time had in great reverence. So that where anye of the clergye or religious person came, he shoulde be joyfully received of all men, like the servaunt of God. Againe if any were mett going on journey, they ranne unto him, and making lowe obeissaunce, desyred gladly to have their benediction ... Upon the Sondayes ordinarely the people flocked to the church or to monasteries, not for bely chere, but to heare the worde of God. And if any priest came by chaunce abrode into the village, the inhabitants thereof would gather about him and desire to have some good lesson or collation made unto them. For the priestes and other of the clergy in those daies used not to come abrode in to villages, but only to preache, to baptise, to visit the sicke, or (to speake all in one worde) for the cure of soules. Who also at that time were so farre from the infection of covetousnes and ambition, they they would not take territories and possessions toward the building of monasteries and erecting of churches, but through the ernest suite, and almost forced of noble and welthy men of the worlde." [1] Nothing more is known of St. Colman except that he died on his remote island in the year 676.

[1] Stapleton's *Bede,* reprinted 1930, pp. 238-40. The Saint's emphasis on "then", "at that time", "in those days" is very significant.

ON the very threshold of Cuthbert's great story there crouches or couches a mischief-making sphinx, with a riddle in its grinning mouth: Which was he, this most famous of the Saxon saints, an Englishman or an Irishman? It is a question to make a man quake in his shoes, but as he is likely to get strangled anyhow, whatever he answers, he may as well put on a brave face and pretend that he doesn't care. The riddle is a very old one, and a few words about it may be found diverting, even if they lead nowhere in particular. Many years ago now, an eminent Irish archbishop complained of the cool way in which the Catholics of Britain, including very much an eminent Scottish archbishop, took it for granted that St. Cuthbert was an Englishman. "We have had so many saints of yore in Ireland," wrote he, trailing his rochet, "that we could very well afford to lend one to Northumbria without saying much about it. But Cuthbert is far too celebrated a saint to part with, especially if we are to get no credit for our generosity." What particularly annoyed His Grace was the assumption, still common in English books, that St. Bede had decided the issue. St. Bede, as everybody knows, was the Boswell of Cuthbert, though he missed by a few years the privilege of personal acquaintance, being only a schoolboy when the great man died. Besides letting Cuthbert monopolize six entire chapters of his *Ecclesiastical History,* a glaring disproportion, he wrote a set life of him in forty-six chapters, and composed a Latin poem celebrating his miracles which runs to about a thousand hexameters. Was not this love indeed? Yet neither Bede nor the anonymous monk of Lindisfarne whose earlier life of the Saint he embodied in his own, with scrupulous acknowledgement, has a single word to say about the birth or parentage of his hero. This is very strange, especially as the models which they faithfully imitated in the construction of their narratives, the ancient lives of St. Anthony the Great and St. Martin of Tours, both begin with a mention of *their* heroes' families and countries. Only in his poem does Bede touch on the delicate question at all, and there in such a way as to leave the careful reader exactly where he was before. Just as Rome, he says, was glorified by Saints Peter and Paul, the Province of Asia by St. John, India by St. Bartholomew, Egypt by St. Mark, Africa by St. Cyprian, Poitiers by St. Hilary, and Constantinople by St. John Chrysostom, so in his own time did Britain bring forth a *fulgur venerabile,* a worshipful splendour, "where Cuthbert on his starlit journey through life taught the English to scale in his footprints the heavenly heights".[1]

Historians have pounced on that solitary crumb from the table of Bede with the avidity of starving men, but whether it is enough to sustain the Englishness of Cuthbert one may, perhaps, doubt, without being too great a heretic. As against the crumb, the Irish claimants offer a banquet of Lucullan richness, the tale of a wicked Connaught king who enslaved and ravished a beautiful young Leinster princess, making her the mother of "a faire knave childe", the future St. Cuthbert. All this was committed to parchment in the twelfth century, not by an Irish scribe, but by an English monk of Durham Cathedral, that glorious fane which was built to be Cuthbert's shrine.[2] Moreover, the Saint's great window in the Cathedral, before the Puritan Vandals destroyed it, told the same "most godly and fine storye" in gleaming blues and purples and gold, while his painted effigy on the screenwork of the altar of SS. Jerome and Benedict bore the inscription: "Sanctus Cuthbertus, patronus ecclesiae, civitatis, et libertatis

[1] Nec jam orbis contenta sinu trans aequora lampas
Spargitur effulgens, hujusque Britannia consors
Temporibus genuit fulgur venerabile nostris,
Aurea qua Cuthbertus agens per sidera vitam,
Scandere celsa suis docuit jam passibus Anglos.
Liber De Miraculis Sancti Cuthberti Episcopi, ed. Stevenson, in *Venerabilis Bedae Opera Historica,* t. ii, London, 1841, p. 4. Of the Saints mentioned above only Cyprian and Hilary belonged by birth to the places they evangelized.
[2] *Libellus de Nativitate S. Cuthberti,* in *Miscellanea Biographica,* Surtees Society, 1838, pp. 63–87.

Dunelmensis, nacione Hibernicus, regiis parentibus ortus ..." [1]
Loving English hands put the story into the popular, jingling
form of verse called for unknown reasons Leonine,

> Sanctus Cuthbertus Anglorum tutor apertus
> Regis erat natus et Hibernicus generatus,

and another such hand wrote on folio 151 of the imperfect
copy of the poem in the British Museum the touching words:
"Hear wants fyve leaves, for which I wold gev fyve oulde
angells." [2] All this Irish propaganda by Englishmen in the
North evoked a protest from a patriotic poet in the South,
who began his rendering of Bede's Life into Old English
rhymes with the line: "Seint Cudbert was i-bore here in
Engelonde". We take off our hat to the sturdy non-conformist,
but the North stood by its tradition and in the fifteenth century
produced a complete metrical version of the Irish story in the
delightful vernacular of the period. [3] Then the Benedictine,
John of Tynemouth, concluded the process by embodying the
Irish tale lock, stock and barrel in his *Nova Legenda Sanctorum
Angliae,* which, when printed at London in 1526 under the
name of its editor, the Augustinian friar John Capgrave, became at once a principal mine and authority of English hagiographers.

So the matter rested for another century, when a third John,
the learned Father Colgan of Louvain, claimed Cuthbert for
Ireland mainly on the strength of Capgrave's *Vita* which he
incorporated, together with Bede's Life, in his *Acta Sanctorum
Hiberniae.* He suggested that Bede's silence on the subject of

---

[1] *A Description of all the Ancient Monuments, Rites, and Customes
within the Monastical Church of Durham,* 1593, Surtees Society, 1842,
pp. 65, 112.

[2] *Miscellanea Biographica,* Surtees Society, p. xi. The Angel was an
old English gold coin showing St. Michael and the Dragon and worth
8s. 6d. when first issued in 1485, but heaven knows how much in our
own degenerate shillings and pence.

[3] Fowler, *The Life of St. Cuthbert in English Verse,* Surtees Society,
1889, pp. 1–28. There are several other versified lives of the Saint in Old
English, further proof of his extraordinary popularity.

Cuthbert's birth may have been due to fear lest its unhappy circumstances "diminish his cult and veneration among the vulgar herd", or that a later lover of the Saint may have removed the story from Bede's text for the same reason, or that this may have been done by some devout but unscrupulous English patriot "so that Cuthbert might appear to have been born in Northumbria". We might call that last provocative idea negative forgery, but if some ancient admirer of the Saint decided to enhance his renown by indulging in a little positive forgery and inventing for him a royal pedigree, he would scarcely have fathered on his hero the blood-and-thunder monster of the Durham tradition. In the middle of the seventeenth century the two formidable Bollandists, Godfrey Henschen and Daniel Papebroch, entered the lists, with Horace for their trumpeter. They dismissed the story of the Irish king as a tissue of contradictions and anachronisms, said that "of course Bede had refused to patch the illustrious purple of his work with those sorry rags", and quoted the "sick man's dreams" of the *Ars Poetica* as their considered judgement on Capgrave, Colgan and all their company. Colgan had interpreted the much-mangled Gaelic name of the Saint which he found in Capgrave as meaning one that wails or laments. "Let the Irish", say the bold Bollandists, "keep their squalling Nulluhoc (*sic*) and leave the Anglo-Saxons their Cuthbert." [1] Those breezy words have been quoted, as though from Holy Writ, by nearly all modern English students of St. Cuthbert, Protestant as well as Catholic—so infallible, occasionally and at a pinch, are the Jesuits.

Wherever he was born, and St. Paul's *nescio, Deus scit* seems to be the safest answer to that question, one likes to think of Cuthbert's function in life and history as being that of a great reconciler, bringing the two peoples whom he loved closer

---

[1] *Acta Sanctorum,* Martii t. iii, Antwerp, 1668, p. 95. Colgan's volume bears on its title-page the emblem of a winged tortoise, closely resembling a modern tank, and the motto, "Cunctando propero", altogether a most excellent device for historians.

together. A few words from the latest and greatest living authority on things Anglo-Saxon may here be in place: "The Roman victory [at Whitby] did not cause a general departure of Irish clergy from England. Many features of Irish Christianity, such as its asceticism and its insistence on penitential discipline, profoundly affected the later develop-ment of the English Church.... The strands of Irish and continental influence were interwoven in every kingdom, and at every stage of the process by which England became Christian. They can be clearly distinguished in the life of the saint who has always symbolized the northern church of the seventh century. Every historian has been conscious of the Celtic influence behind the career of Cuthbert of Lindis-farne.... In his cultivation of the ascetic life, and in the evangelistic journeys through which he impressed Christianity on the imagination of a barbarous people, Cuthbert belongs to the world of ancient Irish saints. But he was never an uncompromising upholder of Celtic usages." [1]

And now that at last we are in sight of the Lammermuir Hills and the winding Tweed, another sphinx confronts us, propounding the fascinating riddle of St. Cuthbert's miracles. [2]

[1] Stenton, *Anglo-Saxon England,* Clarendon Press, 1943, pp. 124-6. Professor Stenton writes less attractively and picturesquely than either of the two Hodgkins of Anglo-Saxon fame, but one somehow feels safer in his company. Still, it must be said that the modern Bollandists, very much including their Celtic expert Père Paul Grosjean, are decidedly of the same opinion as their forbears, that Cuthbert was a Saxon. The indi-cations to the contrary here stated ought not to be taken too seriously. It is a fact, for instance, that the ancient Irish martyrologies which men-tion him list Cuthbert unequivocally as a Saxon.

[2] He was known as the "Wonder-worker of England". Both the Anonymous Life and St. Bede's prose and verse Lives, as well as his six chapters in the *Ecclesiastical History,* consist very largely of stories of miracles. In addition, for good measure, we have the famous twelfth-century *Libellus de admirandis Beati Cuthberti Virtutibus,* which was compiled by Reginald of Durham largely at the instigation and partly with the help of the "intensely human monk", St. Aelred of Rievaulx (Surtees Society, 1835, pp. xviii–292). By Cuthbert's virtues Reginald meant his miracles, of which he provides 141. Some of these he witnessed

But one of those beasts is enough at a time, so we shall resolutely ignore this second challenger, believing that St. Cuthbert himself would have heartily endorsed the sentiments of St. Anschar, the Apostle of the Danes and Swedes, who rebuked a vaunter of his miracles with the remark: "Were I worthy of such favour from my God, I would ask Him to work me this one miracle, that by His grace He would make me a good man." [1] It is Cuthbert the good man, the "child of God", as Bede so frequently and lovingly calls him, not Cuthbert the wonder-worker, who comes home as sweetly as ever he did to our modern business and bosoms. Whether the bones discovered in 1827 under the place of his mediaeval shrine were really his, as seems probable, or whether according to an old Benedictine tradition, which one would be delighted to find authentic, if only for the confusion of all sneering Raines, his sacred body still rests untouched by the centuries in another place, known to three men and the angels,[2] Cuthbert's appeal remains as fresh and compelling as it was on the midnight of 20 March

---

himself and others were witnessed by St. Aelred, "in whose heart the name of Cuthbert always sang". For anything that came under his own eyes, Reginald was an extremely accurate observer, as even the bigoted, monk-despising Raine testifies (*St. Cuthbert,* Durham, 1828, p. 189, note). His stories make splendid reading, whether we believe all of them or not. He tends to be competitive and to pit his beloved Cuthbert against all other saints, English or foreign. It may safely be said that not many of the happenings which he regarded as miraculous would pass the tests of Benedict XIV, or survive the scrutiny of the Congregation of Rites at the present day. But they are grand stories, all the same, and full of instruction.

[1] Migne, *Patrologia Latina,* 118, 1008. Anschar is a most attractive ninth-century saint and closely resembled St. Cuthbert. His life in Migne by his disciple and successor as Archbishop of Hamburg, St. Rembert, is even better done than Bede's Cuthbert, which is saying a great deal.

[2] In his large and handsome *History of St. Cuthbert* (London, 1849), Archbishop Eyre, following Lingard, says all that can be said for the tradition of the removal of the body after 1542 and possibly in the reign of Mary Tudor. His arguments are not very convincing, and Provost Consitt in his more popular, but excellent, Catholic biography published in 1887 rejects them (pp. 226–39). The debate goes on.

in 687, when a monk waved two flaming torches over the darkness of the sea to tell his brethren in Lindisfarne that their Father had at that moment departed *ad Dominum*.

We meet him first in the pages of the Lindisfarne monk and Bede [1] as a child at play, not far apparently from the pleasant place where the modest River Leader marries the lordly Tweed in Berwickshire. The two writers make rather heavy weather of the little fellow's gambols, Bede quoting what was said of the infant Samuel, that "he did not yet know the Lord". However, they take a pride in telling that "he surpassed all of his age in agility and high spirits...whether they were jumping or running or wrestling or exercising their limbs in any other way." For the future dignified, though always dearly human and approachable, Bishop of Lindisfarne, his posture at our first encounter, "pedes ad coelos", is not very pontifical. In fact, he is standing on his head.[2] In a sense, he stood on his head all through life, seeing this world upside down and right side up, with angels managing its traffic rather than policemen. The modern editors of his life, Plummer and Colgrave, tend to think that the angels simply took over from the Irish fairies, but about that there can be two opinions, and Bede who accepted the angels with all his heart was no Irishman. At the age of eight, while larking with the village lads and lasses, Cuthbert was suddenly reprimanded by a small censor of three who bade him desist from tricks unworthy of a holy bishop and priest, and burst into a passion of weeping when he laughed at the odd ad-

[1] Both men have recently been edited in their original Latin, with an excellent translation, by Bertram Colgrave, Reader in English of the University of Durham: *Two Lives of St. Cuthbert,* Cambridge, 1940. An article dealing largely with this valuable book appeared in THE CLERGY REVIEW of June, 1945. A sumptuous translation of the Anonymous Life by Father William Forbes-Leith, S.J., with forty-five delightful illustrations in colour from the Lawson MS., was printed for private circulation at Edinburgh in 1888.

[2] *Vita Anon.,* lib. i, c. 3.

monition. But the words made an impression, and after coaxing away the child's tears, a typically Cuthbertian action, he went home in a thoughtful mood. About that home there clings a beautiful, heaven-lit atmosphere of mystery. No parents awaited him there, but a good unrelated woman named Kenswith who brought him up as her own and whom he loved as his mother.[1]

While still a boy in Kenswith's house, Cuthbert was laid low by an extremely painful swelling of the knee, which no doctor could cure. One day, when servants had carried him out of doors to enjoy the air, he suddenly beheld a white knight riding towards him on a horse of incomparable beauty. This stranger saluted the crippled boy very courteously, dismounted, examined the afflicted knee, and prescribed a poultice of hot flour and milk, which soon healed the trouble. It was an angel, say both biographers, the first of a legion in their story, "and if anyone should think it incredible", adds Bede, "that an angel appeared on horseback, let him read the history of the Maccabees...." But the equestrian messenger of God is not the only interesting and significant character in the incident. There are also the baffled doctors and the servants (*ministri*). Almost to a man, the modern writers who mention Cuthbert say in chorus that he was of humble peasant birth. But Bede never says so, and do peasants usually call in a succession of doctors or employ servants in their cottages? Next, Bede tells the sweet story of how Cuthbert by his "kindly prayer" saved the poor monks who had drifted before a storm so far out to sea on their rafts that "they looked like five tiny birds riding on the waves". After this, we discover with joy our first tangible date in Cuthbert's hazy history, for Bede is as sparing of such useful signposts as a Second Nocturn. One night of summer, on the hills near the River Leader, the Saint, then tending the

[1] This looks suspiciously like the old Irish custom of fosterage! It applied only to children of the well-born who were boarded out with tenants in order to promote tribal unity and harmony. The Brehon Laws regulated the custom in detail.

homely shepherd's trade [1] and praying as was his wont while his companions slept, suddenly beheld "with his mind's eye" the traffic of Jacob's ladder, angels descending and ascending again to Heaven with "a soul of exceeding brightness". At that very moment, as was learnt a few days later, St. Aidan died, lying on the bare earth beside the little wooden church which he had constructed at Bamburgh, and it was 31 August, 651. [2]

The vision splendid did not lead to an immediate renunciation of the world, for some time afterwards Cuthbert is jogging along on horseback far from home, over the Roman road near Chester-le-Street in Durham. It was a wild Friday in winter, and he was wet and weary and exceedingly hungry. He turned aside as night approached to shelter in one of the abandoned shepherds' huts or shielings which were the only refuge in that desolate country, and the first thing he did before he fell to his prayers was to gather a bundle of straw from the dilapidated roof for his horse. Some of the thatch still remained in position, and the ravenous beast while nibbling at this pulled out a little linen bundle containing a fresh loaf and a portion of meat. The starving Cuthbert broke off his rosary of psalms at the good sight and burst into a prayer of gratitude. " 'Thanks be to God,' he said, 'who has deigned to provide a supper for me who am fasting out of love for Him, and also for my comrade.' So he divided the loaf which he found and gave half of it to the horse, and the rest he kept for his own sustenance." A similar story to this is told of him years later when, as a monk, he was "going along the River

[1] Nothing in that to prove him of peasant origin, as many of the best people in Ireland used to tend sheep in their youth. It was provided for by the laws of fosterage.

[2] Bede, *Ecclesiastical History,* iii, 14. In his *Life of St. Cuthbert* the same Bede says that the news reached the shepherds the following morning, but the Lindisfarne monk, who had better sources of information, writes "post paucos dies", a more likely reckoning in any case, as Bamburgh was a good fifty miles from the Leader. The two men also differ about the nature of the vision, the Lindisfarne monk describing it as subjective and Bede, surely off his own bat, giving it an objective character.

Teviot ... teaching the country people among the mountains
and baptizing them." He and the boy accompanying him had
had nothing to eat for some time and were both very hungry,
without any prospect of satisfying their pangs. "Cheer up, my
son," said Cuthbert. "You see that eagle flying in the distance.
It would be easy for God to give us a meal by its ministrations."
And sure enough, a little later, the eagle landed a large fish,
probably a salmon, from the Teviot, which the boy seized
and carried back in triumph to his dear master. "But why",
said Cuthbert, "did you not give our fisherman a part of it
to eat since he was fasting?" So the fish was there and then
cut in two and half returned to the good bird that had provided it.[1] Those are exquisite stories, however interpreted, and
to hide a loaf in the thatch of a hut would certainly not have
been unlike Him who hid the tribute money in the mouth of
a fish and His own divine self in the womb of a maiden. We
have to wait until St. Godric appears in the twelfth century
to meet another saint who had so much sympathy with the
birds and beasts and all wild sentient things of nature.[2] Cuthbert's horse and eagle, his dolphins and ravens and famous
ducks, which loving hands embroidered on the silk robes they
put round his dead body a thousand years ago, are as well worth
knowing as the swan of St. Hugh or the falcon of St. Francis.

When the Saint became a monk of Old Melrose, as most
writers think at about the age of seventeen,[3] he did it in grand
style, riding up to the monastery with spear in hand, and

---

[1] *Vita Anon.*, i, 6; ii, 5. Bede, *Vita*, v, xii.

[2] While being grateful to Mr. Colgrave for his good editing of the
Lives, we may justifiably resent and repudiate his constant insinuations
that because similar stories are told of the Desert Fathers and the ancient
Irish saints, they were invented to accord with a tradition in Cuthbert's
case. What an argument! Because George Washington chopped a tree
with his little axe in carefree youth, the similar exploits of Mr. Glad-
stone in hale old age must be regarded with deepest suspicion by the
historian!

[3] May one mention with one's head in the dust that seventeen was the
age at which, according to the Brehon Laws, the period of fosterage for
boys came to an end?

possibly a squire at his horse's heels. He seems to have been
to the wars beforehand, those wars which fierce old pagan
Penda brought to Northumbria, and his trappings on the
present occasion hardly support the confident theory of his
peasant birth, for only thanes and nobles rode horses when
England was young. Under the gentle abbot, St. Eata, Aidan's
old scholar, and the prior, St. Boswell, who gave his name
to a little town still flourishing near Melrose, Cuthbert revelled
in vigils, fasting, hard manual toil, and service of his neighbour
for thirteen years. It was a life so wholly supernatural, so completely surrendered, so gloriously established in the love of
God and man, that the coming and going of angels, almost
as members of the community, need cause little surprise. They
felt at home in paradise regained. Once, on a snowy winter
morning, when Cuthbert was guest-master at Ripon, a young
man appeared at the monastery, seeking hospitality: "He
welcomed him at once with his usual kindness, gave him
water to wash his hands, and himself washed and dried his
feet, gathering them to his bosom so that he might chafe and
warm them on account of the cold." [1] That it was an angel in
disguise who left no footprints on the snow is not the im-
portant point of this sweet story. Cuthbert himself is angel
enough for anybody, an angel in looks, says the Lindisfarne
monk who knew him, and an angel in deeds.

In 664, just after the Synod of Whitby, the plague struck
Melrose and nearly carried him off, but the prayers of the
monks who loved him and spent the whole night on their
knees praying for his deliverance availed, and St. Boswell was
taken instead. How Cuthbert and he studied the Gospel of
St. John together during the last week of the holy Prior's life
and finished it in time, "because they dealt only with the
simple things of the faith which worketh by love", is a death-
bed story hardly less beautiful than Bede's account of Cuthbert's
own end and another man's account of Bede's. But they have
to be read as they were written, for to curtail them would be a

[1] *Vita Anon.,* ii, 2; Bede, *Vita,* vii.

desecration. Then began the twenty years' epic of Cuthbert's
rural apostolate. He would go out, usually on foot but sometimes on horseback, and be away from the monastery for weeks
together, penetrating into the wildest valleys and breasting the
steepest hills in order to find access to forlorn hamlets which
other teachers had not the courage or love to approach. So winning was his way, so "angelic the light of his smile", that none
could resist him or keep from him the secret of his sins. What
his life was like behind the scenes we know by the favour of
an inquisitive monk of Coldingham who followed him to the
sea-shore one night and watched him with awe enter the icy
waves up to his armpits. In that position "he spent the dark
hours, keeping vigil and singing God's praises to the sound
of the waves". When he was appointed prior of Lindisfarne at
the very difficult time after the departure of St. Colman, Cuthbert made no change in his missionary habits but lavished on
the poor half-heathen people of Northumberland and Durham
the same boundless charities that had transfigured the lands of
Teviot and Tweed and woven his name into the very geography
of Galloway, where the town and shire of Kirkcudbright,
Cuthbert's church, are his memorials. In his island monastery
he achieved by his sweetness and smiling determination a
notable victory. He defeated the Irish moon and prevailed
upon his reluctant brethren to accept the Roman Easter.

But though so great a rover, he hungered all the time for
solitude the completest, to be alone with the Alone, and
attained at last his rocky islet paradise of Farne "in the mayne
Ocean sea". As Chesterton wrote of the Saint's warm lover
and client in after times, King Alfred, there was "always something about him indescribably humble and handy", so that
he could build a wall, manage a boat, till a field or cook a
dinner like an expert. On Farne he built round his little
hermitage a rampart so high "that he could see nothing else out
of it but heaven, which he thirsted and longed to enter". He
built too, though, and this was typical, a house for the visitors
from all parts who constantly disturbed his peace, "taking it

to be another kind of prayer", says Bede, "if he could help the weaker brethren with his exhortations." [1] It is not difficult to picture him there praying among the seagulls or expostulating with the sparrows for stealing his hard-earned crop of barley or pardoning the penitent ravens after they had plundered straw for their nest from the thatched roof of his guest-house. Constrained to be a bishop, he "continued to be the same man that he was before ... of a happy disposition and very friendly ... always cheerful and joyful ... meek and lowly of heart." [2] His episcopal visitations were, like his miracles, all acts of everlasting love unfeigned. A recurrence of the plague saw him daily in the hovels of the poor, ministering to the stricken with such tenderness as they had never guessed this sad world to contain. Once, when a weeping mother brought him her dying child in her arms, he bade her, in the very accents of our Lord, to have no fear, and restored the little boy with a kiss. He often wept himself, for Bede tells us that every time he said Mass it was "with tears poured out from the bottom of his heart". Worn out prematurely by his labours and austerities, he returned to the sweet solitude of Farne to make ready for the last and most desired of his angels, the Angel of Death, and went off happily in his company, "in the very act of praising God", on the night of 20 March, 687, as before mentioned. He is a saint worth knowing, if ever there was one, whose whole existence might be described in a single phrase as the incarnation of the *Benedicite*.

[1] *Ecclesiastical History*, iv, 28.
[2] *Vita Anon.*, iv, i, iii, 7; Bede, *Vita*, xix.

Archbishop of Canterbury

THOUGH in other respects a most courteous and companionable saint, Anselm of Aosta, born to wealth and station under the shadow of the Alps in the year of the Dark Ages 1033, is not too obliging when humbly begged to enter with all his glory a little house of words made of about four thousand half-baked bricks. But then he was not the first to be invited to this modest April bungalow. One has *some* regard for the property of theologians, philosophers, scholars and historians who claim Anselm for their own and resent the trespass of the vulgar herd. Another April saint, Richard of Chichester, English to the bone, who never wrote a thing, seemed a more easily accommodated quest, and he was pursued, even unto headache and exasperation, through the wilds of mediaeval Worcestershire and the schools of Oxford, Paris and Bologna, through the teeming pages of Matthew Paris, the sarcastic O.S.B., and a great tome of the Bollandists, those all-embracing S.J.'s. But Richard eluded capture; he would not materialize; and this was the sadder because the glimpses caught of him ploughing the neglected fields near Droitwich or shivering over his book in an Oxford attic or countering with much courtesy the wiles of a Bolognese Portia or arguing with his shocked almoner in defence of the undeserving poor, were so uncommonly appealing. The blame for his non-appearance rests, one deeply regrets to say, with his dear friend and so-called biographer, Ralph Bocking, that date-despising, rhapsodizing O.P. Friar Ralph's style may be estimated from his excursus on the symbolism of salt, which is the pride of Droitwich, or from his descant on the Saint's name Latinized, wherein he found to his delight elements of the three pleasant words, *ridens, carus* and *dulcis,* a piece of etymology that dumbfounded even the Bollandists, with all their experience of biographers gambolling in the brightest heavens of invention. But, to do him justice, Ralph was probably not much to blame, for his dear, sweet, smiling Richard obviously possessed and practiced the most wonderful gift for lying hid.

St. Anselm, too, in his day two hundred years earlier, had pined for the shadows, but without a hope in the world of being granted them. Genius, like murder, will out, and he was a very great genius, one whose name figures beside that of St. John Chrysostom in Dante's Fourth Heaven of the Sun, whose deeds and sufferings are a part of English history, whose Ontological Argument has teased philosophers for close on nine centuries, whose *Cur Deus Homo* is the most thought-provoking treatise on the Incarnation ever written, whose speculations on Grace and Free Will anticipated by half a millenium the famous theological battle-fronts of Bañes and Molina. It has been said of him that he was "a dialectician even in his prayers", but it would be far truer to say that he was a man of prayer even in his dialectics, and that is why we mere proselytes of the gate think ourselves entitled to do a little eavesdropping while he discourses with the philosophers and theologians. The history of Anselm's "Prayers" is a fascinating subject in itself. Take, for instance, the beautiful tender prayers, one to each day of the week, which the Church in Missal and Breviary invites her priests to say before Mass. They are all given under the confident caption, "Oratio S. Ambrosii Episcopi", but Ambrose, the staid, dry Roman, could not, for all his greatness, have written anything so sweetly expansive. It needed a barbarian to do it, a child of the Goths or Burgundians, and the Middle Ages with one accord voted for St. Anselm. Among the works of Anselm, as edited by the seventeenth-century Maurist, Dom Gabriel Gerberon, and taken over by J. P. Migne (*P.L.*, 158, 921 seq.), the prayers are still to be found. Gerberon relied for his text on the work of the prolific Jesuit, Théophile Raynaud, who was the first to bring all the prayers and meditations attributed to St. Anselm together in one volume. But the most famous of the Maurists, Mabillon, differed from his brother in St. Benedict, Gerberon, and gave good reasons for his conviction that the so-called

"Oratio S. Ambrosii", anonymous in the codex of its origin, came from the devout heart of an obscure monk contemporary with Anselm, named from his lack of inches Joannelinus, or Little John. In our time, the formidable Dom Wilmart of Farnborough has vindicated Little John's authorship beyond further argument, and in the process castigated the unfortunates Raynaud and Gerberon mercilessly. They were, it seems, editors of quite exceptional turpitude.[1]

All that, it may be said, is a highly negative way of doing honour to St. Anselm in his month of April, and the writer who found motes in the kind eyes of Friar Bocking is displaying great baulks of timber in his own. Too true, so here without further ado are some positive Anselmian facts to refresh the memory. He was born, as already stated, in 1033, a bad time in the Church's history. His mother, Ermenberga, is supposed to have been related to the ducal House of Burgundy, largely a dynasty of urbane brigands, but with saints interspersed. His father, Gundulf, a wealthy and worldly Lombard, is given a

---

[1] Mabillon's arguments are given in Migne, *P.L.*, 147, 449 seq. Anselm, he suggested, loved the prayers of Joannelinus so well and used them so much that they came to be attributed to his own pen. Joannelinus, a native of Ravenna who specialized in medicine, became Abbot of Fécamp five years before Anselm was born and died full of years in 1079. Besides many learned articles on the problem contributed to the *Revue Bénédictine,* Dom Wilmart wrote an introduction of sixty-two lively pages for a French translation of the *Meditations and Prayers of St. Anselm,* published at Paris in 1923. This fine analysis of the whole complicated story is made amusingly human by many biting epithets directed to the address of Raynaud and Gerberon, both of them dead for well over two hundred years. It is good to know that the Prayers before Mass, so glowing with love and reverence for Our Lord in the Blessed Sacrament, were written at the very moment when the upstart Berengarius of Tours first denied the Real Presence. Shall we ever be given a Breviary with the Prayers sailing under their right colours: "Oratio Joannelini Abbatis"? For anyone who may care to know, the authentic Meditations of Anselm, according to Dom Wilmart, are those numbered in Migne 2, 3 and 11, and the authentic Prayers are the following nineteen, 9, 20, 23-4, 34, 41, 50-2, 63-5, 67-9, 71-2, 74-5. Not a single one of the sixteen Homilies in Migne is authentic.

peerage and a palace at Aosta by many writers, though not by
the only writer who knew.[1] In his childhood, Anselm used
to imagine from his mother's account of it that Heaven stood
perched on top of the snow-clad mountains which enclose
Aosta, and once in a dream he scaled them and was most
courteously entertained at table by God, the Great King (Rule's
Eadmer, p. 315). The story seems almost like a parable of
his earthly existence which consisted so much of mountaineer-
ing in the high altitudes of the human spirit, invariably with
God for company. The passion for study and speculation which
characterized him even to the hour of his death [2] was early in
evidence, without detracting at all from his boyish charm.
"Crevit ergo puer et ab omnibus diligebatur." Delivered over
at his earnest petition to an enthusiastic but unwise tutor, he
attempted such violent irruptions into the kingdom of knowl-

[1] He, of course, was Eadmer, a monk of Christchurch, Canterbury,
who became the intimate friend and biographer of Anselm. Anselm was
happier than most saints in this biographer, a sensible Saxon who kept
his eyes open and asked plenty of questions. In late life he was deservedly
elected Archbishop of St. Andrews, but prevented by political reasons
from taking possession of his see. Besides his *De Vita et Conversatione
Anselmi,* he wrote also as background a most precious history of the
Saint's time entitled, *Historia Novorum in Anglia.* These are given in
Migne, *P.L.,* tomes 158 and 159, together with Anselm's works, authentic
and spurious. Martin Rule, the author of a very good and solid though
rather long-winded English life of the Saint in two volumes (London,
1883), edited the Latin text of both Eadmer's works for the Rolls Series
in 1884. To this we shall refer as "Rule's *Eadmer*". Another contemporary Benedictine monk, William of Malmesbury, gives a briefer sketch
of Anselm's career in his *De Gestis Pontificum Anglorum* (Rolls Series,
1870).

[2] "When Palm Sunday dawned [A.D. 1109], we were sitting around
his bed as usual. One of our number said to him: 'Father and Lord, as
far as it is given us to know, you are leaving this world and going to
keep the Easter Court with your Lord.' He replied: 'If it is His will I
shall gladly obey, but if He should prefer me to stay with you just long
enough to solve the question of the origin of the soul which I have been
turning over in my mind, I would gratefully accept the chance, for I
do not know whether anybody else will solve it when I am gone'"
(Rule's *Eadmer,* p. 416).

edge that he damaged his young head and nearly lost his senses.[1] It was a happy calamity for other boys, as it turned him into one of the most sympathetic and judicious school-masters of the Christian centuries. Once, an abbot complained to him bitterly about the conduct of the boys at his monastery: "Though we never stop thrashing and restraining them day and night, they only get worse." Anselm looked at him in astonishment. "Tell me, Lord Abbot," said he, "if you planted a sapling in your garden and then walled it all round in such a way that its branches had no chance to expand, what sort of a tree would it be when after years you released it from its confinement?" The abbot answered innocently that it would be a worthless, stunted tree. "Precisely," said Anselm, "and who but you would be to blame? This is exactly what you are doing with your boys. They were planted in the garden of the Church to increase and fructify unto God, but you and your monks so hedge them about with terrors, threats and blows that they have no scope whatever to exercise their liberty.... For the love of God, will you tell me why you are so hostile to them? Are they not human and of the same nature as yourselves? Would you like others to treat you as you treat your boys?" The abbot protested that the only purpose of their severity was to form the rascals to grave and mature behaviour. "Just so," replied Anselm, "bread and other solid foods are fine for the stomach that can manage them, but try them out on an infant at the breast and you will see the little thing strangled rather than strengthened.... Weak souls, as yet young in the service of God, need their own food, just as much as weak bodies, and that food is the milk of others' meekness, kindness, mercy, cheerful encouragement, and loving support." On hearing these words, the good abbot wept and

---

[1] "Pene in amentiam versus est." This interesting detail is from a manuscript in the Vatican Library which belonged to Queen Christina of Sweden. Rule cites it in his *Eadmer,* p. cxix, and thinks it affords corroborative evidence that Anselm's parents were of princely rank—very thin evidence, it must be said.

fell at Anselm's feet, begging absolution for the pedagogical sins of himself and his brethren, which he promised faithfully to amend.[1]

There were Benedictines at Aosta in Anselm's youth,[2] and to their way of life he felt himself irresistibly attracted, though not at first apparently for the highest spiritual reasons. What he hankered after was the freedom of the monastic library. Before he had reached his fifteenth birthday he applied for admission behind his father's back, and on being refused prayed to God for an illness that might soften the abbot's heart. But that cautious man remained obdurate, even when the applicant reported himself to be in danger of death, for the anger of such people as Gundulf was not a thing to be lightly provoked. By a natural revulsion Anselm then took to the primrose path, the only restraint on his dalliance being the love he bore to his holy and unhappy mother. When she died, he seemed, as he said, "to have lost the anchor of his heart", and might have gone to the devil altogether but for the attitude of his extravagant and overbearing father who, possibly because of his pathetic attempt to become a monk, had grown to hate him. So tyrannically was he treated that he determined in his early twenties to run away and seek in a strange land the peace denied him at home. With a single faithful retainer for company and a donkey to carry his few

---

[1] Rule's *Eadmer,* pp. 339-41. John Richard Green, who loved Anselm and described him as "a tender-hearted poet-dreamer, with a soul pure as the Alpine snows above him and an intelligence keen and clear as the mountain air", gives a *résumé* of the passage translated above in his *Short History of the English People* (Chap. II, sec. iii). Even the prejudiced Freeman fell to the charm of this foreigner of pronounced Papistical convictions and declared him to be "the very embodiment of righteousness and mercy" (*History of the Norman Conquest,* vol. iv, p. 444).

[2] The vicar-general of the diocese in those days was the compassionate Bernard of Menthon, Apostle of the Alps, who founded the famous hospices for travellers in the passes now bearing his name. He was declared patron saint of all mountaineers by Pope Pius XI in 1923. As the Benedictines prefer lower altitudes and reasonable temperatures, Bernard put his hospice in charge of the Augustinian canons.

effects, he set out over the snows of Mont Cenis to find his happiness, relinquishing unregretted the wealth and position to which he had been born.

The happiness Anselm yearned for was that of understanding the causes of things, the happiness of a philosophy leaning on Heaven. For nearly three years he eagerly frequented the schools of Burgundy and France, a wandering embodiment of his own famous phrase, *fides quaerens intellectum,* faith in search of understanding. But he sought in vain, and, wearied of dusty answers, at length trudged into Normandy where rumour told of better prospects for learning at Avranches on the sea, so celebrated again for such different reasons in our own mad times, and at mysterious Le Bec, a monastery still building in a little secluded valley without a name, about thirty miles south-west of Rouen. Thither before Anselm was born another such a seeker as himself, and like him, or half of him, a Lombard, had made the same long pilgrimage, the Lanfranc of Pavia who is so much mixed up with 1066 and All That, and whom an old writer described as "the splendid eye of the world" (Migne, *P.L.,* 150, 9). How this famous and saintly man of letters discovered the man of arms turned monk, Herluin, Lord of Brionne, after a terrible night pinioned and blindfolded in the Forest of Ouche, with the wolves howling all around, is memorable even among the finest stories of the Middle Ages.[1] Lanfranc tried to hide at Bec, but his genius could not be kept under and soon transformed the humble wattle and daub monastery into one of the most illustrious schools of Christendom.[2]

[1] Migne, *P.L.,* 150, gives the details, together with Lanfranc's works and an interesting biography of Herluin, whom the author, Anselm's friend, Gilbert Crispin, Abbot of Westminster, calls Saint Herluin. But the founder of Bec, though an exceedingly holy man, was never formally or informally canonized. It is curious that neither he nor Lanfranc should have any real right even to the title of Blessed when that most tempestuous of all Archbishops of Canterbury, Boniface of Savoy, enjoys it.

[2] Bec attracted pupils of the brilliant but showy and conceited Berengarius from Tours. According to the contemporary Guitmund, Arch-

Lanfranc did not take long to discover the worth of his new pupil from across the Alps, and became to him "a friend in a thousand". But Anselm hesitated to commit himself to Bec completely for the endearing reason that he wanted to shine somewhere by his own light and not be merely a pale reflexion of the splendid eye of the world. "How untamed I was in those days!" he used to say long afterwards as an old man to his confidant, Eadmer. He gave Cluny a thought, meditated plunging into the desert altogether as a hermit, and even wondered whether he should not return to Aosta, now that his father was dead, and spend his inheritance in charity. But he could do that wherever he was and the grace of God did the rest. It was in 1060 that he burned his boats, at the age of twenty-seven. Thereafter for thirty-three years Bec was his universe, his purgatory and his paradise. During fifteen of those years he held the office of prior, and then, after Herluin's death in 1078, ruled for another fifteen as abbot. Constantly in his pages Eadmer as it were throws up his hands in despair of being able to do justice to the unearthly beauty of the life which he led all that time, a very angel's life, only that angels feel no pangs of hunger or cold or utter physical exhaustion in their worship of God. We are given glimpses of Prior Anselm wrestling with the embittered, jealous soul of the young monk Osbern who hated him for his very goodness; of Anselm nursing this Osbern, become his dearest friend, day and night during his last illness; and of the desolate Prior weeping his eyes out with sorrow when Osbern dies. Or another time we watch him by the bed of an old paralysed monk named Herewald. "You, Herewald," cries Eadmer suddenly, "know the truth of what I say about his never-ending

bishop of Aversa, it was chagrin at the loss of his men and jealousy of Lanfranc which led the unhappy Archdeacon to deny the Real Presence. If he could not outshine Lanfranc as an orthodox theologian, he would at least make the Catholic world take notice of him as a heterodox one (Mann, *The Lives of the Popes in the Middle Ages,* Vol. VI, pp. 92-4; Migne, *P.L.,* 149, 1428). Both Lanfranc and Guitmund wrote against the new heresy.

charities. You could tell how he nursed you back to health, crushing grapes between his hands so that you might drink the juice from his hollowed palm, when, as you informed me, you could by no other means be refreshed." The Prior haunted the infirmary, ever inventing new ways of alleviating the pain or lassitude of his ailing brethren. "Sicque sanis pater et infirmis erat mater, immo sanis et infirmis pater et mater in commune" (Rule's *Eadmer*, p. 328). That is exactly what he was, a father and mother in one, and that is how he loved to think of God. In one of the many beautiful authentic prayers which he composed at this time for the comfort of friends, he thus addresses Our Lord: "And Thou, Jesus, dear Lord, art Thou not a mother too? ... Indeed Thou art, and the mother of all mothers, who didst taste death in Thy longing to bring forth children unto life.... O Christ, our Mother, see how Thy dead child takes refuge under Thy wings to be cherished out of his fear by Thy loving indulgence and won from his despair by the odour of Thy sweetness.... O Mother, recognize Thy dead child by the sign of Thy Cross which he makes or the voice of his confession. Bring him to life again and justify Thy sinner. Comfort Thy affrighted little one who despairs of himself and looks for his strength to Thee" (Migne, *P.L.*, 158, 981–3).

Some may perhaps detect a streak of sentimentality in such writing, and no doubt Anselm was given to wearing his heart on his sleeve, but the chief characteristic of his spiritual life, marked even in the few lines quoted and dominant in the tenderest and most lyrical of his prayers addressed to the Mother of God, was his piercing sense and horror of sin. So this kindliest of men who put himself at the beck and call of others from morning to night, and often through the night, who wept for the danger of a hunted hare and prayed to God for the liberty of a captive bird,[1] regarded himself first

---

[1] Rule's *Eadmer*, pp. 378-9. Those incidents happened in England and were witnessed by Eadmer, who tells of them delightfully. A boy held a

and foremost as a penitent and practised all his life as a monk
the most rigorous austerities. Sentimentality is mawkish because
it is only a surface emotion, but Anselm's love of God and
man was strong as death and struck down to Hell and up to
Heaven. He is perfectly charming in his letters to his innumerable friends and even mingles tears with the ink when he
writes to one of them (Migne, *P.L.*, 158, 1145), but quite a
different Anselm appears in his dealings with the gay monk
Henry, his procurator in England, who liked a good dinner
and unfortunately was in the habit of getting drunk (Migne,
P.L., 158, 1154-5). On one occasion, the Saint astonished our
excellent Eadmer by telling him that if Hell yawned at his
feet he would gladly jump into it rather than offend God.
"Nihil enim in mundo quantum peccare timebat" (Rule's
Eadmer, p. 374).

It was during the busy crowded years of his rule, when Bec,
for all its seclusion, had become the cynosure of the Western
World and the most hospitable house in Christendom,[1] that
Anselm penned, often at dead of night, the great speculative
works which earned for him the title of "Father of Scho-
lasticism", and the respectful attention of such highly unscho-
lastic metaphysicians as Descartes, Leibniz, Kant and Hegel.
But he was a scholastic with an enormous difference, a philosopher who let cheerfulness constantly break in, and a theologian
so humble and human that his syllogism might at any moment

---

small bird captive by means of a piece of string tied round its leg. This
he would jerk when the bird attempted to fly and then gloat over its
helplessness. Anselm came upon the scene: "Quod Pater aspiciens miserae
avi condoluit, ac ut rupto filo libertati redderetur optavit. Et ecce filum
rumpitur, avis avolat, puer plorat, Pater exsultat." The hare story is too
well known to be repeated, and anyhow there is no room.

[1] Eadmer is at a loss for words to describe Anselm's boundless hospitality but found one good formula: "Se in omni hilaritate, sua in omni
largitate"—that was how he treated his guests high and low, giving himself to them with all cheerfulness and his goods with all generosity
(Rule's *Eadmer,* p. 347).

collapse into a prayer. *Anxie doctus* is the good phrase borrowed from Macrobius which William of Malmesbury applies to him, a man solicitously learned in the sense that his learning was only another facet of his immense charity, questing all the time for means to lighten our common Christian burden of belief. But we must here emulate in a white sheet the same William of Malmesbury who also finding himself behindhand and short of space skipped without a blush from the consecration of Anselm as Abbot of Bec to his consecration as Archbishop of Canterbury.[1]

Anselm as Archbishop is one of the grandest and most heroic figures in the whole of English history. With the deepest misgivings and many a long lingering look behind to the lost paradise of Bec, he consented for the sake of the suffering Church and people of England to be enthroned at Canterbury in September 1093, six months after the famous scene by the sick-bed of the terrible Rufus in Gloucester, when the crozier had been violently thrust into his clenched fingers and himself dragged by main force to the nearest church for a ceremony of thanksgiving which sounded in his appalled ears like the very knell of doom. And indeed that day his peace for thirteen tumultuous years was doomed. In an effort to deter his brother bishops who were entirely under the Red King's thumb, he had protested that they were endeavouring to yoke a poor old sheep, meaning himself, with a ferocious bull. But the poor old sheep become shepherd and guardian of the nation's liberties, temporal as well as spiritual, underwent a third transformation into a proper British lion, a match for the bull any day, despite all that miscreant's loud oaths by the Holy Face of Lucca. The conflict between the gentle scholarly Saint and the blaspheming Tyrant, "a foul incarnation of selfishness in its most abhorrent form, the enemy of God and man,"[2] makes a tremendous story, but all that need be recalled

---

[1] *Gesta Pontificum Anglorum,* ed. Hamilton, in the Rolls Series, p. 77.
[2] So the judicious Stubbs in his *Constitutional History,* i, 302.

of it here is that when Rufus met sudden and unprovided death in the New Forest, probably the only eyes on earth which shed a tear for him were exiled Anselm's (Rule's *Eadmer,* p. 405). It was during his wanderings abroad at this time in search of help from the Holy See that he completed on top of a Campanian mountain the little epoch-making masterpiece in dialogue form, *Cur Deus Homo,* a book destined to keep theologians talking until the end of the world. Specially invited by his good friend Pope Urban II, he attended the Council of Bari in 1098, one of 180 bishops, and covered himself with glory among them, as Eadmer who sat at his feet on the occasion is proud to record. The Saint's small dogmatic treatise, *De Processione Spiritus Sancti contra Graecos,* resulted from this adventure, but dearer to remembrance is the fact that the Red King would have been excommunicated by the Council had not Anselm gone down on his knees and implored the Pope and bishops to withhold their thunderbolt (Rule's *Eadmer,* pp. 104-7).

The six years of conflict with Rufus were followed by seven of even more painful strife with his less violent but equally totalitarian brother, Henry I, from all of which Anselm emerged a scarred and exhausted warrior, still clasping and holding high, untattered and untarnished, the banner of the Church's freedom. He stood for freedom of the body as well as of the soul, and, a pioneer in this as in so many other respects, explicitly condemned and prohibited "the nefarious traffic of slavery, hitherto prevalent in England," at the national synod convened and presided over by him at Westminster in 1102 (Rule's *Eadmer,* p. 143; William of Malmesbury, *Gesta,* p. 120). He died with sackcloth and ashes spread under his wasted body on 21 April, 1109, "just as the dawn was breaking". Nine years later St. Thomas Becket was born. If we would seek for the sources of that giant's strength, we might find a clue by watching him on his throne at Canterbury during the singing of the capitular Mass, absorbed—and may apostles of the liturgy forgive the reference—not in his Missal or Pontifical, but in the genuine *Orationes Sancti Anselmi*.[1]

[1] So Herbert of Bosham, St. Thomas's secretary and biographer (Robertson, *Materials for the History of Thomas Becket,* Rolls Series, 1877, vol. iii, p. 210). In his attractive life of Anselm published in 1873, Dean Church makes the surprising statement that he "suffered the indignity of a canonization at the hands of Borgia". There would have been no indignity about it, but in fact Anselm was never formally canonized at all. He did not need to be, as the devotion of the faithful had seen to it almost from the day he died. He was formally declared a Doctor of the Church by Pope Clement XI in 1720. No saint is more alive and dateless. Reading him, we can imagine ourselves lying in the infirmary at Bec, watching the sweet face lined with thought and suffering which used to bring tenderness into the eyes of the stern old Conqueror, or listening to the voice of infinite sympathy, telling how good a place Heaven is and how friendly God wants to be even with the blackest of sinners.

Hermit

MAY is a month embarrassingly rich in well-documented English saints. On the 7th occurs the feast of the very attractive John of Beverley, who ordained St. Bede, and whose genial kindness to the young and the afflicted is immortalized in Bede's *Ecclesiastical History*. The 19th is the day of the splendid Dunstan, "the first prime minister of England, great alike as statesman, reformer and saint", who if he did not tweak the devil's nose with a material red-hot tongs, as the Middle Ages loved to think, certainly put it badly out of joint by strictly spiritual means.[1] Dunstan at school with the Irish monks of Glastonbury, or playing anthems on his harp and being taught new ones by the angels, or driving his procurator wild during their journey to Rome by his inveterate habit of distributing everything he possessed to the poor,[2] or

[1] Dr. Armitage Robinson considered that the tongs story, unheard of until a century after the Saint's death, had been "the ruin of Dunstan's reputation", for it tended to make people forget that he was "one of the makers of England" (*The Times of St. Dunstan*, Oxford, 1923, p. 81). The story occurs for the first time in the life of Dunstan, who died in 988, by Osbern, a monk, musician and scholar of Canterbury during the pontificate of Lanfranc who died in 1089. The Devil, it will be remembered, poked his head in at the window one evening while Dunstan was engaged in his favourite hobby of working metals, and, like the fool he is, made some remarks which enabled the Saint to identify him. Thereupon, Dunstan, "sancto actus furore", whipped the glowing tongs out of the fire, seized the Devil with them, and by main force dragged him into his cell. After a brief struggle the Devil managed to break loose, and rushed through Glastonbury, for it was there it happened, bellowing in the most frightful fashion, "O what has that bald-head done to me! O what has that bald-head done to me!" For, says Osbern, Dunstan "had few hairs but they were beautiful" (Stubbs, *Memorials of St. Dunstan*, Rolls Series, 1874, pp. 84–5. Of the story Bishop Stubbs writes: "One can hardly doubt that it had some foundation. . . . It seems not unlikely that Dunstan may have taken someone by the nose, and that the identification was an afterthought." The *Memorials* include five biographies, one by a contemporary of the Saint who knew him personally).

[2] "He said to his procurator: 'What are you going to give us for supper tonight?' That worthy replied in a fume: 'Nothing, absolutely nothing,

singing Mass so devoutly that he "seemed to be talking to Our Lord face to face", or, as Archbishop of Canterbury, guiding the destinies of England with one hand and comforting the sorrow, suffering and perplexity of all comers with the other, or telling the Canterbury schoolboys stories round the fire in his old age—"Sweet Father Dunstan" is endlessly enticing, and far too great a man to be subjected to the Procrustean indignities of these pages.

Another skilled musician and counsellor of kings was St. Aldhelm, Abbot of Malmesbury and Bishop of Sherborne, who died in 709 and is commemorated on 25 May. He, too, received his early education under Irish auspices, and he was the first Englishman to attain celebrity as a scholar both at home and abroad. Bede speaks of him as "undecunque doctissimus". Himself of semi-royal birth, he dearly loved the poor country folk of Wessex, and composed songs, hymns and ballads for their instruction and entertainment, which were afterwards great favourites of King Alfred. Alas, they have perished,[1] but there

---

since you won't keep anything for your own use.' The Bishop said to him: 'Now please don't be too troubled on that account, as Christ Our Lord is rich and generous to those who believe in Him.' Then he rose as it was evening and retired some distance to say Vespers. But the said procurator continued to mutter foolishly: 'That's right; go and adore your Christ as if nothing else mattered, never giving a thought to our predicament.' Before he had finished Vespers, there came a certain venerable abbot, bringing with him all the delicacies of those parts, upon which the Bishop and his train fared splendidly for many days, thus stopping the grumbling of that saucy procurator" (*Vita, auctore "B,"* that is, the unidentified writer who knew Dunstan personally, in Stubbs, *Memorials,* p. 39).

[1] His other works, of which the most influential was the *De Laudibus Virginitatis,* written in both prose and verse for the nuns of Barking, are given in Migne, *P.L.,* t. 89. Unfortunately, though a sweet, unassuming and lovable man, Aldhelm picked up from his Irish teacher, Maildubh, at Malmesbury, and from his Italian professor, Adrian of Monte Cassino, at Canterbury, a most extravagant Latin style, a kind of *stribiligo* or secret jargon, made popular by the extraordinary seventh-century Gaulish humbug calling himself Virgilius Maro Grammaticus. But Aldhelm knew the genuine Virgilius Maro also and quotes him. Among the men of his time whom he greatly influenced was St. Boniface, the Devonian Apostle

remains as his monument, in despite of the devouring centuries, the little Saxon church dedicated to St. Lawrence, unique now in Europe, which he built at Bradford-on-Avon in Wiltshire.[1] Next, in the bright firmament of May rises the Sirius of the Saxon stars, "l'ardente spiro di Beda". The fact that St. Bede is the only Englishman to be honoured with a place in Dante's *Paradiso* is significant. Dante obviously knew little and cared less about England and her history, but he could not ignore Bede, the "disciple of Rome inspired by the intellectual passion of Ireland",[2] for the simple reason that Bede, in a true and deep sense, was so largely the creator of the Poet's own

---

of Germany. Hodgkin, in his *History of the Anglo-Saxons,* Oxford, 1939, devotes several sympathetic pages to our Aldhelm, and so does Stenton in his *Anglo-Saxon England,* Oxford, 1943, but not so understandingly.

[1] In his time, and he died more than eight centuries ago, the famous chronicler, William of Malmesbury, expressed astonishment that the little church should have survived until then, when not a trace of the monasteries founded by St. Aldhelm at Frome and Bradford remained. William, who esteemed Aldhelm to be his greatest benefactor after God, is our chief authority for the Saint's life (*Gesta Pontificum Anglorum,* ed. Hamilton, Rolls Series, 1870, pp. 330-443). One of many miracles recounted of his hero is the following. While in Rome on a visit to Pope Sergius I, Aldhelm used to sing Mass daily at the Lateran Basilica. Once, after Mass, when he was generally in an ecstasy, he doffed his chasuble and threw it behind him as usual, expecting his chaplain to catch it. But on this occasion the chaplain was missing, having gone off to study the sights, when, lo, a sunbeam shot through the sacristy window, caught the chasuble, and held it suspended in mid-air, like a clothes-hanger. In case you might be tempted to doubt this miracle, a favourite one, by the way, with the saints of Ireland, William states that they had the identical chasuble right there at Malmesbury and proceeds to describe it minutely.

[2] So Bishop Hensley Henson in *Bede: His Life, Times and Writings,* edited by A. Hamilton Thompson, Oxford, 1935, p. xiv. The Bishop continues: "Great in his works, Bede is greater in himself. The example of the man is more precious than the achievement of the scholar. . . . Every circumstance of human living has altered in the course of twelve centuries. The whole aspect and outlook of English society have been transformed; and yet the moral beauty of Bede's life holds us, and we cannot dispute its appeal." The book to which those words are an introduction was written by a group of English and foreign scholars, all non-Catholics, in commemoration of the twelfth centenary of the exceedingly Catholic Saint's death, and is very valuable.

mediaeval world. It was the genius of this stay-at-home recluse who never crossed the Channel nor even got so near afield as London that started in his cell by the Tyne the long process of education which made Dante's brilliant age possible. Poet, scholar, theologian, master of the Scriptures, man of science, Father of English History, but first and foremost and all the time sweet saint of God, "the most beloved of all the monks in the world",[1] Bede fertilized the slow mind of the barbarian West, set a standard and ideal for all who aspired to learning, and consecrated the pursuit of knowledge by his exquisite holiness.[2] As St. Boniface said of him, he was "the candle of the Church lit by the Holy Ghost", and has thrown his beams through the darkness of twelve centuries, even as far as our own naughty world.

St. Bede's feast falls on 27 May.[3] The following day brings for our devotion a man of very different stamp, St. Augustine, the Apostle of England. Compared with the warm-hearted Anglican and Saxon saints. Roman Augustine may strike us as having been a somewhat frosty and aloof man of God. But the truth is that we know very little of his character except what may be precariously deduced from his actions, and those actions remain to this day enveloped in a beautiful south-coast fog. One thing, however, seems plain enough in the murk, that the quiet, dignified monk from St. Gregory's monastery on the Coelian Hill must have been uncommonly brave to persist with his mission, after the hair-raising stories he had heard in Provence about the savagery and wickedness of the pagan English. What a change was that, from the peace and

[1] To change one word of his own tribute to St. Acca (Migne, *P.L.,* 91, 500).

[2] The extraordinarily wide scope of his interests and reading is well shown in two articles of the book mentioned above, "Bede as Historian", by Dr. Wilhelm Levison of Bonn, and "The Library of the Venerable Bede", by Professor M. L. Laistner of Cornell University.

[3] Curiously, he had no feast in the Church's universal calendar until 1899, when Pope Leo XIII declared him a Doctor. But he was universally venerated even in his lifetime.

refinement of a cloister looking out upon the capital of civilization to the rude barbarism and squalor of Jutish Kent, where
even the king knew no better than to receive distinguished
strangers under a tree, for fear that if he took them into his
house they might bewitch him! We are often told, especially
by our good friends the Anglicans, who tend to regard
Augustine's mission as the first step in Papal aggression, that
the Saint behaved overbearingly and tactlessly in his dealings
with the native British bishops, but the evidence for the charge,
an obviously cock-and-bull "Canterbury Tale" about a hermit
and an alleged prophecy, is slender indeed.[1] Against it we can
put the questions of moral theology, liturgy, and canon law sent
by Augustine to his friend and mentor, St. Gregory the Great,
the other Apostle of England, which do not give the impression
of a haughty, self-assertive prelate, but rather of a truly humble
man, very diffident of his own judgement and even scrupulous
to a fault.[2]

All the saints so far mentioned in these pages were ecclesiastics of one kind or another, and it is time that the lay world
had a representative. None better could be chosen than St.
Godric the Hermit, who died, probably a centenarian, in 1170,
the year St. Thomas Becket was martyred, and is commemorated on 21 May. Godric, a Norfolk man, passes with uncommonly high marks all the traditional tests for Englishness. The
English are reputed, on illustrious home and foreign authority,

[1] Bede, *Historia Ecclesiastica,* ii, 2. The dear Bede always becomes a
little excited and less his urbane and charming self whenever the
wretched Paschal controversy arises, as it did on this occasion. But he is
careful to prefix an "ut perhibent" to the story of the hermit and a
"fertur" to the subsequent alleged prophecy of Augustine that divine
vengeance would overtake the Britons for their obstinacy and unwilling-
ness to co-operate. Bede was writing a good hundred years after Augustine's death, which gave plenty of time for legends to grow.

[2] Bede, *Historia Ecclesiastica,* i, 27. This is a very precious chapter.
Gregory was never greater than in the answers he returned. They prove
the marvellous breadth and tolerance of his mind, and more than compensate for some of those Homilies which, perhaps, irritate us occasionally
in the Breviary.

to be a nation of shopkeepers, even keepers of empty shops at moments in their history; Godric kept a shop, or at any rate, a warehouse, and became a sort of Selfridge of East Anglia. The English are a seafaring race; Godric went to sea and showed so much aptitude for the life that he rose to be captain and part owner of the merchant-ships which he sailed to Scotland, Flanders and Scandinavia. The English are inveterate travellers; Godric travelled on his two feet all the way to Rome (thrice), Jerusalem (twice), the shrine of St. Giles in Provence, and the shrine of St. James in Santiago de Compostela. The English are a reserved people who do not talk to one another in trains and make their homes into castles to keep out bureaucrats and other busybodies; Godric felt so strongly in this respect that he made his home for sixty years in a virgin forest near Durham, abounding in wolves and snakes to protect his privacy. The English are famous lovers of birds and beasts, dead or alive; Godric surpassed all other saints, not excluding the Irish ones nor even St. Francis, in his extraordinary tenderness for the shy wild creatures of his woodland retreat. Such a man is well worth knowing, and happily the wolves and snakes did not deter a valiant Boswell of Durham named Reginald from visiting him often and worming out of him the details of his picturesque career, which he committed to writing for our benefit at the urgent entreaty of another of Godric's friends and visitors, St. Aelred.[1]

[1] Reginald's work, *Libellus de Vita et Miraculis S. Godrici,* was printed for the first time in 1845, from a manuscript in the Bodleian, under the auspices of the Surtees Society and the editorship of the Rev. Joseph Stevenson, Librarian and Keeper of Records to the Dean and Chapter of Durham. This editor was almost as interesting a character as the Saint whose life he edited. Presbyterian minister, foundation-member and vice-president of the Surtees Society (other vice-presidents in their time were such men as the scholar-bishops, J. B. Lightfoot, Mandell Creighton, Brooke Westcott and William Stubbs, the historians John Lingard and Thomas Hodgkin, the poet Robert Southey, the Catholic antiquary Daniel Rock, etc.), Sub-Commissioner for Public Records at the British Museum and the Record Office, Anglican Vicar of Leighton Buzzard with wife and family, Catholic priest of Oscott, and Jesuit novice of

Godric was born of very poor parents named Aylward and Edwenna at the little Norfolk town of Walpole, about nine miles from King's Lynn, which is mentioned by the large-minded Bradshaw but despised by all except the most condescending of cartographers and makers of gazetteers. The year of his birth is unknown, but it must have been close to that tiresomely well-known year, 1066. Though of lowly condition, the family cannot have been mere serfs, tied to a particular manor, for they seem to have migrated in Godric's childhood to a new home near Spalding in Lincolnshire. The Saint's own youthful decision against work in the fields in favour of trade points also to a certain independence of status. He began operations by peddling small wares in the neighbouring villages, hoping thus to relieve the bleak poverty of his father, mother, brother and sister, to whom all the days of their lives he remained most tenderly devoted. Once, when hunger invaded the house, he set off barefooted for the estuary of the River Welland, where sometimes a dilatory crab or other

---

Manresa House, Roehampton, at the age of seventy-two; such was Joseph Stevenson's extraordinary spiritual Odyssey. To him more than to any other, historians are indebted for the British Government's decision to launch the famous Rolls Series in 1857, and as a Catholic priest he produced for the Government in the sweat of his brow thirteen huge folio volumes of transcripts from the Vatican Archives, ever since one of the treasures of the Record Office in Chancery Lane. Altogether, he edited some fifty large tomes for various learned societies. As a Jesuit, he worked with unflagging energy for fifteen years at Farm Street. When eighty-five, he made a pilgrimage to the home of his beloved St. Cuthbert at Lindisfarne. His two great profane loves in life (and not so very profane either) were children and animals, and he generally kept his pockets stuffed with sweets and nuts for those privileged parties. At eighty-eight, he walked part of the way from Farm Street to the Zoo in Regent's Park, distributed largesse to his many friends there, and then walked all the way back. It was too much even for the "youngest old man" in England and he had to take to his bed shortly afterwards. Someone mentioned the name of his little son Robert, the light of his eyes, whom he had lost nearly sixty years earlier. At the word, the dying man threw up his hands and cried joyfully, "I shall see him again! I shall see him again!" He saw him again on 8 February, 1895. He was a fit person to edit the life of St. Godric.

eatable thing would be left behind by the receding tide. The sands near the shore yielded nothing, but a few miles out in The Wash he came upon a prize in the shape of three stranded dolphins,[1] one dead and the others still palpitating or doing whatever dolphins usually do in such distressing circumstances. "He was touched with pity for the living ones," writes Reginald, "for he considered it cruel to deprive any breathing creature of its joy in existence" (*Libellus,* p. 27). But he had no scruple about spoiling the dead, and set off for home heavily laden with steaks of dolphin. While more than a mile from land, the returning sea caught and overwhelmed him, so that eventually he was completely submerged. However, strong in limb and stronger in faith, he battled his way through, "nor did he once in that predicament", says Reginald proudly, "let go of his booty." He said himself that he felt no fear because God was as near under the waves as over them.

Gradually business in the world of pedlary improved, and then our enterprising Saint formed partnerships with other traders, set up well-stocked booths at country fairs, and opened depots in the Lindsey and Norfolk towns. All this was more for the fun of the thing than for gain. He was completely unworldly, and while he journeyed from place to place entertained himself with ruminations on the *Pater Noster* and the Creed rather than with thoughts of profits and percentages. The chronology of his life is as vague as we have learned resignedly to expect from old-time hagiographers, who were more concerned to find the devil under every stone, or a miracle in every coincidence, than to give us an occasional date. So it is impossible to say when Godric first footed the long road to Rome, except that it was in the midst of his trafficking. On his return

[1] The writer on Godric in the *Dictionary of National Biography* seemed to think that dolphins are only heraldic fish. He accordingly swathed the word in inverted commas and suggested porpoises as an alternative. But dolphins eight to ten feet long are much more than *entia rationis,* as North Sea fishermen will feelingly and profanely testify, and as anyone can see for himself who makes the short crossing from Gibraltar to Tangier.

he took to the sea, and for about twelve years sailed his ship to the ports of Brittany, Flanders, Denmark and Scotland. His favourite resort was St. Andrews, not so much for purposes of business as of devotion,[1] and when voyaging thither he used always to call at the little island of Farne to pay his respects to the memory of St. Cuthbert. Many a tear he shed on those occasions, as he afterwards confessed to Reginald, thinking while he wandered about of Cuthbert's tears and prayers, or seeing him in the mind's eye bent over his spade, or stretched for a brief, begrudged hour on his stony couch asleep. Cuthbert laid a spell upon him then which changed the whole course of his existence.

It would probably have been at the dawn of the twelfth century, just after the warriors of the First Crusade had captured Jerusalem, that Godric abandoned trade, distributed the bulk of his wealth to the poor, and set off on foot as a pilgrim to Palestine.[2] On the journey home he took in Compostela for good measure. Reginald frequently tells us that he was "robustissimus", as strong as they are made, of medium build, with powerful chest and shoulders, and a fine shaggy head from which looked out two very bright and shrewd blue eyes (*Libellus*, p. 212; also Geoffrey, another Durham monk who knew the Saint, in *Acta Sanctorum*, Maii t.v, p. 70 D). He needed his strength for soon he was to feel again the pull of St.

[1] According to legend, a certain St. Regulus of Constantinople brought relics of the first-called of the Apostles to Fife in the fourth century. Round these grew up the city of St. Andrews as a place of pilgrimage, and the story may also partly account for the adoption of the Apostle as the national Saint of Scotland. Merely to scoff at such a traveller's tale is no help to explaining the existence of St. Andrews or the devotion to St. Andrew.

[2] An amusing reference to him occurs in Albert of Aix's History of the First Crusade. Piracy and trading by sea were in those times closely related, which accounts for the following statement of Albert, after he had described the defeat of Baldwin I, King of Jerusalem, on the plains of Ramlah: "The King leaving Arsuf boarded a ship called a *buza* and sailed for Jaffa, accompanied by Godric, a pirate from England" (Migne, *P.L.,* 166, 629). Godric's prowess on the sea must have become known, and no doubt he piloted the fugitive King to safety.

Peter's tomb. Hardly was he back from this second pilgrimage to Rome when the magnet drew him a third time. His mother, who must have been nearly as sturdy as himself, expressed a wish to go with him, and once out of England insisted on making the whole journey barefooted. When rivers had to be forded Godric would pick her up in his great arms and carry her across (*Libellus,* p. 38). They make an appealing picture, that rustic mother and son, trudging a thousand difficult miles to pay their humble duty to St. Peter.

After returning to England and "restoring his mother safe and sound to his father", he begged their permission to enter on a hermit's life and set off north to find his desert. But this was not so easy as he had imagined. We first hear of him at Carlisle, haunting the churches and diligently learning the Psalms by heart from a Latin Psalter given him as a present, which became his most treasured possession. Then, with St. John the Baptist and St. Cuthbert leading, he plunged into the wilds of Durham, which were worth calling wilds in those days, until at Wolsingham, ten miles north-west of Bishop Auckland, he found an aged anchorite named Aelric to be his novice-master. For two happy, suffering years, the last of Aelric's life, they clubbed together in their forest among the wolves and vipers, "having everything in common, which consisted of nothing except the poor rags on their backs" (*Libellus,* p. 45). Aelric taught Godric all that he knew of heavenly wisdom, and Godric waited upon Aelric hand and foot, hunting for the roots and berries on which they subsisted, watching by the old man's pallet day and night at the end until his eyes nearly dropped out from weariness, and fetching a priest through the dangerous jungle to give him the Last Sacraments. Desolate at the loss of his friend, for whose soul he offered to God four months of constant prayer and terrible austerities, he once again set his face steadfastly towards Jerusalem, living on bread and water all the way, never once removing the penitential shoes of matting which tortured his feet, and apparently thoroughly enjoying himself. He visited all the Holy Places, bathed in the Jordan, spent whole nights of prayer on the Mount of Olives, nursed sick pilgrims with tireless devotion in the Hospital of St. John, and learned everything he could about Christian perfection from the friendly hermits of Judea. But though sorely tempted, he would not take a cave out there himself, for, as Reginald naïvely puts it, "he did not think that an English talent ought to be buried in foreign ground" (*Libellus*, p. 58).

After his return to England, Godric searched long and anxiously, with many disappointments, for the ideal solitude which St. Cuthbert had promised him in a vision or dream. He found it eventually at Finchale, a small clearing amid woods and rocks, close by the River Wear and only three miles or so from Cuthbert's shrine at Durham. There, having obtained the sanction of the Durham Benedictines, he joyfully set up his everlasting rest, and in sixty years was not absent more than three or four days all told from his hermitage. He built himself a hut roofed with sods, a little wooden oratory dedicated to the Blessed Virgin, and finally a miniature stone church "in honour of the Holy Sepulchre and St. John the Baptist". While so engaged, villagers in bed two miles away would hear through the stillness of moonlit nights the sound of his axe or the tap of his hammer (*Libellus*, p. 84). The Benedictines who knew him for a saint used to come as often as they could to say Mass in his chapel and that was how Reginald eventually made his acquaintance in his hale old age. Very timidly, the good monk broached the question of writing his life. After staring at him for a while Godric said: "You would attempt to write the life of a bawdy rascal? Very good, here are the heads. Godric is a country clod and fat. He used to be a fornicator, adulterer, and dirty hound, who practised usury in his business dealings, and gave false measure and deceived the unwary. Now he is a hermit, but a hypocrite; a solitary, forsooth, whose head is crowded with vile thoughts; a glutton and covetous fellow who here devours and dissipates the alms of the charitable. Godric likes his ease and can often be found both day and night snoring luxuriously. He is also very fond of the praises of men. Write these and worse things about Godric, if you would show him to the world truly for the monster he is" (*Libellus*, p. 269). That is a picture of Godric but for the grace of God, who knew his own raging passions and consequently practised over many years austerities that would have killed in a month any man less powerfully constituted.

But under his hair-shirt and terrible iron cuirass beat the tenderest and most compassionate heart. In spite of his craving for solitude, he was but a hermit north-north-west, not having it in him to repel any intruder, human or animal. His mother, his brother, his sister, all were welcomed to Finchale and looked after with unflagging love and devotion. When they died he wept for them bitterly and redoubled his prayers and penances until sure that they had passed into Heaven. Hundreds of sorrowing people used to come to him and none ever went away uncomforted.[1] As for the lower creation, he is singular even among the animal-loving saints in his genuine liking for snakes. A man who likes snakes may be expected to like almost anything. Vipers were the terror of Finchale, but Godric lived with them on the friendliest terms, allowing them to stretch out by his fire in cold weather, to curl around his feet, to coil themselves up in his pots and pans, and generally to make themselves perfectly at home. He could pick them up and stroke them with complete immunity, and their antics, says Reginald, "used to fill him with admiration and amusement" (*Libellus*, pp. 67–9). At length, however, after many years, he felt obliged most reluctantly to tell them to go, "because they distracted him too much at his prayers". His relations with such soft-eyed marauders as deer and hares were a little more controversial, though equally charming, as when he

---

[1] Among his more distinguished visitors, besides St. Aelred of Rievaulx, was that other lovable Cistercian abbot, St. Robert of Newminster. When Robert died, Godric had a vision of him ascending to Heaven like a glorious flame of fire.

lectured an offending hare among his cabbages, but before ordering it away tied a bundle of green stuff on its back. In the winter it was his habit to go out barefooted in the snow, searching for any poor bird or beast that had come to grief. These he would physic and feed with the kindliest solicitude until they were well enough to fend for themselves again. Foxes, hares and stags hunted by his good friend and spiritual lord, the Bishop of Durham, used to fly to his hut for protection, knowing by instinct that there they would be safe. He did much hunting on his own account, but it was for the traps and gins laid against his comrades of the forest, so as to release whatever captives he might find in them (*Libellus,* pp. 98–9).

Godric's excessive austerities eventually wrecked even his giant's strength and the last eight years of his life were spent in almost uninterrupted suffering, heroically borne. It was then that seeing Reginald's sad reproachful face he relented in sheer kindness of heart and gave him the biographical details for which he craved. As the end approached, he was heard whispering about a passage "over the borders of the Great Sea" that he soon must make. He had been accustomed to pray daily for those who went down to the sea in ships. Now, he was putting out to sea again as he had so often done of old, but this time it was on the last voyage home. He died on 21 May, 1170, and round his tomb in the little church he had himself constructed grew up the stately Priory of Finchale, whose ruins today are among the most hauntingly beautiful in England. He shares with Our Lady, who once appeared to him as the Mother of Mercy and taught him a holy song (*Libellus,* p. 118), the dedication of a Catholic parish church in the city of Durham.

Apostle of Germany

A VERY strong case indeed could be made out for regarding St. Boniface as the greatest Englishman that ever was born, even though he might not have been able to write *Hamlet* or to win the Battle of Trafalgar. Yet of the 2665 Catholic churches and public oratories in England only about seven are dedicated to him, as compared with scores and scores built to the honour and glory of St. Patrick, St. Anthony of Padua and St. Teresa of the Child Jesus. Even St. Philomena with all her notes of interrogation leaves him nowhere. This is the more strange because he was an uncommonly lovable great man, as we may judge by the number of his devoted friends, both men and women, who cheerfully sacrified the happiness and security of their English cloisters to follow him into the wilderness. It is like a miracle that we should still, after twelve centuries, have the privilege of looking straight into his heart as revealed in the charming letters which he wrote to his friends and their no less charming answers. He belongs to the small dear company of the saints who were not afraid to be humanly affectionate, such people as Paulinus of Nola, Anselm, Aelred and Catherine of Siena. When Papal Legate in Germany and the foremost ecclesiastical figure of the Frankish dominions, he wrote with the simplicity of a child to ask advice from his friend Egbert, Archbishop of York. "My letter has to be short," he says, "so I have no room to tell you all my troubles within and without; but it is with intense desire that I beg you to console me again in the way you have already done, that is by sending me some particle or spark of the candle of the Church which the Holy Ghost has lighted in your Northumbria, the writings, I mean, of the holy priest and scholar Bede.... Instead of the kiss which I am prevented from giving you, I am sending you by the bearer of this letter two little kegs of wine. As you love me, I beg you to use it for a

day of rejoicing with your friends." [1] Who would not want
to know more of the Saint who wrote and acted in that fashion,
especially as he never touched anything stronger than water
himself?

Boniface was born of a noble West Saxon family at Crediton,
near Exeter, about the year 680.[2] Devon in those days was
still a part of the British kingdom of Dumnonia, but some
hardy and enterprising Saxons had sailed up the rivers Exe and
Creedy to establish a small outpost of Wessex in the Cymric
world. This happened only a decade or two before Boniface
was born, so we can see at once where he obtained that "spirit
of adventure and determination which is not excelled by

[1] Migne, *P.L.,* 89, 756–8. The eighth-century life of St. Boniface by the
monk Willibald, on which all subsequent lives are based, was printed
for the first time at Ingolstadt in 1603 by Henry Canisius, nephew of St.
Peter Canisius, second Apostle of Germany. It has been reprinted many
times, as by the Bollandists and in the volume of Migne cited above. St.
Boniface's letters to the number of thirty-nine, and thirty-three letters
written to him were first published at Mainz in 1605 by the Jesuit Nicholas Serarius. The Oxford scholar Giles republished them in his *Sancti
Bonifacii Opera* (London, 1844), and this is the edition, very faulty but
very convenient, to be found in Migne. The reader must beware of
Gile's dates as so much chronological poison. A far better edition is that
by Philip Jaffé in the *Bibliotheca Rerum Germanicarum,* vol. iii, Berlin,
1866. And even superior to that is Michael Tangl's *Briefe des heiligen
Bonifatius und Lullus,* Berlin, 1916. Of Catholic lives of Boniface the
best by far is that from the attractive pen of Professor Godefroi Kurth,
of the University of Liége (second edition, 1902), written for the series,
"Les Saints". A good Anglican life, *Boniface of Crediton and his Companions,* by Dr. G. F. Browne, Bishop of Bristol, appeared in 1910. Some
of the letters are translated in *The English Correspondence of St.
Boniface,* by E. Kylie, London, 1911.

[2] Willibald, as is the way of his kind, mentions neither place nor date.
Stenton in his *Anglo-Saxon England* states that Boniface was born
"shortly before 675", but he gives no evidence, and other scholars are
content with the less precise "c. 680". Crediton, once a bishopric and
still a seat of the Protestant bishops of Exeter, is assigned in all the books
since the fourteenth century as the Saint's birthplace, very late but the
best that can be done in the matter. Anyhow, it must have been near
Crediton, as he was sent to school at Exeter.

Gilbert or Drake or Raleigh",[1] three other fearless Devonians. The family was already Christian, possibly converts of the wide-ranging St. Birinus, and our Saint received in baptism the name of Wynfrith or Winfrid, which he retained for nearly forty years, until at the beginning of his missionary career in Germany Pope St. Gregory II imposed on him as a symbol of his dependence on the Holy See the new Latin name of Boniface.[2] Boniface, however, we may call him from the outset. He found his vocation very precociously, for we are told that he made up his mind to be a monk "cum esset annorum circiter quatuor seu quinque" (Migne, *P.L.,* 89, 605). And a monk he became, or at any rate a monk in embryo, an oblate of St. Benedict, at the age of seven, to the great sorrow of his father who had pinned all his wordly hopes on this extraordinary child. Through the seventy years that remained to him Boniface never once faltered or looked back, though the glittering prizes of his victorious people were his for the taking. If ever the fine Roman phrase "integer vitae" applied in its fullness to a human being it was to this Saxon lad only two removes from barbarism.

After some years at a poor monastery near Exeter, Boniface was transferred to the better equipped Benedictine house of Nursling in the diocese of Winchester, whose bishop, named Daniel, became one of his dearest friends, as he was also a friend and adviser of St. Bede.[3] Long afterwards, he would write to this good old man from Germany for counsel in his many difficulties, send him in token of his love a woollen rug "ad tegendos pedes dilectionis vestrae",[4] and console him on

---

[1] Hodgkin, *A History of the Anglo-Saxons,* vol. i, p. 327.

[2] Gregory seems to have been fond of Latinizing his Saxon visitors for he imposed the name Clement on Boniface's elder contemporary and friend, Northumbrian St. Willibrord, the Apostle of the Frisians who inhabited the country we now call Holland.

[3] St. Bede records his indebtedness to Bishop Daniel in the Preface to the *Ecclesiastical History.*

[4] Or it may have been a woollen towel for wiping (*tergendos*) the episcopal feet.

his blindness with the reflection borrowed from St. Jerome: "My Father, you still have eyes wherewith to see God and His angels, and to contemplate the glories of the Heavenly Jerusalem" (Migne, *P.L.*, 89, 702–3). At Nursling, of which now no trace seems to be left, and whose name and site even are doubtful, the great intellectual influence was that of charming, acrostic-loving St. Aldhelm, Bishop of the adjoining diocese of Sherborne and Abbot of Malmesbury. Aldhelm was a portent in Saxon England, the first man of the invaders in whom the genius of Ireland, Rome and Germany fused to produce a new and exciting type of Latin poetry and prose. The Latin language affected him, and through him Boniface and many others, very much including the nuns, like a heady wine, and they all got slightly tipsy on it, playing with the grand sonorous words as though at a marvellous new game, weaving them into strange, amusing patterns, or indulging in terrific feats of alliteration. Those were the times when two grammarians of Gaul named Galbungus and Terrentius argued for a solid fortnight about the vocative case of *ego*. Boniface fell so much in love with the new learning of Aldhelm that he continued to write hexameters almost to the day of his martyrdom, and even in a letter to Pope St. Zachary (elected in 741) could not refrain from bursting into song. Though such efforts are not to our taste, we ought to be able to sympathize with them, remembering that the poor Saxons had no Itma or Brains Trust to forward their education. Neither had they crosswords, in place of which Boniface invented a very ingenious system of cryptography.[1] He and his friends had come out of the Teutonic darkness into the Roman day, and who will blame them for romping a little while like schoolboys in the sunlight? The mention of schoolboys is a reminder to say that the first Latin grammar to be composed or compiled in England came from the pen of Boniface during his Nursling

---

[1] Some examples are given in that fascinating book, Dr. Wilhelm Levison's *England and the Continent in the Eighth Century*. The Ford Lectures, 1943, Oxford, 1946, pp. 291–2.

period when he was headmaster of the monastic school.[1] He won fame and many friendships as a Latinist, especially in the convent circles for whose learned ladies St. Aldhelm had written his *De Laudibus Virginitatis,* but his principal addiction all through life was to the study of the Scriptures. During the last period of his missionary career, when, like his old friend Bishop Daniel, he was going blind, he begged that dear centenarian[2] as a great favour to send him a manuscript of six of the Prophets which his revered master, Winbrecht, Abbot of Nursling, had written in fine, bold uncial characters. "You could give me no greater solace in my old age," he says, "for I am unable to procure a similar manuscript of the Prophets in this country, and owing to failing eyesight I can no longer read small cursive writing" (Migne, *P.L.,* 89, 702).

After his ordination by Bishop Daniel at the then canonical age of thirty, Boniface was chosen in a synod of the West Saxon Church to conduct some delicate negotiations with Berchwald, Archbishop of Canterbury, a rather difficult prelate who plays such a curious changing rôle in the stormy life of St. Wilfrid. The studious monk of Nursling, all inexperienced in the ways of the world, proved himself a born diplomat and acquitted himself to the satisfaction of everybody, including the Archbishop and the great law-maker, Ine, King of Wessex, whom the *Catholic Encyclopedia* has canonized. Almost overnight our Boniface became a personage in England, and who can say to what heights of ecclesiastical glory he might not have attained just by staying at home? But glory was the last thing this loving, lowly-hearted Saxon wanted. Time enough for that in Heaven. We are not told how long his missionary vocation had been maturing in the quiet of his Hampshire monastery, but it may be significant that ten years before he sailed away a

---

[1] It was discovered by Cardinal Mai in a palimpsest of the Vatican Library and published by him in Volume VII of the ten volumes of his *Classici Auctores,* 1825–38.

[2] He *must* have been a centenarian if he was already bishop when Boniface first went to Nursling. Bede hints at his great age.

friend dedicated to him a poem entitled, "The Pilgrimage beyond the Seas". By the dawn of the eighth century England
had been almost entirely converted, and generous hearts were
thinking more and more in terms of such a pilgrimage to places
where other peoples, their kinsmen by race, still sat in darkness
and the shadow of death. St. Willibrord had been labouring for
years with small success among the Frisians, north and south of
the Zuider Zee, the toughest pagans of the Continent but the
nearest in blood and language to the English. Boniface determined to go to the assistance of Willibrord.[1]

Very reluctantly his abbot, who loved and valued him, gave
permission, and he sailed from London for the mouths of the
Rhine and up the River to Wijk bij Duurstede near Utrecht
with three companions in the year 716, when he was about
thirty-six. Everything points to the fact that he did not intend
this to be a final good-bye to his native land, but rather in the
nature of a reconnaissance. And a disconcerting reconnaissance
it proved, for unknown to Boniface the Frisians, under a fierce
leader named Radbold, had recently defeated the Franks led
by the great Charles Martel himself. That meant the destruction
of St. Willibrord's patient laborious achievement. It gives us
some measure of Boniface's quality to know that he fearlessly
bearded the terrible Radbold in his stronghold of Utrecht and
so much impressed the champion of the pagan gods as to be
allowed to depart, not only with his head still on his shoulders,
but with an actual licence to preach. Boniface soon saw, however, that preaching in the wild conditions then prevalent
would be waste of breath, so he retired for a time to his Hampshire base in order to think out a new plan of campaign. He
has been called, with good reason, a great missionary statesman.
"The most striking feature in Boniface's career is the way in
which while never waiting for circumstances he was quick to
seize each circumstance and use it to the utmost good. He never

---

[1] "Willibrord was to England what Columbanus had been to Ireland.
He inaugurated a century of English spiritual influence on the Continent"
(Levison, loc. laud., p. 60).

lost sight of any work he had ever planned and begun; if he turned aside for some pressing need he wove that special work into his general plan".[1] His return to Nursling nearly proved his undoing as a missionary, for the monks with enthusiastic accord elected him their new abbot, and he was able to escape the dignity only by the strong personal intervention of his friend Bishop Daniel.

With letters of commendation from Daniel as his passport Boniface left England for ever in 718 and set his face towards Rome. The days of missionary freelances, such as had been many of the great Irish apostles of the Continent, were fast drawing to a close, and Boniface had determined to appear this time among his pagans as the direct delegate of that Holy See which had so marvellously planned and carried through the conversion of his own dear country.[2] The Pope, bearing the name of good omen, St. Gregory II, loved him at sight and kept him many months near him, planning the great new assault on the hoary paganism of Germany. Boniface began again with his first and most difficult love, Friesland, where now a more tolerant ruler than the ferocious Radbold held sway, and for three years laboured might and main, under the direction of the old hero, St. Willibrord.[3] But when Willibrord, then near his end, would have made him his coadjutor and successor in the see of Utrecht, Boniface retired into the wilds of Hesse. On his way thither, a refugee from preferment, he encountered at an abbey near Trier the grandson of the unhappy Merovingian King, Dagobert II, a boy of fourteen named Gregory. Gregory was so fascinated by the wonderful visitor

[1] Whitney, in *The Cambridge Medieval History,* vol. ii (1913), p. 539.

[2] The hundreds of English slaves on the Continent prepared the way for the English saints. The most remarkable and romantic case was that of the Saxon girl Balthild, who by her beauty and charm won the love of King Clovis II, became his Queen, regent of Gaul after his death, and foundress of the famous monastery of Corbie. St. Wilfrid, it seems, did not like her at all!

[3] After ten years of study in Ireland, Willibrord spent no less than forty-nine years on the Continent, dying in harness at the age of 81— a glorious old missionary warrior.

from England that he insisted there and then on becoming his disciple, and never after parted from him during the thirty remaining years of Boniface's life. This delightful boy is known in the Church's calendar as St. Gregory of Utrecht, for Boniface was like that, not only an outstanding saint himself but a cause of sanctity in others.

He was now fully launched on the great work of his life, the making and organization of Catholic Germany. The details of the mighty achievement, the grandest surely in missionary history, are too well known to need more than the briefest mention here, especially as they can be found in a hundred books—his second and third visits to Rome; his consecration as bishop of Central Europe by the Pope, and subsequent appointment as Legate and Archbishop of Mainz; his famous, superlatively brave action in hewing down with his own hands the oak-tree that was the symbol of German paganism and building with planks sawn from it a little church in honour of the Prince of the Apostles; his foundation of monasteries as fortresses and power-houses for the faith throughout Hesse, Thuringia, Württemberg and Bavaria; his establishment of dioceses which have survived all the changes and turmoil of twelve centuries; the synods he convened for the restoration of church discipline and the forging of those links with Rome which not even the terrible assaults of Lutheranism and Nazism have been able to break; his great reform in old age of the Church of France; and finally his return to Friesland with all his years and labour weighing him down to sign in his English blood the last testament of his love for Europe.

What was the secret of Boniface's marvellous and enduring success? "Apart from his burning zeal and his capacity for work, which for so many years he strained to its utmost tension, one of the chief ones was the amiability of his character. This it was before which opposition melted away, this made all wishful to work with him, this attached all men to him. Not only was he beloved by the Popes, who would have had him always with them, but he was dear to the whole Roman

Church. Its deacons and its archdeacons were constantly writing to him the kindest of letters, and sending him presents.
He had the greatest influence with the 'Princes of the Franks',
who ever showed themselves ready to do all he wanted; and
the people of this country, whether men or women, were always
most devoted to him. Every letter that is addressed to him is full
of affectionate language." [1] Boniface's foundation of Fulda,
the Monte Cassino of the North and to this day the very *foyer*
of German Catholicism, "in eremo vastissimae solitudinis in
medio nationum praedicationis nostrae", is one of the great
romances of religion and civilization.[2] Seven years after that
epoch-making event, the Saint's dearly loved cousin Lioba,
who is also in the Church's calendar, came with a group of nuns
from her cloister at Wimborne near Bournemouth to start the
abbey of Bischofsheim in the same vast wilderness. "It would
be difficult," wrote the profound scholar Edmund Bishop on
one occasion, "to exaggerate the praises of these valiant and
devoted women, who faced the dangers of a distant journey
only to bury themselves in wild and savage regions, exposed to
hardships from which even strong men had shrunk." Lioba,
who is hardly known at all and commemorated in no English
diocese, was yet one of the most attractive of the English saints,
beautiful in both body and soul. Here she is writing to Boniface
from Wimborne before she set out on her great adventure for
love of him: "I beg you in your kindness to remember your old
friendship with my father Tinne. He died eight years ago in the
West Country, and you will not refuse him your prayers, nor
my mother Ebba either, your relative, who is still alive but

[1] Mann, *The Lives of the Popes in the Early Middle Ages,* vol. i, part
ii (1902), p. 251.
[2] In the year 741 he sent his young Bavarian disciple St. Sturm or
Sturmi, a man addicted to solitude whom he used to call affectionately
"my hermit", to search for a good site for the monastery. Sturmi's adventures as he roamed alone with his donkey through the virgin forests
of Hesse, "where nothing was to be seen but the sky and the giant trees",
are related in his life by Eigil, the fourth abbot of Fulda (Migne, *P.L.,*
105, 425–44).

suffering greatly. I am their only daughter, and would, though all unworthy, that I might deserve to have you for my brother, for in none of my kindred do I place my hopes and trust as I do in you. I am sending you a little gift, unworthy indeed of your notice, but it will remind you of your little kinswoman, who hopes that the long distance between will not cause you to forget her but that we shall love one another truly for ever. I most earnestly beg you, dear brother, to defend me with your prayers against the assaults of the unseen enemy. And I also ask you please to correct the rusticity of the Latin of this letter, sending me in your goodness a few words of the counsel which I hungrily long for. I wrote the enclosed verses for you, but they need your polishing. . . . I learned the art from my mistress Edburga who never ceases studying the Scriptures . . ." (Migne, *P.L.*, 89, 720–1). Lioba became famous in Germany not only for learning but for the better gifts, kindness and hospitality. She ruled her nuns by love in the true spirit of St. Benedict. St. Boniface regarded her with deep affection and often visited her at Bischofsheim, where she lived so austerely that the small cup she used at meals was known as "the Beloved's little one". When death came in 780, she begged to be buried alongside the dear man who had drawn her to the missions and to the very top of the holy mountain of God. Among her other close friends were Charlemagne and his Queen, St. Hildegard.

The St. Edburga mentioned by Lioba was another of Boniface's devoted correspondents who delighted to supply him with books and anything else he needed from her abbey of Minster-in-Thanet. But the most famous of his nun friends and disciples was the great lady whom many think to have been his niece, St. Walburga of Wimborne, abbess of the double monastery of Heidenheim in the diocese of Eichstätt, Bavaria. Walburga was sister of the adventurous St. Willibald who travelled over much of Europe and the Near East before he eventually settled down by Boniface's appointment as the first bishop of Eichstätt. Even dearer than these to the Apostle of

Germany was the Wiltshire man St. Lull, his chosen successor in the see of Mainz, where he laboured in all holiness and simplicity of life for thirty years. Many of Lull's letters are extant and in them we may discern something of the profound love and veneration which the English people of that epoch bore to his master, St. Boniface, as well as the very considerable effect which the counsels and admonitions of Boniface had on the religious life of England. For he was an apostle of England, too, as of France, Holland and Germany. These were but a few of the brave English souls, men and women, who dared everything to be near him and to work under his inspiration.

And now to conclude these ramblings which are so ludicrously inadequate to their theme, here are a few lines from Bede's disciple and close friend, Cuthbert, Archbishop of Canterbury, written to console St. Lull on the death of St. Boniface: "Though I too was at first stricken to the heart by the news, my sorrow was relieved and turned to joy and exultation by the memory of what this glorious and outstanding soldier of Christ had achieved ... in places and among savage peoples where none before him were brave enough to venture ... We in England lovingly reckon him among the best and most splendid teachers of the true faith, and in our national synod we have decreed that his feast is to be solemnly celebrated every year on the day of his martyrdom, as in a special sense our patron together with Blessed Gregory and Blessed Augustine." [1] Boniface overthrew Thor and Woden and made of the German Church the nursing mother of such exquisite saints and mystics as Mechtilde and Gertrude, Bruno and Albert the Great, Eckhart, Suso and Tauler. She also gave us the *Imitation of Christ*. Who knows but that she might defeat Thor and Woden again, whether with a swastika or a hammer and sickle on their banners, and produce fruits of divine grace as lovely as in the past, if only we prayed hard enough to her great English Apostle, St. Boniface?

[1] Migne, *P.L.*, 96, 829 (*S. Lulli Moguntini Episcopi Epistolae*). Cuthbert is not easy to translate as he affected the turgid Aldhelmian Latinity.

A MONG the swarm of Johns in the Martyrologies, and they more than double in number the Peters and Jameses,[1] thus attesting the devotion of Christian hearts to the Precursor of Our Lord, as also, though in lesser measure, to His Beloved Disciple, none more closely resembled those two primary Saints in "trade of life" and circumstances of death than the sixteenth-century son of a Yorkshire mercer [2] whose virtues during his years on earth spread their fragrance from the smallest and poorest diocese in England over the universal Church. Before Anne Boleyn started her mischief, even old Bluebeard, who from the beginning had plenty of faith but next to no good works, was proud of him and used to boast to visitors from abroad that no other country could produce the match of his Rochester. "Once when I was with others in the King's company", wrote Cardinal Pole, "I recollect him turning to me, whom he considered to have a greater acquaintance with men of learning owing to my long sojourn in foreign parts as a student, and saying that he felt confident I had discovered nobody in all my travels to be compared with Rochester for learning and holiness." [3] The very Lutherans whom he

[1] The Johns are so abundant that most of them had to be given distinguishing sobriquets of one kind or another, with such pleasing results as St. John in the Well, St. John the Skipper (one would like to have known him!), St. John the Mower, St. John the Hairy, St. John the Woman-hater (one would not care so much to have known *him*), St. John who saw an Angel, St. John the Despot (nor him), St. John the Dwarf, St. John of the Grating, etc. Of the fifty martyrs under Henry VIII sixteen were Johns to ten Thomases and four Richards, the next most numerous names.

[2] In a small way, for he was able to leave to each of his three children only the sum of £2 13s. 4d., which, even if multiplied by twenty, was a very modest fortune.

[3] *Epistolae Reginaldi Poli,* ed. Quirino, Brescia, 1744, t. i, p. 95. Pole, who was so good a man himself and who enjoyed the familiar friendship of such admirable scholar-bishops as Sadoleto and Ghiberti and of the ideal layman Gaspar Contarini, all three afterwards cardinals, practically endorsed the King's sweeping judgement, writing with reference to Fisher in his famous book, *Pro Unitate Ecclesiae* (1536): "If search were

fought tooth and nail on every front admired him, and expressed their indignation in no uncertain terms when Henry,
become the Boleyn's slave, had him killed.[1] It is safe to say
that his only real peer in the world of his time was his good
friend, the perfect, gentle knight, St. Thomas More, who wrote
of him: "I reckon in this realm no one man in wisdom, learning and long approved virtue together, mete to be matched and
compared with him."[2] Lovely and pleasant in their lives, in
their death they were not divided, and will now for ever keep
each other company in the Church's remembrance.

The superhuman grandeur of John Fisher's character is
almost frightening when deeply meditated, like as if the
Medway under the windows of his ramshackle, ill-furnished
palace, where Erasmus was so uncomfortable, had suddenly
become the Jordan that day the heavens were opened, or shabby
Rochester had faded into shining Ephesus and there could be
heard the very accents of a tired old man who had once rested
his head on the bosom of Jesus. Long before this other St. John
rested his head on the block for the love of Jesus, he guessed
how it would be with him and saw undismayed his life con-
verging to the dungeon of a new Herod and the vengeance of
his Herodias. After the Bishop's final imprisonment in the
Tower in April 1534,[3] for refusing to take the Oath of Succes-

to be made through every corner of Christendom in this our age, it
would not be easy to find another such perfect bishop as he."
[1] Friedmann, *Anne Boleyn,* London, 1884, vol. ii, p. 83–6. This remarkable book has worn better than most of its kind and is still both
readable and valuable. The King was disconcerted by the storm which
his execution of Fisher and More had roused on the Continent among
Protestants as well as Catholics and set his propaganda machine at work
to assuage it. He took great credit to himself for not having poisoned
Fisher (though it is on the cards that he, or the Boleyn gang, had a
good try!), or boiled him in lead, or hanged him in a halter, "what best
agrees for a traitor", or burned him at the stake, but only struck off his
head, "the which death is most easy".
[2] *The Workes of Sir Thomas More wrytten in the Englishe tongue,*
London, 1557, p. 1437.
[3] He had already been twice arrested, in October 1530, and in April
1533.

sion because it included a repudiation of the authority of the Holy See, the King sent commissioners to make an inventory of his poor confiscated chattels at Rochester. Among "divers old trash" listed by those careful if disappointed men, who left not so much as a poker or a broken looking-glass out of their reckoning, they mention, referring to the contents of the broad gallery of the palace, "a St. John's head standing at the end of the altar".[1] This was a coloured representation in wood or plaster of the head of the Baptist on a dish, and the Bishop seems to have substituted it in his later years for the ordinary skull which he used to have placed on the altar during his Mass and on his table when he sat down to his frugal meal, "lest that the memory of death might hap to slip from his minde".[2]

[1] Gairdner, *Letters and Papers of the Reign of Henry VIII,* vol. vii (1883), p. 222. The complete contents of the Bishop's bedroom were as follows: "A bedstead with a mattrass, a counterpoint [counterpane] of red cloth lined with canvas. A celer and tester [a canopy and its supports] of old red velvet nothing worth. An altar with a hanging of white and green satin ... with our Lord embroidered on it. 2 blue sarcenet curtains. A cupboard with a cloth. A little chair covered with leather, and a cushion. A close stool [commode] and an old cushion upon it. An andiron, a fire pan and a fire shovel." The Bishop's plate, mostly cheap stuff, except a few good chalices which had been presented to him, included his only mitre, "set with counterfeit stone and pearl" (ibid., viii, p. 352).

[2] Van Ortroy, *Vie du Bienheureux Martyr Jean Fisher:* Texte Anglais et Traduction Latine du XVIe Siècle, Brussels, 1893, p. 100. This is the first complete publication in book form, edited and annotated with the full panoply of Bollandist learning, of the earliest life of St. John Fisher, put together with consummate skill from a mass of carefully sifted documentary and other evidence by some still unidentified genius, during the decade 1566–76. One of the Latin translations of the English original was made by the Jesuits of St. Omer for the use of their eminent brother, Jean Bolland, the eponymous founder of the Bollandists, from a manuscript which subsequently passed into the Stonyhurst Archives. This document provides the foundation of van Ortroy's text. A very convenient reprint of it, with an excellent notice of van Ortroy's life and labours, was published by Father Philip Hughes in 1935, but his Bollandist would have been shocked to find no index provided, judging by his gentle reproach to Father Bridgett, whose classical modern *Life of Blessed John Fisher* (2nd ed., 1890) he so much admired, for the same sin of omission (*Vie,* p. 2, n. 1).

John Fisher was born at Beverley, in the East Riding of Yorkshire, eight miles north of Hull, in the year 1469, when the White and Red Roses were fighting it out and preparing the way for the Tudor despotism that he would die in opposing. His parents, Robert and Agnes, "of honest state and condition, and by trade of marchandise," had him christened John very likely in honour of the local Saint, who, according to William of Malmesbury, enjoyed great posthumous fame as a tamér of wild bulls. John of Beverley's little client did not inherit this charism, and a wild bull eventually killed him. He probably learned his three R's at the grammar school attached to the splendid Beverley Minster, his patron's shrine, and then, at the age of fourteen, on a red-letter day for the University, was sent to Cambridge, where he matriculated at Michaelhouse, a foundation subsequently incorporated in Trinity College. Though Cambridge has long been as famous for its sturdy and vociferous Protestants as for its mathematicians, historians and poets, the memory of John Fisher, who was none of these things, is still cherished by the Cam, in spite of the best efforts of omnipotent Cromwell, his successor as Chancellor of the University, to efface it.[1]

A lecture delivered on 24 July, 1935, by Mr. E. A. Benians, Master of St. John's College, began and ended as follows: "Four colleges unite today to pay homage to the memory of John Fisher. In the noble list of founders and benefactors which

---

[1] "All the stalles endes in the Queare of that college [St. John's] had graven in them by the joyner a fyshe and an erre of wheat. But after he [Fisher] had suffered at London, my lord Crumwell then commaunded the same armes to be defaced, and monstrous and ugly antiks to be put in their places" (Van Ortroy, *Vie,* p. 45). However, the quaint rebus of the fish and ear of corn survived or reappeared in a window of the College chapel, to distract a certain young undergraduate named T. E. Bridgett at his prayers and to make him curious to know more about the Founder of his College. He read all that he could find on the subject, and Fisher's spotless character and heroic death gave weight to other arguments which caused him to refuse the oath of royal supremacy in 1850, thus sacrificing his degree, and to become a Catholic and Redemptorist, one of the brightest ornaments of the Church in modern times.

our University and our colleges preserve, few names stand out
with the eminence of his. He was Master of Michaelhouse and
President of Queen's College; and, with the Lady Margaret,[1]
a founder of Christ's College and St. John's. In the University
he held the offices of Senior Proctor, Lady Margaret Professor,
Vice-Chancellor and Chancellor—that of Chancellor for thirty-
one years. . . . Fisher is endeared to every son of Cambridge by
his services to collegiate life. In learning he mediated between
the old and the new. On the stem of the mediaeval university
he grafted the colleges of the Renaissance. The University had
no more faithful servant. Unsparing of effort, and ever loyal to
its interests, he exalted the place of Cambridge in the national
life. To the problems of Church and State he brought an un-
yielding integrity of mind and a character steeled in the
austerities of the Middle Ages. For him the times were out of
joint, but he surrendered neither faith nor courage. English
liberty was not bound up with the preservation of papal power,
yet if none had challenged Henry, how many would have re-
sisted Charles? It is a key to his place in our history that in
learning he promoted the work of Erasmus and in politics he
shared the fate of More. . . . To the conduct and pattern of his
life the Church which he defended and adorns has paid its
highest tribute, and we, not less mindful of his virtue and
service, in this Hall which knew his presence, remember today,
with gratitude and humility, one who has placed us for ever in
his debt." [2]

[1] The Lady Margaret Beaufort, Countess of Richmond and Derby,
mother of King Henry VII, who chose Fisher for her chaplain and confessor in 1502. It was through his influence that she devoted so much of
her wealth to Cambridge. She made provision in her will for the foundation of St. John's, but after her death in 1509 her grandson, Henry VIII,
deflected the money to his own purse. Fisher then made over to St. John's
a legacy which she had left him for his private use.

[2] Benians, *John Fisher,* Cambridge University Press, 1935, pp. 5,
40–41. To that noble and moving tribute it need only be added that St.
John Fisher's devoted services to learning had the entirely spiritual aim
of producing efficient and holy priests. He was not a humanist, and,
though an immensely learned man, probably for learning as such cared

Fisher was appointed bishop of Rochester in 1504 by Margaret Beaufort's hard-headed, unromantic son, the victor of Bosworth, Henry VII, "for none other cause", as he explained to that valiant and saintly Lady in a charming letter, "but for the grete and singular virtue that I know and see in hym." [1] We have the advantage of knowing almost exactly what he looked like in his later years, not only from Holbein's crayon sketch of his honest Yorkshire face, with its sunken cheeks and gentle, "anxiously conscientious" expression, but also from an admirable pen-picture of his earliest biographer who shows him "tall and comlye, six foot in height, verie slender and leane, nevertheless upright and well formed, straight backed, bigg joynted and strongly sinewed; his hair through age and imprisonment turned to whiteness; his eyes nether full blacke nor full graye but of a mixt colour betweene; his forehead smooth and large, his nose of a good and even proportion, somewhat wide mowthed, and bigg jawed as one ordained to utter speech and speak much: wherein was notwithstandinge a certaine comlyness; his skin somwhat tannie, mixt with many blew vaines; his face, hands and all his bodye so bare of flesh as is almost incredible, which came ... by the great abstinance and pennance he used upon himself many yeres together, even from his youth ..." [2]

To read of the Bishop's austerities is almost to feel oneself back in the desert with the first St. John: "His dyett at table was for all such as thither resorted plentifull and good, but for himself verie meane ... The most of his sustinance was

nothing at all. Of one of his many erudite controversial works he said that he wished he had spent the time employed on it in prayer, which is the most effective form of controversy. The famous sad words, spoken with reference to the Apostolic Age, indicate perfectly where lay all his concern: "In that tyme were no chalyses of golde, but then was many golden prestes, now be many chalyses of golde, and almost no golden prestes" (*The English Works of John Fisher*, ed. Mayor, E.E.T.S., 1876, p. 181).

[1] Cooper, *Memoir of Margaret, Countess of Richmond and Derby*, Cambridge, 1874, pp. 95–6.

[2] Van Ortroy, *Vie*, pp. 355–6.

thinne pottage, sodden with flesh ... The ordinarie fasts appointed by the Church he kept verie soundly, and to them he joyned many other perticular fasts of his owne devotion, as appeared well by his thinne and weake body, wherupon though much flesh was not left, yet would he punish the verie skynne and bones upon his backe." The commissioners sent by the King in 1534 pounced upon a securely locked chest which they discovered in the Bishop's private oratory, thinking that in this surely must be his missing hoard. But when they smashed the lock they found "instead of gould and silver which they looked for, a shirt of haire and two or three whips, wherwith he used full often to punish himself, as some of his chaplyns and servants would reporte that were about him and curyously marked his doings. And other treasure than that found they none at all." [1]

Finally, here is a glimpse of the Saint after dark: "When night was come, which comonly brings rest to all creatures, then would he many times dispatch awaie his servants and fall to his praiers a long space. And after he had ended the same, he laid him downe upon a poore hard cowch of strawe and matts; ... and he never rested above 4 howres at one time, but straight waies rose and ended the rest of his devout praiers" (*Vie*, pp. 103–4).

The Bishop's austerities were the consequence of his overwhelming personal love of Jesus Crucified and of his unappeasable longing to make reparation for his own piercingly felt unworthiness and for the sins of all mankind. *Cor Joannis cor mundi,* we might truly say of him. In a far nobler sense than his friend Erasmus he was a great European and looked beyond his England to mourn the folly of kings and princes, who fought among themselves while the Turk devoured apace and made ready to overwhelm Christendom. "Almighty God

[1] Van Ortroy, *Vie*, pp. 103, 317. The Saint had two hair shirts, for he wore one day and night all through the fourteen months of his incarceration in the Tower, and only put it away on the morning of his execution.

knoweth", he said, 'how grete nede we have to praye ... None ordre, none integryty is now kepte. It semeth Almyghty God to be in a maner in a dead slepe, suffrynge these grete enormytees so longe. Now we must do as the discyples did then in the ship; they awaked Jhesu their master from slepe with cryings and grete noyses, saying, *Magister, non ad te pertinet quod perimus? ...* Our relygion of Crysten fayth is gretely diminished; we be very fewe, ... so that scant the sixth parte of that we had in possession before is left unto us. Therfore, good Lord, without Thou helpe the name of Crysten men shall utterly be destroyed and fordone." [1] When we look East today and see a worse and more ruthless enemy than the Turk, not at the gates of Vienna, but well within the gates, and with Poland, which the Turk never conquered, under his heel, might we not think that St. John Fisher was speaking in 1946 rather than in 1505? And the remedies he proposes, the well-tried ones of penance and prayer preached by the great prophets of Israel in times of national peril or disaster, are still the way of salvation. He would exempt none from the duty of helping Jesus, like another Simon of Cyrene, to carry His cross: "Let no creature thinke in hymselfe and saye, I am not within holy orders, I am not professed to any relygion ... The least Crysten persone, the poorest and most lowe in degree, is nigh in kindred to Almyghty God." So, as he said in his great moving sermon on the Passion, preached on a Good Friday morning: "A man may easily say and think with himself, beholding in his hart the Image of the Crucifixe, Who art Thou, and who am I? Thus every person, both ryche and poore, may thinke, not onely in the church here, but in every other place, and in hys businesse where about he goeth. Thus the poore laborer maye thinke, when he is at plough earing his grounde, and when he goeth to his pastures to see his cattle, or when he is sitting at home by hys fire side, or else when he lyeth in hys bed waking and can not sleepe ... If eyther love or hope or joy or comfort wil

---

[1] *The English Works of John Fisher,* ed. Mayor, E.E.T.S., London, 1876, part i, 170–2. Spelling slightly modernized in places.

make us sing, here in this booke of the Crucifixe is great occasion of song." [1]

Despite his austerities, St. John was the very soul of gentleness and compassion. "In speech he was very milde, temperate and modest, saving in matters of God and His Church ... and therein he would be ernest above his accustomed order" (*Vie,* p. 357). When compelled by his pastoral solicitude to pronounce sentence of excommunication on a propagator of heresy at Cambridge, "after he had proceeded a space in the readinge thereof, he stayed and began again to consider the great waight of his greevous sentence, which so much pearced his hart that even before them all he could not refraine weepinge, ... and so left off without further proceeding in the excommunication for that time" (*Vie,* pp. 112–13). The poorest bishop in England by his own free choice, for the King had offered him Ely in 1505, with five times the revenues of Rochester, and Lincoln in 1514, with eight times those revenues, he beggared himself

---

[1] *English Works,* ed. Mayor, pp. 159, 391, 420. Everybody knows that John Fisher was one of the most learned men of his generation. Father Bridgett goes so far as to say that "there is scarcely a Greek or Latin Christian writer, now contained in the great collection of Migne, ... from whom he does not make apt citations, which he could not have borrowed from other writers since they regarded new controversies, and are introduced by remarks which show conclusively that they were the fruit of his own reading" (*Life,* 2nd ed., p. 93). But perhaps not so many are aware that this retiring Saint, who rarely left his diocese and only once crossed the Channel to be present, under compulsion, on the Field of the Cloth of Gold, was the most famous and popular preacher of his age. In his *Short History of English Literature* (1905, p. 212), Professor George Saintsbury maintained that Fisher wrote incomparably finer English prose than St. Thomas More. That provocative statement brought Professor R. W. Chambers into battle, but even while slaughtering Saintsbury he allowed that "the most finished pulpit eloquence of the day is to be found in the sermons of Fisher" (*The Continuity of English Prose,* written as an introduction to Dr. Elsie Vaughan Hitchcock's fine edition of Harpsfield's *Life and Death of Sir Thomas More,* E.E.T.S., London, 1932, pp. cliv sqq.). Fisher's published sermons were, of course, merely those preached on state occasions. There were thousands of others preached all the year round and every year to his homely flock at Rochester and to the rustics of his many country parishes.

still further by his incessant charities, so that when led back to the Tower after his condemnation to the rope and knife of Tyburn, he was obliged to say to his guards: "My masters, ... I am not able to geve you any thinge in recompence, for I have nothing lefte, and therfore I pray you accept in good part my harty thankes" (*Vie,* pp. 94, 333). So far as is known, St. John never worked a miracle, but his charity attested the mercy and love of God more beautifully than any miracle: "Wheresoever he lay, ether at Rochester or elswhere, his order was to inquire where any poore sicke folkes lay neare him, which after he once knewe, he would diligently visit them. And where he sawe any of them lykely to die, he would preach to them, teaching them the way to die... Many times it was his chaunce to come to such poore howses as for want of chymneys were verie smokie, and therby so noisome that scant any man could abide in them. Nevertheles himself would there sitt by the sicke patient many times the space of three or foure howres together in the smoke, when none of his servants were able to abide in the howse, but were faine to tarrie without till his cominge abroade. And in some other poore howses, where stayres were wantinge, he would never dysdain to clymbe up by a ladder for such a good purpose. And when he had given them ghostly comfort, ... he would at his departure leave behind him his charitable almes, giving charge to his steward or other officers dayly to prepare meate convenient for them (if they were poore) and send it unto them" (*Vie,* pp. 101–2).

Last scene of all, St. John in Herod's dungeon and at the block. The Acts of his Martyrdom, so to call them, rival in pathos and splendour the few gems of such literature which have come down from the Ancient Church, the *Martyrdom of Polycarp,* the *Epistle of the Gallican Churches,* and the *Passion of St. Perpetua.* How like across the centuries and seas our English John was to the disciple of the Beloved Disciple, who would not "swear by the genius of Caesar"! Two broken old men standing up, at peril of stake and rope, for the dignity of man, these were the ultimate heroes. Of St. John's stand the ineffable Froude wrote in his unspeakable *History*: "The peers swore; bishops, abbots, priors, heads of colleges, swore with scarcely an exception—the nation seemed to unite in an unanimous declaration of freedom (*sic!*). In one quarter only, and that a very painful one, was there refusal." In fact, it was all wonderfully like the freedom-loving plebiscites of Stalin and Tito. Long before his death, the Bishop was heard by his household to say that "he should not die in his bedde, ... but alwaies he would utter his wordes with such a cheerfull countenance as they might easily perceive him rather to conceive joy than sorrowe therat" (*Vie,* p. 58). On the eve of his last journey to London, when he was gravely ill, he had written a noble letter to Cromwell, who, like the Proconsul at Smyrna with Polycarp, used all his cunning to persuade him to take the oath. In it occurred a sentence that became a kind of slogan on the lips of St. Thomas More: "Not that I condemn any other men's conscience; their conscience may save them, and mine must save me." He had fainted on the way to London, and in the Tower we find him so weak and wasted that, as the King's chaplain who came to tempt him reported, "his body could not bear the clothes on his back". Near the Christmas of 1534, when he had been eight months in close confinement, grievously ill from liver-disease and suffering tortures in his old bones from the terrible cold of his cell, he wrote again to Cromwell begging for a few clothes to keep him warm and a little food better suited to his ailing condition than the grim prison fare, as well as for the following two favours: "That I may take some preest with me in the Tower ... to hear my confession againste this holy time, and that I may borrow some bookes to styr my devotion more effectually these holy dayes for the comfort of my soul ... And thus our Lord send you a merrie Christenmass and a comfortable, to your hart's desyre" (Bridgett, *Life,* pp. 291–2).

Cromwell's "pore Beadsman", as he signed himself, was created a cardinal on 20 May, 1535, by Pope Paul III, "on account of his fame for virtue and learning". On 17 June he was brought to trial at Westminster and condemned to be hanged, drawn and quartered for treason, the death which, until the last moment five days later, he believed he was going to endure. "Yet could ye not have perceived him one whitt dismaide or disquieted therat, neither in worde nor countenance; but still continewed his former trade of constancie and patience, and that rather with a more joyfull cheere and free minde than ever he had done before" (*Vie,* p. 334). He even jested pleasantly with his gaolers, much in the spirit of the other "bird of Paradise" then held by the King in his cage. When, at dawn on 22 June, the feast of England's first martyr, the Lieutenant of the Tower came to announce to him that it was the King's gracious pleasure he should die that morning by the axe rather than by the rope, he answered: *"I most humbly thanke the King's majestie that it pleaseth him to ridd me from all this worldly business; and I thanke you also for your tydings. But I pray you, Mr. Leiftennant, when is mine howre that I must go hence?—Your howre* (said the Leiftennant) *must be nine of the clocke.—And what howre is it now* (sayd he)?—*It is now about five,* said the Leiftennant.—*Well,* then said he, *let me by your patience sleepe an howre or two; for I have slept verie little this night; and yet, to tell you the truth, not for any fear of death, I thanke God, but by reason of my great infirmitie and weakness."*

Like St. Peter on the night before he was to have been beheaded, he slept soundly for two hours and more, thus paying to God the last and loveliest tribute of his trust. When waked by an attendant, he gave the man his hair shirt and begged him to convey it out of the Tower secretly. Then he dressed himself in "a cleane white shirt and all the best apparrell he had, as cleanly brushed as might be". On the attendant expressing astonishment at those festive preparations, he said gaily: "Dost thou not marke that this is our marriage daie?" At nine the Lieutenant came, and hearing him say to his man, "Reach me my furred typpet to put about my necke," exclaimed: "Oh, my Lord, what need you be so careful for your health for this little time, not much above an hour?" To that he answered: "I thinke no otherwise, but ... though I have, I thanke our Lord, a verie good stomacke and willing minde to die, ... yet will I not hinder my health in the meane time one minute of an howre." Too weak to walk to the scaffold on Tower Hill, he was carried there, but when the soldiers would have helped him up the steps, he said to them: "Nay, masters, seeing I am come so farre, let me aloane, and ye shall see me shifte for myself well enough." [1] As he was mounting the steps, "so lively it was marvaile to them that knew before of his debility and weakness, ... the south east sun shined verie bright in his face, whercupon he said to himself these wordes, lyfting up his hands: *Accedite ad eum et illuminamini, et facies vestrae non confundentur*." And so "with a bold courage and a loving chere" he laid his neck on the block and died "for the fayth of Christes Catholyke Church." [2] The clue to the perfect beauty of his character is best found in the little book of the love of Jesus, *The Wayes to Perfect Religion,* which he composed for his half-sister Elizabeth, a nun, during his imprisonment. "Consider the love of your spouse the sweet Jesu," he wrote, "how excelent it is, how sure, how fast, how constantly abiding. Martirs innumerable both men and women for His love have shead theyr blood ... No paine, no tormentrie, might compell them to forsake His love ... Rather than they would forgo it, they gave no force of the losse of all this world beside, and theyr owne life also." It was the story of his own heart that he there unfolded.

[1] Cf. St. Polycarp: "They were about to nail him to the stake, when he said, 'Let me be as I am. He that granted me to endure the fire will grant me also to remain at the pyre unmoved.' "

[2] Van Ortroy, *Vie,* pp. 337–9, 342, 411–13. It is a noteworthy fact, and such a one as St. Thomas More might have planned from Heaven, that the only fragments surviving of the great life of him written by his nephew, William Rastell, deal almost exclusively with the martyrdom of St. John Fisher, which Rastell witnessed. They were published by van Ortroy and have been re-edited with even greater precision by Dr. Hitchcock in her admirable edition of Harpsfield's *Life and Death of Sir Thomas More* (pp. 221–52).

ST. AIDAN AND HIS ROYAL FRIENDS
ST. OSWALD AND ST. OSWIN

ST. AIDAN and St. Oswald have already been saluted in these pages, but they deserve much more than a passing reverence, for they are two of the dearest great men to be met with in the pages of history, English, Irish or European.[1] St. Oswin, every inch a king, was their match in sanctity and charm of character, a man so winning that Bede, writing eighty years after his tragic death, must sorrow for it as though it had happened that morning. From the way he speaks his sudden "heu, pro dolor!" it would not be surprising to learn that tears had blotted his parchment. "Now there are three kinds of martyrdom," reads an old Irish homily of Bede's time, "to wit, white martyrdom, green martyrdom, and red martyrdom. White martyrdom consists in a man's abandoning everything he loves for God's sake. Green martyrdom consists in this, that by means of fasting and labour he frees himself from his evil desires, or suffers toil in penance and repentance. Red martyrdom consists in the endurance of a cross or death for Christ's sake, as happened to the Apostles." [2] St. Oswald and St. Oswin are accounted red martyrs; their friend St. Aidan was a white and green one.

Nothing whatever seems to be known about his Irish beginnings. We meet him first in the pages of Bede at Iona, about

[1] If anyone thinks that such praise is extravagant let him blame the Venerable Bede and not the present poor copyist. The Saints of England, whether Saxon, Norman, Plantagenet or Tudor, were peculiarly lovable. About that there can be no two opinions, and the more's the pity that they are not better known and honoured.

[2] Ryan, *Irish Monasticism,* London, 1931, p. 197. The immense learning of this invaluable book is worn with the easiest air, and Father Ryan is never far away from the humour that lurks in such a reference as he makes to the numerous Britons in Irish monasteries: "They were celebrated in Irish monastic tradition for their short tempers, which must have been very short indeed to attract attention in a land where the average native temper was short enough!" (p. 206).

the year 635, with the crown of his white and green martyrdom already upon his head. He may have gone to Iona in boyhood, and in that case it is possible that he had the privilege of looking upon the "glad angelic" face of St. Columba, who died in 597, the year St. Augustine came to England. Though so little is known about him personally, the pattern of his life in the great monastery is easy enough to trace. Nearly all the Irish monks of those days came from prosperous families, and Aidan, quite apart from the aristocracy of soul conferred by his holiness, was undoubtedly a man of fine breeding. Otherwise, two kings, themselves the flower and perfection of Anglian nobility, could hardly have loved him so dearly. We take too much for granted if we think that such a man did not feel keenly the pang of parting from kindred and country, for, as an eminent English scholar has said, the lives of the Irish saints "illustrate that homesickness, so characteristic in all ages of the Irish exile, which it sometimes required a miracle to cure".[1] That was the first step in his white martyrdom, and one so generously taken that it has blanked out his early life completely. But to become an exile for the love of God was not merely an exercise in renunciation. English and Continental observers said that the "consuetudo peregrinandi" had become "a second nature with the Irish", but this inveterate habit of wandering abroad came from a kind of divine restlessness of missionary zeal "to which was due the fact that so large a portion of the Continent owed their first knowledge of the glad tidings to Irishmen".[2] Those itinerant Irish monks of long ago were in their own humble fashion Xaviers, saints in a hurry, not much good at organizing things, but great at opening doors for other men, the Theodores and Bonifaces, to enter by and prevail.

The austerities of Iona, though extensive, were not, like those

[1] Plummer, *Vitae Sanctorum Hiberniae*, Oxford, 1910, vol. i, p. cxxiii. In her famous *Wandering Scholars*, Miss Helen Waddell gives a few touching examples of the exiled Irish Monks' nostalgia (7th edition, 1934, pp. 31–2).

[2] Plummer, *Venerabilis Baedae Opera Historica*, Oxford, 1896, vol. ii, p. 170.

of the Egyptian monks, excessive. St. Columba slept on the bare rock with a stone under his head, but he allowed his disciples to have beds with straw palliasses and pillows of sorts, to make easier their heavily rationed slumbers. It is probable, though not certain, that two modest meals, a dinner at noon and a supper at sunset, were allowed daily, except on Wednesdays and Fridays, and during Lent, when the famished monks had to wait until night for their only refection. The *daemonium meridianum* of the Psalmist, who incidentally has gone into retirement in the new Latin version of the Psalter, was to them primarily the devil of hunger, that brought on lassitude and threatened vocations. But with Aidan, as we learn from Bede, this particular fiend never had a chance. The repasts at Iona, if quite as small, may have been a little more varied than those of other Irish monasteries, in which bread and vegetables were the staple fare, for St. Adamnan in his life of St. Columba mentions milk, fish, seal-meat and even beef as being occasionally served. "To the question whether intoxicating drink should be allowed at meals or no, the Irish monastic fathers returned no unanimous answer, but public opinion on the whole seems to have been against the teetotallers. The monk who drank nothing but water for thirty years was regarded as a great exception and his example was not followed with enthusiasm. Beer was used in Columba's monasteries, and the sternness of the Saint stopped short at the decree that he who had spilled any should drink water only until the amount spared equalled the amount wasted. Cronan of Roscrea worked a miracle to provide his guests with beer, and the result was so successful that they all became inebriated!" [1]

---

[1] Ryan, *Irish Monasticism,* pp. 338–9. Father Ryan tells in his notes about a certain Abbot Maelruain of Tallaght who was one of the mysterious Culdees and as rabid a teetotaller as St. Jerome. One day, his friend, another abbot named Duiblitir, begged him to allow the Tallaght monks beer on Easter Sunday, Whit Sunday and Christmas Day. Maelruain flatly refused, saying: "As long as my injunctions are obeyed in this place, the liquor that causes forgetfulness of God shall not be drunk in this place." The good Duiblitir was not for accepting that new definition of

The monks of Iona, as indeed monks everywhere and all good Christians too, conceived themselves to be primarily soldiers on campaign, fighting a hard, unending battle, not only with the powers of darkness, but even more against the eight leagued enemies of God in their own hearts: pride, vanity, anger, lust, gluttony, covetousness, dejection, and perhaps worst of the lot, *acedia* or spiritual tedium.[1] That explains all their hard ways with themselves, their fastings, vigils, other macerations, incessant prayers, and toil in field or workshop, so that, in St. Jérome's words, the monk would be "tired out before he goes to rest and half-asleep while still on his feet". That was the price they paid humbly and gladly for "the prize of learning love", and the sweet paradox of it is that by all their conflict with human nature they became only the more exquisitely human, men of limitless sympathy and compassion who could not see so much as a beast or bird in trouble without wanting to help it. Referring to Columba, Adamnan his biographer writes: "One time when he was dwelling on Iona,[2] the Saint called

beer, and replied: "Well, my monks shall drink it, and they shall be in heaven along with yours." To this Maelruain retorted rather nastily: "My monks, who shall keep my rule, shall not need to be cleansed by the fire of Doom, for they shall be clean already. Your monks, however, may perchance have something for the fire of Doom to cleanse." Very different from the censorious Maelruain was the delightful Abbot Ruadán of Lothra who had a fine elm tree from which flowed a beautiful beer. And "the monks of Ireland yearned to Ruadán".

[1] Those eight *fontes peccatorum* are the ancestors of our Seven Deadly Sins. It will be noticed that envy has no place among them but that vanity has—the *caenodoxia* of Abbot Joannelinus's Sunday preparation for Mass. Benjamin Franklin, while strong for the Particular Examen, was tenderer to vanity than the ancient monks. "I give it fair quarter wherever I meet with it," he wrote in his *Autobiography*, "being persuaded that it is often productive of good; therefore, in many cases, it would not be altogether absurd if a man were to thank God for his vanity among the other comforts of life."

[2] Adamnan calls the Island *Iova insula,* the first word being an adjective derived from its Irish name of I or Y or Hi. Some distracted or sleepy scribe of later times wrote Iona for Iova, and so by the double happy mistake of taking an adjective for a noun and then mis-spelling it we got our musical Iona. The mistake became stereotyped "by the fancy

one of the brethren and thus addressed him: 'At dawn three
days hence you will go to the western part of this island and
wait there, sitting down by the sea shore. A certain crane will
come as your guest, carried by the force of the wind all the long
way from the north of Ireland. It will arrive after midday, very
spent and weary, almost at the end of its strength, and fall down
before you there on the sea shore. You will be solicitous to lift
it compassionately and carry it to the nearest house, where for
three days and nights you will carefully feed it and minister to
it as to a guest. Then, its strength completely restored, it will
not wish to tarry away from home among us any longer, and
will fly back to the sweet coast of Ireland from whence it
came.' " [1]

Thirty-eight years after the death of Columba the Beloved,
"omnibus carus, hilarem semper faciem ostendens," Oswald,
son of Ethelfrith the Destroyer, the fierce Anglian king who
had slaughtered the poor unarmed British monks at the Battle
of Chester, emerged from his retreat at Iona, where he had
learned the Irish language and the ways of Christian holiness,
to join issue with the marauding Briton Cadwallon, a Christian
in name but a black pagan at heart.[2] Supported by twelve devoted thanes, who had shared his exile and acquired his faith,
Oswald gathered around him a small Anglian army, erected as
a rallying-point a great wooden cross on a hill a few miles north
of Hexham where the Roman Wall dips steeply into the valley
of the Tyne, and in its shadow made ready with many prayers
for the last decisive encounter between the old order and the
new. Memories of Iona must have crowded on him at that critical time, for, as already mentioned, even his dreams, while he

which saw in Iona the Hebrew equivalent for the name Columba"
(Plummer, *Venerabilis Baedae Opera Historica,* II, 127).

[1] Migne, *Patrologia Latina,* vol. 88, col. 741.

[2] At least so says Bede, but he did not like Britons, and Cadwallon,
King of Gwynedd, may not have been quite such a thundering villain
as he is painted. Anyhow, he had many real wrongs to avenge, and if he
allied himself with the enemies of the faith, that is only what many
"Most Christian" kings would do afterwards, with less excuse.

snatched a brief sleep in his tent the night before the battle, were invaded by Columba, whom he saw spreading his Irish cloak protectingly over the little English army.[1] The great victory followed, and soon he was master of England from the Humber to the Forth, even if old Penda the Pagan remained a menace in the south. His first care in that glorious hour, and it proves the quality of his faith, was to send to Iona for missionaries to evangelize his backsliding or unconverted Northumbrians, among whom the achievement of Roman Paulinus had been largely undone by the depredations of Penda and Cadwallon.

In those days monks were mostly laymen, only a few chosen spirits being promoted to the priesthood in order that their brethren might have the comfort of Mass and the Sacraments. Each large monastery took care also as a rule to have a bishop in the community who would ordain such priests as were necessary, so Seghine, the Abbot of Iona, had a man ready at Oswald's call. Now, painful though it is to admit it, some evidence exists that not *all* Irishmen at all times have been paragons of the patient, kind, forbearing, courteous, hopeful charity which St. Paul hymned in his First Epistle to the Corinthians, and, alas, Abbot Seghine's first choice for Northumbria fell short of the beautiful standard. He was a brusque old gentleman, it seems, of an "austere stomacke", who soon returned to Iona to report that the English were "folkes that might not be reclaymed, of a hard capacity and fierce nature". When he had said his say and put the English in their place, Aidan spoke: "Me thinketh, brother, that you have been more rigorous than reason would with that unlerned audience, and that you have not, according to the Apostle's instruction, first given them milke of milde doctrine untill being by litle and litle nourished and weaned with the worde of God, they were

---

[1] This incident is not to be found in Migne's deplorably defective edition of Adamnan's Columba, but is in the great edition of Reeves reissued in the "Historians of Scotland" series, vol. vi, Edinburgh, 1874, pp. 5–6 (English), 112–3 (Latin).

able to understand the more perfect misteries and fulfill the greater commaundementes of God." Thus did Aidan, the true disciple of Columba, make his appearance in history. All eyes were turned upon him, says Bede, and the monks quickly concluded that he was the best man among them to be "sent to instruct those unlerned paynims,... for he was chiefly garnished with the grace of discretion,... and did afterward show him selfe to be beautified with all other vertues." [1]

Of Aidan and Oswald it could truly be said that the soul of the Irish monk was knit with the soul of the English king and he loved him as his own soul. Nothing in religious history is more attractive than the covenant of those two wonderful men to bring to the rude clients of Thor and Woden a knowledge of the goodness and kindness of God our Saviour. Every Irish

---

[1] *The History of the Church of Englande,* compiled by Venerable Bede, Englishman. Translated by Thomas Stapleton, Student in Divinitie. Antwerp, 1565. Oxford, 1930, pp. 173–4. Some Anglican scholars in the past, including, strange to say, the great Bishop Lightfoot, were in the habit of invoking Aidan as a witness to their theory of continuity. Thus in his otherwise admirable *Chapters of Early English Church History* (2nd ed., Oxford, 1888, p. 144) Professor Bright ventured the statement that Aidan "would never have admitted the principle that all episcopal jurisdiction must be derived from Rome." But only three pages earlier he had invoked the witness of Bede, the noblest Roman of them all, to the validity of Aidan's episcopal consecration. Would Bede, who was as much a "Romanist" as Wilfrid or Theodore or Augustine himself or even Cardinal Manning, have lauded Aidan to the skies if he had had the slightest suspicion that he did not hold with the Pope? The idea is preposterous, and anyhow it is funny, when one comes to think of it, that defenders of Anglican continuity should have to go begging in Ireland of all places for an alms in support of a theory without other visible means of subsistence. There is, however, in Migne (*P.L.,* 80, 21–4) a famous piece of evidence for continuity, namely the letter of Abbot Dinoot of Bangor, in Flint, to St. Augustine of Canterbury, in which he decisively rejects the papal claims. The only trouble is that the learned world of our time, Protestant no less than Catholic, decisively rejects Dinoot's letter as the clever forgery of some Welsh Protestant in the sixteenth century, who deceived Spelman, the discoverer of the document, Wilkins in his *Concilia,* and finally J. P. Migne himself (cf. Haddon and Stubbs, *Councils and Ecclesiastical Documents,* vol. i, 1896, p. 122; Gougaud, *Christianity in Celtic Lands,* Eng. tr., 1932, p. 215).

monk, even though he might live in community, was by disposition more than half a hermit, in love with solitude, so Aidan passed by busy imperial York, the see of Paulinus, to search for some equivalent of the rocky island paradise he had lost. It was there to his hand in Lindisfarne, another island of destiny that only awaited his coming to take its place with Lérins and Iona as a marvellous seed-plot of religion and civilization. At Lindisfarne he gathered round him helpers from Iona, and formed a school of English boys, twelve in number, like the Apostles,[1] whom he trained with loving care that they might in due course preach to their own countrymen. Among them were the future Bishops Chad and Eata, two saints in a mist, about whom Bede tells us just enough to whet our baulked appetites for a great deal more. Perhaps they were some of the many youths Aidan had ransomed from slavery, which was one of his favourite charities.

When he speaks of Aidan Bede's language begins to glow: "This thing did chiefly commend his doctrine to all men, that the lerning which he taught was correspondent to the life that he led. He was not desyrous after worldly goods; he was not enamoured with present vanitees. His joy and comfort was foorthwyth to distribute to the pooue that met him all that was given him of kinges or other wealthy men of the worlde. He used to travel continually,...never on horse backe but allways on foote, except peradventure greate neede had forced him to ryde. And in his travel what dyd he? Forsoothe whome so ever he mette, riche or poore, incontinent abyding for a time with them either he allured them to receive the faythe if they were out of the faythe, or strengthened them in the faythe

---

[1] Whenever the Irish monks could manage it, they liked to do things by dozens. St. Columba came to Iona with twelve companions and St. Oswald left it with the same number. The idea behind such expressions as a baker's dozen, consisting of thirteen loaves or cakes, and a sitting of hen's eggs, which is usually thirteen, seems to have been to honour our Lord and His Apostles. The supposed unluckiness of thirteen may have been due at least partly to Protestant propaganda against Catholic customs.

if they were in it, exhorting them eftsoones no less in works than wordes to alms giving and other good deedes. And his religious life so farre passed the slackness and key-colde devotion of our time that all they which went with him, were they professed into religion or were they lay brethren, gave themselves continually to contemplation ... Every devout man and woman taught by his ensamples tooke up a custome all the whole year through, saving between Easter and Whitsontyde, upon Wensday and Friday to continew in fasting untill three of the clocke in the afternoon. If rych men had done any thing amisse, he never for hope of honour or feare of displeasure spared to tell them of it, but with sharpe rebuking amended them. As for such gyftes as in money were liberally given him by rich men, he dyd either (as we have sayed) give them in a dole for the reliefe of the poore, or else he laid it out for the raunsoming of those that had been wrongfully solde. Finally, many of such as by money he had redeemed, he made after his scholars, bringing them up in learning and vertue and exalting them to the highe dignitie of priesthood." [1]

In his book of lectures, *Leaders of the Northern Church,* published posthumously in 1890, Bishop Lightfoot delivered himself of the statement that "it was not Augustine, but Aidan, who was the true apostle of England", a remarkable bouquet for Ireland, if it was not rather intended as a brickbat for Rome. Still, Oswald must not be left out of the picture, who "being advaunced to so royall majesty, was ever notwithstanding lowly to all, gracious to the poore, and bountifull to all pilgrimes and strangers," a prince more ideal than Plato dreamed of, combining the valour and wisdom of an Alfred with the deep personal piety of a St. Louis. Out of respect for his ascetic habits, Oswald did not often invite his friend Aidan to dinner, but one such occasion Bede has made memorable. It was an Easter Sunday, and "a silver dish replenished with princely deintees" had been set in front of the King and the Bishop. Before they could partake of it

[1] Stapleton's *Bede,* pp. 172–3.

the royal almoner hurried in to say that "a very great number
of poore people flocking from all places did sit in the courte,
looking for some almes from the Kinge". Oswald at once
ordered that the delicacies "be bestowed on the poore and
the dishe of silver broken and by peecemeale parted among
them, at the sight whereof the Bishop who sate by the Kinge,
being delited with such a worke of mercy, took him by the
right hand and said: I praie God this hand be never consumed." [1]

Bede says explicitly that Oswald caught his holiness from
Aidan, listening to his words and watching him day by day
so quietly and perfectly fulfilling the divine injunction to do
justly, to love mercy, and to walk humbly with his God.
"This was a gracious and pleasaunt sight that, whereas the
Bishop was unskillfull of the English tongue and the Kinge by
reason of his longe banishement in Scotland understode and
spake the Scottish [Irish] very well, when the Bishop preached
the faith of Christ, the King was interpreter of the heavenly
worde to his dukes and subjects," namely the Angles of the
Yorkshire dales and the Picts or "Redshankes", as Stapleton
likes to call them, of the country beyond the Cheviots and
Tweed It was a sight those sturdy, uncouth conquerors and
conquered could not get over, and so they flocked to baptism,
drawn half and half by Aidan's story and Oswald's example.
They were thorough in whatever they did, good or bad, and
made splendid Christians, even if it was necessary, as Gregory
the Great allowed [2] and Gregory the Wonder-Worker practised,

[1] Bede, iii, 6; Stapleton, 175-6. "Which thinge came even so to passe."
Five centuries later, Simeon of Durham produced good evidence that the
hand was still undecayed, and William of Malmesbury, about the same
time, contributed the information that Oswald was the first English saint
whose relics worked miracles (*Gesta Regum,* ed. Stubbs, Rolls Series,
1887, p. 54), a priority of no small distinction in that chronicler's eyes.

[2] "No doubt at all," he instructed St. Mellitus to tell St. Augustine at
Canterbury, "but that it is impossible to cut off everything at once from
rough natures, because he who would climb to a height must ascend step
by step and cannot jump the whole distance" (Bede, i, 30; Stapleton,
p. 77).

to leave them many of their traditional customs, with the saints substituted for their gods and fairies, and our Lady taking over from the rather attractive spouse of Woden who gave her name to Friday. That was not to paganize Christianity but, the very opposite, to Christianize paganism.[1]

The "pulcherrimum spectaculum" of monarch and monk evangelizing the people shoulder to shoulder was brought to an end in August, 642, by the implacable old foe of the Christian name, Penda of Mercia, who waylaid and slew the Northumbrian King at the Battle of Maserfield. "Oswald of the Fair Hand", as men would afterwards lovingly call him, died with a prayer for his soldiers on his lips. He was only thirty-eight years old. Penda exposed his severed head and arms on wooden stakes, but they were rescued the following year and taken home, the arms to Bamburgh and the head to Lindisfarne, where Aidan sorrowfully interred it in his little monastery church. Afterwards it was placed in the coffin of St. Cuthbert and shared the famous Odyssey of his relics until they came to rest in Durham Cathedral. Oswald, Aidan, Cuthbert, they are names to conjure with, and they did some remarkable conjuring from heaven, such as bringing Penda's whole family to baptism and Christianizing all England from the Forth to the Severn. "The corpse of St. Oswald, decapitated and dismembered, helped to propagate the new religion as effectually as Oswald the living king",[2] and Aidan's Irish disciple and successor, Finan, had the sweet triumph of converting Penda's son, Paeda, and marrying him to the daughter of Oswald's brother, Oswy. Thirty years after Maserfield, the lady in question, then Queen of the Mercians, had her uncle's sacred remains translated from Bamburgh to the great monastery of Bardney, in Lincolnshire. But the good monks of that place were stout local patriots and refused at first to harbour the

[1] Bright (*Chapters of Early English Church History,* pp. 72–6) is excellent on this question which Frazer in his massive volumes discusses with so much learned obtuseness.

[2] Hodgkin, *A History of the Anglo-Saxons,* 1930, vol. i, p. 289.

bones of Mercia's one-time enemy, though, as Bede reports, "they knew him to be a saint". The relics were accordingly left unhonoured in the waggon that brought them at the monastery door, and the monks went to bed thinking they had struck a blow for the glory of Mercia. But next day they changed their tune when they heard the whole county talking with awe of the great pillar of light which had shone to heaven all night long from the waggon, and "began now to desyre earnestly that the same holy relikes might be laied up in their house" (Stapleton's *Bede*, p. 188). Many are the fine stories which Bede and others tell of the miracles wrought by the martyred king, who was a real king of hearts and captured the imagination and love of Christian men all over Europe.[1]

Oswald gone, Northumbria fell asunder into its well-known but confusing component parts, Deira and Bernicia, which was a bad thing, regretted by countless schoolboys ever since. But it had one splendid result in bringing Oswin from his exile in Wessex to the throne of Deira, the southern of the two kingdoms with its capital at York. Oswin was a second Oswald, and became even dearer to Aidan, if that was possible. Here is Bede's portrait of him: "A marvaylous devoute and godly man, ... of countenance beautifull, of stature high, in talke courtyous and gentle, in all pointes civill and amiable, no lesse honourable and bountifull to the noble, than free and liberal to persons of lowe degree. Whereby it happened that for his outward personage, inward hart, and princely port he had the love of all men ... Among other his rare vertues, his humilitie and passing lowlynesse excelled." Then Bede tells of Oswin and

[1] Plummer in his edition of Bede mentions centres of devotion to Oswald at Utrecht, Soissons, Lisbon, Udine, Venice, Vicenza, Cologne, Constance, Mainz, Münster, Ratisbon, Salzburg and Prague (vol. ii, pp. 159–60). One of the best of the miracle stories, "a lesson for ungodly students" Stapleton calls it, is about a learned but wicked monk of Ireland who was converted to God "in all hart and deede" by drinking a cup of water containing a chip of the tree on which Oswald's head had been impaled, the tree that is supposed to have given Oswestry its name on the map.

Aidan perhaps the most charming story in the whole of his wonderful book: "He had given to Bishop Aidan a very faire and proper gelding...to passe over waters and ditches, or when any other necessitie constrained. It fortuned shortly after, a certaine poor weake man met the Bishop, riding on his gelding, and craved an almes of him. The Bishop as he was a passing pitefull man and a very father to needy persons, [alighted] and gave the poore man the gelding, gorgeously trapped as he was. The King hearing after hereof, talked of it with the Bishop, as they were entering the palace to dinner, and saied, What meaned you, my Lord, to give awaie to the beggar that faire gelding which we gave you for your own use? Have we no other horses of lesse price...to bestowe upon the poore, but that you must give awaie that princely horse? To whom the Bishop answered, Why talketh your Grace thus? Is that broode of the mare dearer in your sight than that son of God, the poore man? Which being said they entered for to dine. The Bishop took his place appointed, but the King would stand a while by the fire, ...where musing with himself upon the wordes which the Bishop had spoken, suddenly put off his sword and came in great haste to the Bishop, falling downe at his feete, and beseeching him not to be displeased with him for the wordes he had spoken, saying he would never...measure any more hereafter what or how much he should bestow of his goods upon the sonnes of God, the poore" (Stapleton's *Bede*, 197–8). With something of awe in his heart, Aidan helped Oswin to his feet and lovingly comforted him, but as the meal proceeded became more and more sad himself until at last he burst into tears. He foresaw then what the end would be, and shortly afterwards Oswy, the Bernician king, on his march to power, caused Oswin to be assassinated. The crime broke Aidan's heart. He survived his friend less than a fortnight, dying suddenly, as he had mostly lived, without a roof over his head or anything but the bare ground to lie on. Such was what the Irish annals called touchingly the *Quies Aidani episcopi Saxonum*. The night he breathed his last,

31 August, 651, a young shepherd on the Lammermuir Hills saw a multitude of angels escorting his glorious soul to Heaven, and thereupon promptly renounced the world to become St. Cuthbert of Lindisfarne.

OFTEN enough the lives of the great Saints only serve to make us who read them feel like worms. We hear of their long prayers, their miracles, their incredible labours and terrifying austerities, and we say, perhaps, with a despondent shrug—*"Gigantes erant in diebus illis"*. But let us take courage because there are many ways of going to Heaven besides in a fiery chariot, and at the time when Francis de Sales, Vincent de Paul, and other mighty men of God were changing the face of the earth there also lived in such homely, familiar places as Kildare and Durham an authentic saint who never worked a miracle or did a famous thing in his life, except to get hanged. The name of this quiet, physically weak, cheery nonentity was Ralph Corby. Ralph was the apotheosis of the average man, so little distinguished for anything, even brains, that his superior wrote about him in the following terms when he first came on the English Mission in 1632: "His abilities are utterly mediocre and both judgment and prudence are wanting to him. He has had very little experience and made but small progress in his studies. How he gets on in his dealings with the neighbour time will tell, as he is by nature slow and of a pensive cast of mind. In other respects, too, he appears to be little fitted for most of our ministerial duties." That, then, was that, and yet this half of a broken hope is crowned now with a glory which not even St. Francis or St. Vincent was granted to attain, a glory purchased by faithful traffic with the one real talent he possessed—a great love for his fellow men.

The Corbys, or Corbingtons, as the name was often written, belonged to the prosperous yeoman classes of County Durham. Ralph's grandfather had conformed to the requirements of the Elizabethan Government in matters of religion, and brought up his only son, Gerard, according to the Thirty-nine Articles. Gerard, however, was born with a Catholic soul that could not assimilate those ingenious formularies, but only when a grown man did he finally reject them. His own son, Ambrose, reports that he was then disinherited and cast penniless upon a hostile world, but from evidence in the Record Office, London, we may take a much more charitable view of the elder Corby's behaviour. There can be no doubt at all that he loved his boy, and what he did was probably to give him some money and explain that, as the presence of a recusant in the house would very likely be the ruin of them all, it would be better if he tried to establish his fortunes elsewhere.

Gerard accordingly said good-bye to home and obtained a post as serving-man in some Catholic family. But the long arm of the law found him out even in that lowly disguise, and, probably about the time of the Spanish Armada's sailing, he decided to take refuge in Ireland. There his good address and pleasant manners won him entrance to Maynooth Castle, the ancestral home of the Geraldines. His mistress was "the beautiful Mabel Browne", daughter of Sir Anthony Browne, Master of the Horse to King Edward VI, who had married the restored eleventh Earl of Kildare. The Fitzgeralds had not yet been robbed of their faith and very probably the Countess, too, was a Catholic. At any rate, she took a great liking for the young exile whom loyalty to the Church had brought to her doors. It would seem that Gerard's sister was there also, and doubtless for the same reason, because on 9 May, 1591, their father addressed to Maynooth a letter, from which the following is an extract:—"Son Garrat my hartie commendations to you ... and I doth desire God to bless you and to make you His servant and to prosper all your doings. The cause of my writing to you at this time is to certifie you that I have been before the great commission divers times ... for mantaninge of you and yr sister, for the doe charge me that I do know wher you and she is and allso do almoste forse me to be bounde in an hundred markes that nather I nor your mother shall entertain nather of you, nor have no maintenance by me." [1]

Meantime in England there was a girl named Isabella Richardson, to whom Gerard had given his heart. After a while at Maynooth he crossed over to claim her, and had the joy of seeing her received into the Church before they got married. There followed what we must suppose to have been a very precarious and modest honeymoon and then Maynooth once more, "where they lived some twelve years in very good esteem with my Lady of Kildare, serving in her house". At Maynooth, probably in a cottage on the beautiful estate, were born their children Robert, Ralph, Richard, Mary, Ambrose and Catherine. Ralph appeared on Lady Day, 1598, in the middle of Hugh O'Neill's glorious rebellion. It was a great time and a great place to grow up in, and the little fellow must have been familiar almost from his cradle with the thrilling story of the Geraldines, whose Castle walls and wide, green acres formed the whole of his world. Like O'Neill, to whom the Pope had granted the high privileges of the old crusaders, they too were renowned for their staunch Catholicism, pathetic evidence of which lay before the Corbys' door in the ruins of "St. Mary's College", founded by them to propagate the Faith and destroyed by Henry VIII. Young as he was, Ralph would certainly have been told of the superb defiance hurled at that tyrant by Lord Thomas Fitzgerald, gallant Silken Thomas, and how the poor boy, for he was little more, ended his brief episode of glory on a gallows at a place called Tyburn, near London. Without any great stretch of imagination we can

[1] Record Office, *Dom. Eliz.*, 238, 148. The old man goes on to say that he was yet "in great estemation" with the Dean of Durham and "Doer" or manager of his coal-mines at Rawton and Spenneymoor. It shows how thorough was the Elizabethan persecution that not even the influence of a powerful prelate such as the Dean availed to save the most harmless people from molestation. The next letter in the series is also addressed to Maynooth by a certain very lovable Thomas Awde who tells how hard he found it to keep his two little shops open in villages near Durham City, because he was a Catholic.

picture Gerard Corby showing his son the yew tree under which Lord Thomas played his harp so wistfully on his last evening at Maynooth, the yew tree that still stands at the entrance to the great new St. Mary's College which a later generation of the Geraldines, Protestants through no fault of their own, did much to help into existence.

Thus with brave and holy memories to mould him did Ralph's childhood pass. Ireland did not retain him long, for though Rye Water that glides by at Maynooth might be a very pleasant stream, it was Derwent and Tyne that flowed through his father's dreams. Gerard also had news that old Grandfather Corby was near his end and dissipating the family property at a ruinous pace, so, on the death of Queen Elizabeth, he returned with his wife and children to Durham, where he had the great happiness of bringing his father into the Church before he left them at the age of a hundred.

Now began ten years of hide and seek for the family, during the course of which Gerard crossed the Irish Sea several times, and, still oftener, the North Sea, "living", says his son Ambrose, "in a manner in continual travel to provide as best he could for his children and family, which he did abundantly." In Durham he was not left in peace very long but driven into Lancashire, where also the zealous officials of King James harried him from place to place. Only once, however, did they succeed in laying him by the heels, when he was promptly cast into prison. How his wife and children fared during his absence is not indicated but easy enough to guess, and it was in such conditions of hardship and hourly tension that Ralph went through his boyhood. No wonder, then, that his health should have suffered and the seeds of a crippling disease have been laid in him which must have ended his days prematurely, had the rope of Tyburn not anticipated it.

By his brother's account he was a quiet and most peaceable lad, utterly devoted to his parents and with a strangely unboyish indifference to the attractions of money. Whenever a copper or two came to him he would at once make them over to his younger brother. There is only one more trait, namely that on Sundays and holydays it was his custom to recite the Little Office of the Blessed Virgin with great devotion. At the age of fifteen a big change came over his life as his father then decided, for the sake of the children's education, to seek a permanent asylum on the Continent.

The place selected was St. Omer, now in France but then in Flanders, principally because of the flourishing College which Father Robert Persons, that bravest of men, had started there in 1592 to save the faith of English boys debarred from all educational facilities at home. How the Corby family managed their escape abroad is not recorded, but, as there were spies at every port, it cannot have been an easy exploit. Perhaps they got away through Scotland, which country is reported in the State papers of the time to have been "the common passage for English caterpillars into foreign parts". On arrival, Ralph and his two brothers, Robert and Richard, were entered at the College, while their parents, with the three younger children, established themselves modestly in the town. It was just as well that the whole family had come over, because two years later King James issued an edict, in which the St. Omer College had the honour of special mention, ordering the immediate return of all English children who did not wish to see their parents' property confiscated. As far as the Corbys were concerned, that unpleasant despot might now confiscate to his heart's content.

Of Ralph's life at the College next to nothing is known except that he went arrayed in a uniform of canvas doublet with knee breeches and worsted stockings, so distinctive in appearance that the dramatist Massenger made a joking reference to it in his play, *The Fatal Dowry*. His prefect of studies was a certain Father Thunder, whose name suited him down to the ground. According to the spy Wadsworth, who knew the College life intimately, this vigorous man used to exercise "many of his claps" upon the aforesaid breeches, and doubtless Ralph had his fair share of them, being so little good at his books. As all the boys were, in a sense, outlaws for their faith, the religious spirit of the place flourished mightily. Ralph soon made up his mind to be a priest and, having battled as well as he could with Latin and Greek, passed at the age of twenty-one to Seville, where Father Persons had established a seminary. Owing to a breakdown in health, due, no doubt, to the murderous Seville sun, he was obliged to leave after a year, and we next find him at yet another College of the great Persons, that of Valladolid, where he remained for five years and received his ordination. Immediately afterwards, he joined the Society of Jesus and made his novitiate at Watten, a little place about twenty miles inland from Calais and about five miles north of St. Omer. That over, he was sent to finish his theology at the Jesuit College in Liége, and then for two years to the "House of Tertians" in Ghent, where the final touches were put to his religious formation.

England came next, but before accompanying him thither we may take a brief look at the other members of his family. Of his three brothers, two joined the Jesuits shortly after himself, and the remaining one died while preparing to enter the novitiate. Both his sisters became Benedictine nuns at Brussels, so by 1628 Gerard and Isabella Corby were alone in the house, their respective ages being sixty and sixty-five. Great-souled pair that they were, they decided to follow their children's example, Gerard going to the Jesuits as a laybrother and his wife to the Benedictines in Ghent. As Sister Benedicta she lived to be a hundred and up to her last Advent kept the Church's fasts very strictly, "saying daily a world of prayers and practising austerities with constant zeal". Despite her great age she used to sweep her cell, make her bed and mend her clothes with her own hands right to the very end.

As for her husband, after his death at Watten in 1637, his Rector, Father Robert Stafford, spoke with feeling of the old man's "golden charity". For the last five years of his life he was totally blind, "all which time it is wonderful how saintly and how laudably he carried himself and more than once hath told me that he was so well content with his lot as that he wished for no other." Like his beloved Isabella, "he was not more solicitous of anything than not to be troublesome to anyone", so he, too, up to the end, "made his own bed, swept his chamber, and went from place to place in the house without any guide." The Rector thought it unnecessary to speak of his piety, "being that he spent daily, both forenoon and afternoon, many hours with exceeding reverence upon his knees, either before the Blessed Sacrament or Our Lady's altar."

One would certainly have to go far to parallel such a family record, but the brightest part of the story has still to be told. The English Jesuits of those days parcelled out their country into twelve districts, and these again into a certain number of "Residences", each with a specific name. In 1632 Father Ralph Corby was appointed to the Residence of St. Michael the Archangel, by which was meant the Yorkshire area. Possibly because his superior, who wrote the report quoted at the beginning of this sketch, did not think much of him, he remained only a short time attached to St. Michael's, and in 1634 was at work in the adjoining Residence of St. John the Evangelist. This extensive district included his native county of Durham, to which the Jesuits used to refer in their letters as "Mrs. Durham" or the "Bishoprick". The Bishoprick had the advantage for Catholics of being far removed from London, so throughout the reign of Charles I the priests working in it appear to have suffered comparatively little molestation. Writing on this point when a prisoner in Newgate, Father Corby said that all his time in England, "through God's infinite goodness and love towards me and friends' good help, hath fallen out with great facility, especially considering the few talents I have and the infirmity of my corporal health."

The Jesuits on the English Mission, of whom there were surprising numbers, had come to be divided into three classes: (1) those who led an entirely private life as chaplains to noble or wealthy families, because, through infirmity or age, they could not undertake more active work; (2) those who lived

in Catholic areas or with families exempted from the pressure
of the penal laws, and so could freely receive people at home
or visit them out-of-doors; (3) the free-lances, who lived as
best they could in hiding, and carried on their apostolate at
the risk of their lives. It was to this third heroic class that
Father Corby belonged, as we learn from a little book entitled
Certamen Triplex, which his brother Ambrose published at
Antwerp within a year of his martyrdom:

"In the neighbourhood where he lived were many Catholics
of narrow means and obscure station, who could neither main-
tain priests at their houses, by reason of their poverty, nor go
to them elsewhere, on account of the danger they would incur.
These Ralph always thought it his special province to console,
help in every way, provide with the Sacraments and visit at
their homes in the villages. He was quite indefatigable at this
work, going about it not only during the daytime but towards
dusk or late at night, in the heats of summer and the cold and
rain of winter. He made his journeys on foot, carrying a stick
in his hand, which he used jestingly to call his horse and, on
entering a house, would commend it accordingly to the care
of those within. That he might the more freely visit the
cottages of the poor without arousing suspicion he used to go
in a very humble guise, wearing no tunic or cloak, so that
he might have been taken for a common servant, or farm-hand,
or letter-carrier. His lodging, too, and meals were such as
poor people are accustomed to, unprepared and haphazard, and
he used always to say, looking very pleased and with a grateful
and joyous heart, that he was as much delighted with them as
with the greatest luxuries. It is no wonder, then, that, for
labours carried on in this apostolic spirit during twelve con-
tinuous years, and considering also his modest and gentle
manners, he should have been commonly called by the poor
Catholics their 'dearest Father' and 'the Apostle' of that
district."

Among many other tributes paid to Father Ralph after his
death is this exquisite one from a brother Jesuit who knew

him well: "He was in his paradise when he was with the poore Catholics at Durham and in the villages." The Martyr's own account of his labours, written while in prison at the behest of his superiors, is pitched in just such a minor key as we should have expected:

"Since I came into England (the rest of my life you know) I have, thanks be to God, been helping and comforting people according to my vocation and ability, in administering the Sacraments and instructing privately, for preaching in public I could never do, which hath sometimes caused in me great grief but always kept me in humility, so as I lived in a mean state, going ordinarily on foot from place to place, which I had near one another. Concerning the state of my soul, I hope I am well, and hath striven daily to go forward in virtue, considering my infirm health, bleeding in great quantity in spring and fall of the leaf for this eight years' space, which hath not only altered my bodily constitution, but weakened my head very much, so as I can neither meditate nor read much, but spend my time in good thoughts as ejaculatory prayers, and saying my Office and beads. Neither have I been of late able to go on foot, but forced to use a horse, which was no little trouble, especially these dangerous times, all which hath increased my desire to end my life by suffering for God's sake, which He of His infinite goodness grant me."

It now remains to be seen how this gentle, sweet-souled saint, who throughout the whole course of his life was never known to breathe a single unkindly word about anybody, came to be herded with thieves and murderers in the vilest of English prisons. This was how it happened. King Charles had fallen foul successively of the City of London, the Scots, and his Puritan Parliament. In August, 1640, the Scots crossed the Border and took possession of Newcastle, on which occasion Father Corby had his first premonition of impending martyrdom. Hatred of Catholicism was largely the reason why Puritans and Presbyterians flew to arms. Events moved rapidly after the Scots' first foray, and by the beginning of 1644 the Civil War was in full swing. In January that year, the Covenanters once more invaded Durham and occupied Sunderland, from which place the King's Commander-in-Chief in the North, the gallant and generous Marquess of Newcastle, tried to dislodge them with an army only a third as large as theirs. Eventually bottled up in York by the combined forces of the Scots and Parliamentarians, he was in desperate straits when, on 1 July, Prince Rupert came to his assistance. That "impetuous sprig of royalty" was spoiling for a fight and persuaded Newcastle, against his better judgement, to engage the enemy at their camp on Marston Moor. The battle resulted in total defeat for the Royalist army, and then practically all Durham came under the power of the Parliamentarians, who at once settled down to the congenial occupation of priest-hunting.

On 8 July, 1644, five days after the catastrophe of Marston Moor, Father Ralph Corby was saying Mass "in a lonely house surrounded by a wood at Hamsterley, a place in Co. Durham near Newcastle." These words are from the *Certamen Triplex*. In the Newcastle area, however, Hamsterley is not the name of a place but of a house, Hamsterley Hall, Lintz Green, on the River Derwent, and, as another account says that Father Ralph was taken at "Lintzford", we may assume that Hamsterley Hall, then and to the present day associated with a branch of the wide-spreading Surtees family, was the actual scene of his capture. He had just finished reading the Epistle when a party of Puritan soldiers burst into the house. Quick as lightning he was out of his vestments but had not time to reach a hiding-place before they were upon him. He had paid to prudence all the tribute that could be demanded, and now it was the turn of her sister virtue, fortitude. As the altar, dressed for Mass, would have convicted him in any case, he readily admitted his priesthood and thereupon was led away in triumph to Sunderland, where a branch of the Grand Committee for Religion set up by Parliament held its sessions.

When informed by his captors that he admitted being a

priest, the Committee requested him to put the confession in writing, which he did in the following manner: "I, Ralph Corby, a priest resident in the Bishopric of Durham, was this day taken by the Parliamentarians at Hamsterley about nine o'clock in the morning, while saying Mass, and at the same place were seized my priestly vestments and other effects." At the top of the paper he had drawn a little cross, to the great indignation of his examiners who thereupon asked him whether he was a Jesuit. "By the great goodness of God I am," he answered, and that detail, too, was added to the confession. They kept him until eleven o'clock that night, when he was hustled on board a vessel bound for London. From Sunderland to London by sea is some three hundred and fifty miles, and it was on no "luxury liner" that Father Ralph made the journey. To mention only one point, even the best equipped ships of those days were so notorious for their smells that old travellers, such as Fynes Moryson, regularly recommended the neophyte to take with him a quantity of angelica, cloves, rosemary, etc., for the comfort of his heavily assaulted nose.

During the first day at sea Ralph was kept under hatches, but after that received what he considered the very kindly and humane permission of walking about on deck. There, to his exceeding joy, he met another priest, a secular named John Duckett, who had been seized near Durham on 2 July. "After their first meeting on board ship," says the record, "they lived together like twin brothers and kindred souls," which latter in very truth they were. It took the old tub of a vessel a whole fortnight to make London, but the voyage held no tedium for the two men since every mile of it brought them nearer to the desire of their hearts. Despite Father Corby's gentle reference to their guards, there is good evidence to prove that the soldiers on the ship treated them with great brutality, acting, says the contemporary account, "like those leopards which brought St. Ignatius to Rome".

What happened at the end of the journey is told in the following matter-of-fact way by Father Corby himself: "Landing at London, I was guarded to the examiners where, showing me my writing, I acknowledged it, so as they examined me very little, as where I was born. I told them in Ireland, my father being fled thither for his conscience. [Then came] some other frivolous questions, as whether I knew Dr. Cosin or were in the King's army or no, to which I answered negatively although they have put it here affirmatively. And so they committed me to Newgate." The Dr. Cosin here mentioned was the dispossessed Dean of Durham and a staunch Royalist, which fact would seem to show that the commissioners designed a double charge against the two prisoners. It was even boldly stated by the London news-sheets that they had been "taken as they fled upon Prince Rupert's rout near York, and were priests in the regiment of the Popish party, employed to settle the Protestant religion".

Their commitment to Newgate was made the occasion for a display of brutality, "for a troop of about forty armed soldiers, with a captain at their head, was ordered out, and, as a military escort, half in derision, with drums beating and guns firing, led these innocent and peaceful confessors of Christ as though they had been malefactors, traitors and disturbers of the peace of the Kingdom." [1]

They had to wait about six weeks for their trial, as the Old Bailey Sessions did not begin until 4 September. During that time they were lovingly cared for by two fellow-prisoners and confessors, Mr. John Horsley, a cousin of Father Ralph, and Cuthbert Prescott, the brave Jesuit laybrother, whose perilous duty it had been during many years to collect Catholic boys and get them across the sea to St. Omer. These wonderful men lived, in the expressive words of Mr. Horsley, "as the birds and beasts, merely upon God's providence," and as for the two priests, they seemed "to have entered into a sort of holy emulation which of them should excel in humility, charity, patience, zeal for the glory of God, and all other heroic virtues; yet so as always to preserve the most perfect mutual

[1] *Certamen Triplex,* p. 59.

love and harmony." They never had much doubt as to the result of their trial and, "though many other proofs existed of the great desire of martyrdom that consumed them, the greatest was the exceeding joy of each and the marvellous serenity of their countenances while in prison, so much noticed by those who were with them that some, on parting, bore testimony to it with words and tears of joy and admiration." Friends outside thought that they might save Father Corby if they obtained an authentic certificate of his birth in Ireland. He became very downcast when he heard of their efforts, but, relates his brother, Providence so arranged it "that a notary at Ghent made out the certificate of his birthplace on the same day and almost at the same hour that he, being hanged in London, began to be born in Heaven." Scrupulous that he was not to run ahead of God's intentions, he felt obliged at his trial to put forward this poor argument of his Irish birth, only, as we shall see, to have it laughed out of court.

In connection with these efforts to save him there is a beautiful story to be told. During some skirmish of the Thirty Years' War in Germany the Imperial troops had captured a Scottish colonel whose release the Parliament men were endeavouring to negotiate. The Emperor's representative in London now urged on them that they should offer to exchange Father Corby for the prisoner, whereupon the martyr addressed the following lines to his would-be saviour: "As for your kind offer of freeing me by the man of Germany, I thank you, and have given it freely to Mr. Duckett, for I shall allege I was borne in Ireland, which if it does not prevail, I find myself more willing, thank God, to die for so glorious a cause than to live. And truly since the Scotts came in about four years ago, I have had this desire, and asked God Almighty that He would effect it in me, if it were His blessed will." Over this matter of the exchange there ensued between the two priests "a humble, charitable and fervent contention", which Mr. Horsley, who witnessed it, described in the following way:

"Mr. Corby never ceased until he had procured it to be

conferred on Mr. Ducket but nothing else could have effected it, had he not served himself of his being borne in Ireland, and therefore not believed to be lyable to the law of death for priesthood; for unto all the rest Mr. Ducket found ready answers, retorting with like humility, fervor and charity Mr. Corby's allegations for his enjoying that benefit. As when Mr. Corby pressed his owne being in yeares, sickly, and quite spent, Mr. Ducket yonge and, in respect of his talents also, being still able to endure greate labours for the goode of many soules, for all which and what els Mr. Corby could urge, Mr. Ducket would not acknowledge any preeminence at all, the eye of their truly humble soules being fastened upon what might postpose each one of them to the other."

From prison Father Corby wrote some letters which, as one recipient put it, "would joy any heart and set on fire anything fireable". A little note addressed to his "dear and loving Sisters", the Benedictines, says: "As you have heard of my imprisonment, so I make no doubt but you esteem it (as I hope it is) a great favour and benefit of God Almighty bestowed upon me. . . . I was committed the 22 of July, being St. Mary Magdalene's day, to Newgate, where, thanks be to God, I, with five others, are very well and merry as ever I have been." Another letter, written on the morrow of his trial, explains what happened when he was put in the dock:

"The Sessions being the 4th of September, I was called second, where, reading my accusation, the chief whereof was 'that Ralph Corby, being an Englishman, went overseas and was made priest and Jesuit against the laws,' the Recorder asked, 'Guilty or Not Guilty.' To which I answered, 'For being priest and Jesuit I confess myself or rather think it an honour than a crime.' He pressed me to answer directly. I still replied twice or thrice I was a priest and Jesuit, and if he would have that to be guilty he had my confession, which, when he could get no other answer, he asked what I had to say for myself. I said I was not born in England, as was alleged in the indictment. 'Where then?' quoth he. . . . I answered, in Ireland.

'Oh,' quoth he, after a gibing manner, 'that will be no evasion, for know you not the Statute?' Which presently he caused to be read. I do not well remember what it was, but he extended it not only to England but to all Queen Elizabeth's Dominions, in which Ireland was, and so he said, 'If you be so courageous you must suffer.'

"Then the jury came and found me guilty, and so bade them take me away. The next day I was called to judgment, where, standing at the Bar, he asked what I had to say for myself. I said I had yesterday alleged I was an Irishman borne, and desired to be tried by my Country.... He said that he had sufficiently answered yesterday, for the Statute included both England and Ireland, and so he pronounced sentence, that I was to go back again to Prison, to be carried on a hurdle to Tyburn, where, being half hanged, I should be cut down, bowelled and quartered into four parts, which being brought back again to Newgate should be hung where it pleased the King. Which being said I came back again to Newgate where I expect that good Sabbath which is the Eve of her glorious Nativity by whose holy intercession I hope to be borne to a new and everlasting life, which God of His infinite goodness grant by the intercession of her and of all His glorious Saints. Amen."

Father Duckett was condemned at the same time as Father Corby, so having loved one another during life in death they were not to be divided. When removed from the bar they were thrust for a time "into a vile and filthy dungeon, amongst a rabble of murderers, thieves and malefactors, loaded with chains and otherwise shamefully treated, all which they endured with placid countenance and mind at peace, without making complaint against anyone." But the prison governor, who was a kindly man, soon had them released and restored to their own cell. There they were visited, both at night and during the day, by the ambassadors of Catholic princes and other eminent people, such as the Duchess of Guise, whom they endeavoured to satisfy "by the humble and sedulous exercise of their priestly office, in every mode of gratifying them and alacrity in serving them that they could show". Father Ralph, who never forgot a kindness done him, promised in particular to pray earnestly in life and after death for the King of Spain and the Elector of Bavaria, through whose munificence the English Jesuits had been able to establish the four colleges at which he made his studies. The Ambassador of France, the Marquis de Sabran, was not content until he had acquired the martyr's rosary and a little paper thus inscribed: "I, Ralph Corby, priest of the Society of Jesus, promise to pray for the welfare of the most Christian King of France, for her Majesty the Queen and her family, and for the French nation."

It had been noticed that, after his condemnation, the Father often melted into tears and displayed an ever-deepening tenderness towards all who came in contact with him. That his thoughts were full of his mother and sisters at the last we know from a little note which he addressed to a lady who had been good to him. "I doubt not", he said, "you will write to comfort them in my behalf, and, if you please, send them some little token, as also to my brother Ambrose. Thus, with tears in my eyes, not of sorrow but of joy, once again, dear Sister, farewell." On the day before he died he wrote directly to his dear ones, but unfortunately the letter has been lost.

Amongst others who heard the Father's last Mass and received Holy Communion at his hands were a man and his wife with whom the martyr had lived a number of years. Their evidence, tendered at the time, is put down as follows in the record:

"They much respected him, both for the happy passage in which he was and for his known virtues in former times, especially two very remarkable, the one that notwithstanding many occasions they had of conversing with him very intimately they never heard him bring forth any one word which might touch disgustfully any other person, nor would he permit any to be so touched in his presence, so careful he was of charitable union. The other was his own moderation and composure of his passions (if there could be said to be any where no effect appeared), always so present to himself, or rather to Almighty God, that they could never for any rarity of accident perceive in him the least change from his tranquility to anger or discontent, a virtue most suitable to the other of his charity.

"These persons of near acquaintance, having taken up their place the most commodious that their respect to the Mysteries they assisted at, and to others, would permit, to behold the good man's actions and countenance in that his last offering, when he was now come to the altar, prepared for that Mystery, perceived in him, as also others did, an unusual tied kind of posture, without freedom of action or pronunciation, the one defective as out of bashfulness, the other interrupted as by a mind strongly diverted, and accompanied with tears. The Duchess of Guise, after the Offertory, asked one who knelt by her what it was. He answered, some transport of tenderness or devotion. They afterwards asked Father Corby what the matter was. He said some thoughts came to his mind which he begged Almighty God to take from him. Mass being ended and he restored to his former alacrity, he came unto two parties and in a friendly familiarity told them that the occasion of that change was that, having cast his eyes upon them, he fell into a lively apprehension and feeling of his approaching departure from them, his intimate friends, which struck so deeply with him that it provoked tears and hindered the freedom of his action."

That they might the more openly confess their priesthood, both Fathers found means to get a tonsure shaven on their heads, and they were also permitted, by unusual good fortune, to go to the gallows in their cassocks. Just before they left, Father Corby received the following letter from another English priest, the Rev. George Gage, brother of the good and brave Sir Henry Gage, Governor of Oxford:

"Hon. Sir,—The same noble person who sent you by my

means 20s. at your first coming into Newgate sends you likewise as much more at your going out, and begs that this his
charity may kiss your dying hands, and be part of what your
piety intends to bestow on the way, or at the place of execution,
where no doubt you will have many needy spectators, amongst
others whose mere devotion will carry them to attend you
there. And now give me leave, I beseech you, to beg part of
your sufferings for my own necessities . . . since I am sure next
unto the dreadful sacrifice of the holy Altar there is nothing
more acceptable to Almighty God than the sacrifice of martyrs'
blood. . . . Sr. Your devoted servant, G.G. I may not seal up
this before I beg your blessing, which on my bended knees
I would do if the times permitted."

Then began the procession to Tyburn through the midst
of a great concourse of people, many of whom said openly,
"it was a wonder to see and observe the great courage and
constancy of such men as these when they came to die for
their religion." According to the relation of an eye witness,
"They were both placed on the same hurdle, the one close by
the other, sitting upon straw, as the custom is, and Father
Corby sitting at the right hand of Mr. Duckett. . . . Father Corby
was the elder and of a sickly and wan complexion, his face
being, after his imprisonment and former hard usage, very
thin and pale, and also by reason of a long infirmity, inclining
him to a consumption, all which caused him to seem the sadder
of the two, though those that had occasion to discourse with
him found him always of a quick and lively spirit. But Mr.
Duckett was a handsome young gentleman, of a sanguine,
cheerful and smiling countenance, very affable and pleasing to
all that did behold him. They had both no other cause but
to be cheerful and courageous, the one being still the other's
good example, reciprocally comforting one another all the way
they passed." Of Mr. Duckett it is said that he did not wait
to be placed on the hurdle "but of himself leapt into the straw
and composed himself upon it as if he had been riding in
triumph". All the way to execution he had "a continual smile

in his look" and, together with Father Corby, gave a loving benediction to any who signified a desire for it.

Arrived at Tyburn, the holy martyrs reverently kissed the gallows and then in ringing tones Father Corby suddenly cried out: "Mr. Sheriff, Mr. Sheriff, why do we come hither to die?" When that official made no answer, he continued: "Mr. Sheriff, we were apprehended in the Bishoprick of Durham and brought hither, which methinks is a great way to be brought, and here we are to suffer and to die, but we do not know for what, nor nobody doth come against us." After that he went on to prove that religion, and religion alone, was their crime, and concluded with the words: "Mr. Sheriff, we die for our Saviour, and, as our Saviour died willingly for us, do not think, Mr. Sheriff, that we are afraid of death. We die willingly and with all our hearts for our Saviour." On the evidence of the man who took them down, these words were said "with a much more smiling countenance than was according to his natural strain". For fear that Father Duckett might speak too persuasively "out of the abundant joy that appeared in him," he was at once half-throttled with the rope but had time to say to a minister who wanted to argue with him, "Sir, I come not hither to be taught my faith but to die for the profession of it." As the cart was drawn away the two friends clasped one another in a last embrace and so went side by side to Heaven.

THOMAS CANTILUPE, Bishop of Hereford in the thirteenth century, is in the curious and interesting position for a canonized saint of having been solemnly excommunicated shortly before his death by his metropolitan, the Archbishop of Canterbury, himself a man with a considerable and deserved reputation for holiness. The Archbishop described him as a wolf in sheep's clothing, a perjurer, a contumacious rebel, and various other uncomplimentary things, but King Edward I who had known him intimately told Pope Clement V that he was the walking embodiment of all Eight Beatitudes, and Pope John XXII finally estopped Canterbury's charges in A.D. 1320 by raising him to the altars of the Church, the last Englishman but one to be so honoured until the apotheosis of St. John Fisher and St. Thomas More in our own day.[1] "Natione Anglicus, angelicus homo ipse," wrote the Pope in his Bull, plagiarizing St. Gregory the Great. Plainly, we have here the elements of a very good story if we could disentangle them and enter a little by an effort of sympathetic understanding into the peculiar psychology of great mediaeval ecclesiastics. At any rate, we can try.

As his surname vaguely indicates, Thomas was of Norman blood. Some writers have seen in it visions of a field and a wolf, *Champ de Loup,* but that derivation belongs probably to the wonderland of puns and heraldry. In the world of fact, the Cantilupes came over with the Conqueror and received from him for services rendered generous portions of England's green and pleasant land. Several of the family are commemorated in the *Dictionary of National Biography,* e.g. Grandfather William, the first Baron, who stood by and even encouraged King John in all his iniquities, was his seneschal, and likewise

---

[1] There is a good presumption that John Thwing, an Augustinian canon now known as St. John of Bridlington, was formally canonized by a Bull of Pope Boniface IX, in 1403, during the Great Schism. St. Osmund of Salisbury was canonized in 1457, but he was a Norman.

sheriff for the counties of Warwick, Leicester, Worcester and Hereford, with his residence at Kenilworth Castle, a bold, bad Baron of the original vintage; his son William, the second Baron and father of St. Thomas, a chip of the old block who found great favour with the young Henry III, abetted him as his father had abetted his father, held the Great Seal for a time, and was appointed guardian of England during the King's absence in 1242, altogether an unpromising parent for a saint; Walter, the younger brother of the second William, an eminent and excellent churchman though an inveterate pluralist, who became bishop of Worcester, and reversed the family tradition of royalism by acting as spiritual director of the barons in their revolt against Henry III, "with the exception of Bishop Grosseteste . . . decidedly the greatest bishop of his time." [1] Our Saint's mother, Millicent de Gournay, had been married to Almeric de Montfort, Earl of Evreux in Normandy and of Gloucester in England, before she became the wife of Cantilupe, and so Thomas was a relative-in-law of the famous Simon de Montfort who triumphed at Lewes and fell at Evesham. Other marriage alliances connected with him with the Marshalls, Fitzwalters and a few more illustrious heirs of 1066.[2]

[1] Walter was an intimate friend of Grosseteste, as well as of Adam Marsh, which by itself is proof of his quality. The article on St. Thomas in the D.N.B. was entrusted to the most accomplished of mediaeval historians, Professor Tout. The tiny Warwickshire village of Aston Cantlow is the only geographical memorial of the family now remaining.

[2] The best and, in many respects, the only source for the life of St. Thomas is the long account (166 folio pages in double columns) compiled from the process of canonization by the Bollandist Constantine Suyskens and published in the *Acta Sanctorum,* Octobris t.i, Antwerp, 1765. A century earlier, the English Jesuit Richard Strange, who figured prominently in Titus Oates' accusations and spent some lively months evading pursuivants, brought out an enthusiastic life of the Saint in his native tongue (Ghent, 1674). This remains the only life of him ever written in English, which is curious seeing that he enjoyed a pre-Reformation popularity second only to St. Thomas Becket's. Father Strange's book contained enough charm of style, though not nearly enough honest, hard facts, to merit republication in the "Quarterly Series" in 1879.

St. Thomas came into this world at the little Buckingham-shire village of Hambleden, three miles north-east of Henley-on-Thames, where the Cantilupes had one of their numerous baronial mansions. Most probably that event took place in the year 1218, an ill-starred date when the country was seething with discontent owing to the presence of hordes of rapacious foreigners, and to the exactions of hard-pressed impecunious Popes, at grips with the Hohenstauffen. Thomas had four brothers, among them an elder one, Hugh, afterwards Arch-deacon of Gloucester, who shared most of his thoughts and ideals, and three sisters who were not permitted to share anything with him, even a roof over their heads at night. However, as they all married barons they stood in no great need of his hospitality, but he might have been more civil and fraternal towards them without any particular damage to his angelhood. He used to say that women's talk was silly, and he never let any of the girls give him a sisterly kiss, even when their tears pleaded for such a small token of family affection.[1] In this respect, we may fairly say, he wore his halo somewhat askew. During his childhood he was cared for by "a devoted, noble and saintly matron", and she, rather than his mother, appears to have laid the foundations of his holiness. His father and mother do not come into the picture at all and he never speaks of them, though they did their duty at least to the extent of paying others well to look after him.

Valuable additional, confirmatory or corrective information is to be found in *A Roll of the Household Expenses of Richard de Swinfield, Bishop of Hereford,* published in two volumes by the Camden Society in 1855. Swinfield was one of St. Thomas's closest friends and succeeded to his dignity. The most interesting and astonishing documents about the Saint are contained in the *Registrum Epistolarum Fratris Johannis Peckham Archiepiscopi Cantuariensis,* edited in three volumes for the Rolls Series by Charles Trice Martin, London, 1882–5. Many of the Chronicles pub-lished in this Series also refer to our hero, but not very helpfully. None of his own writings appears to be extant, except two letters given in Peckham's Register and Webb's abstract of Swinfield's Roll.

[1] *Acta Sanctorum,* Octobris t. i, p. 553.

Perhaps that was the custom among the nobility of Angevin times.

At the age of seven, Thomas was delivered over to an able and conscientious tutor who grounded him thoroughly in classical learning and also fostered in him a deep devotion to Mass and the Divine Office. While still small boys, he and Hugh used to attend the singing of the entire Office daily at some religious house, and many years before they became priests took to saying it privately on their own account. No doubt they also hunted, hawked, fished, and, let us hope, romped, like other boys of their age and station, but of this we are told nothing. As Oxford at the time was no place for two earnest students bent on improving their minds,[1] they went to Paris instead and there set up house in some style, with an imposing retinue of tutors, chaplains and domestics. The contrast between their condition and that of Richard de Wyche, starving in an Oxford garret a little earlier, is interesting, though far less uncommon than might be imagined, and shows that saints can make the most of any circumstances. St. Thomas used his chances to befriend people of St. Richard's class. He would have as many as thirteen poor students to dine with him daily, and embarrassed professors also, such as the great John Peckham, who afterwards excommunicated him, gratefully acknowledged his benefactions. When his ready money failed, as it often did owing to his boundless liberality, he used to beg for his distressed dependants from affluent people in his own circle. So he advanced in grace and learning, like Shakespeare's winter, frosty, at least towards women, but kindly. In due course he took his Master's degree, and in 1245

---

[1] Town and Gown riots were endemic. On St. George's Day, 1238, a Welsh undergraduate shot dead with an arrow the brother of the recently arrived Papal Legate, Cardinal Otto, who immediately put the University under an interdict, suspended all lectures, cast thirty masters into prison, and excommunicated the Chancellor, Simon de Boville, O.P. Matthew Paris, O.S.B., who detested foreigners only less than he did the Mendicant Friars, tells the story with immense gusto and a quotation from Ovid (*Chronica Majora*, vol. iii, Rolls Series, 1876, pp. 481–4).

proceeded to the first General Council of Lyons, whither his father had been dispatched by King Henry to protest against the exactions of the Roman Curia. Pope Innocent IV, then in the thick of his great struggle with the portentous Frederick II, had come to the Council at the peril of his life, and our Saint very probably listened with awed attention while he pronounced his moving opening discourse on the "Five Wounds of the Church", namely, the sins of the higher and lower clergy and the spread of heresy; the aggression of the Saracens who had again captured Jerusalem; the schism of the Greeks and their attacks on the Latin Kingdom; the savage invasions of Christendom by the Tartars; and the persecution of the Church by the Emperor.[1]

Very likely St. Thomas was ordained by the Pope at Lyons, and it is certain that he there obtained from His Holiness the rather peculiar favour of a dispensation to hold several benefices simultaneously, a right which he afterwards freely used. But we must not be too quick to raise shocked eyes to heaven, for

---

[1] This outstanding Pope, one of the greatest in history, has been very harshly handled by historians, Catholics no less than others. Thus Canon Barry, following tamely in the wake of that cross-grained bigot, Matthew Paris, who attributed everything Innocent did to a greed for gold, wrote of him in his *Papal Monarchy*: "To speak of Innocent with respect for his person would be in defiance of the multiplied proofs which exhibit him as grasping, cold-hearted, insincere, and a nepotist" (p. 347). For Innocent's enemy, Frederick, on the other hand, Canon Barry, who was an excellent priest but too prone, it seems to me, to play up to his Protestant audience, has nothing but tenderness: "The Alcibiades of the century ... he sleeps with his royal robes about him in the Cathedral at Palermo ... truly a spirit misunderstood, never wisely handled, full of mysterious charm and powers wasted, the most captivating, enigmatic, and unhappy of Christian Emperors" (p. 350). As against that pleasant rhetoric, the searcher for truth should read the calm, factual, thoroughly documented pages of Monsignor Mann, who devoted the entire fourteenth volume of his *Lives of the Popes in the Middle Ages* to Innocent the Magnificent. By a misprint of almost prophetic implication, Canon Barry's preface is dated "Dorchester, 9 November, 1001." Mgr. Mann's volume appeared in 1928. The truth is that Innocent saved the Church, at infinite cost to himself of danger and misery, from complete domination by the Hitler, not the Alcibiades, of the thirteenth century.

Thomas was a pluralist of no ordinary kind. Two motives inspired him, first, as a good Englishman to keep foreigners out of English benefices, which at the time was a sorely needed reform, and secondly, to instal in the livings poor native clerks of proved worth whose services might otherwise have been lost to the Church. He always kept a most vigilant eye on his appointees, and his pluralism, like that of his saintly and patriotic uncle Walter who undoubtedly inspired it, resulted in nothing but good to souls. Walter, who superintended his education, seems to have been his ideal in matters ecclesiastical, and he could hardly have chosen a better model, even though the good Bollandist concerned with the nephew is reluctant to admit the uncle's sanctity and reputed miracles on account of his support to the Barons in their revolt against Henry III. Belgian Jesuits of the eighteenth century had a strong sense of the subject's duty to his prince under practically all circumstances. Another very good friend and counsellor whom Thomas discovered during his university career was the Dominican Robert Kilwardby, an eminent professor at both Paris and Oxford, destined in due course to be the first friar—and how Matthew Paris hated it!—to sit on the throne of St. Augustine at Canterbury. Thomas chose this excellent unworldly man, who ended his days in Rome as a cardinal, for his confessor and spiritual director. Many years later it became Archbishop Kilwardby's pleasant task to induct his penitent as Chancellor of Oxford University, on which occasion he covered him with confusion by publicly announcing before all the robed dons and hilarious clerks that, to his certain knowledge, their new ruler had never stained his baptismal innocence.[1]

The thirteenth century, the age of Bracton, was a great time for the study of civil law, a discipline, however, forbidden to clerks in orders. But our Thomas, a jurist born and "valde legalis", as his brother reported of him, obtained a second dispensation from Innocent IV to spend some years at Orléans, the foremost centre of juristic learning, where he progressed

[1] *Acta Sanctorum,* Octobris t. i, p. 552.

so rapidly through the dark forest of the codes that he was frequently invited to deputize for his professor. Thence he returned to Paris to plunge enthusiastically into the jungle of canon law, and was honoured in the midst of his labours, austerities and charities by a visit from no less a person than King St. Louis IX.

About the year 1257, he took up duty as professor of canon law at Oxford, and five years later was elected Chancellor of that turbulent University. An under graduate who was there during his period of office, Hugh Barber, testified as follows in the process of his canonization: "Valde bene regebat Studium Oxoniense, et valde bene puniebat scholares delinquentes." But his severity was tempered by his never-failing charity, which made allowance for the high spirits of youth and only con-fiscated its weapons when they became a menace to life and limb. Even so, we are told, his house at times resembled a small arsenal, so full was it of bows, arrows, swords and daggers. His period as Chancellor coincided with the beginnings of the national revolt against the misrule of Henry III, and, following the example of his uncle Walter, the intimate friend of Simon de Montfort, he cast in his lot with the Barons. It says something for his influence and popularity at Oxford that the whole University went over to the same side. When Henry's son, Prince Edward, later the great King Edward I, approached the City in 1263, the students in a body demanded to be allowed to sally forth and attack his camp. The Chancellor sternly refused and had all the gates locked and guarded, whereupon the bold spirits, thirsting for a fight, stormed a wine-shop, became uproariously drunk, and started one of the worst Town and Gown riots in Oxford's history.[1]

[1] Wood, *Historia et Antiquitates Universitatis Oxoniensis,* Oxford, 1674, t. i, p. 111. The editor of Strange's life of St. Thomas, following the mediaeval chroniclers who believed in giving good round numbers, asserts that he had 20,000 students under him. In fact, as Rashdall shows, the number, with servants included, never in mediaeval times exceeded 3,000. The Saint's action on this occasion may partly account for the excellent relations between himself and Prince Edward, who afterwards,

At the end of the year, St. Thomas, probably to his relief, was chosen with a few other eminent men to speak for the Barons at Amiens, where St. Louis had agreed to arbitrate in England's controversy. Henry and Prince Edward were there, too, as well as Henry's wife Eleanor, sister of the Queen of France. Even a saint's judgment could hardly escape being warped in the presence of so much majesty, and Louis pronounced entirely in favour of his brother monarch. The Barons repudiated the award, sprang to arms, and by the great victory of Lewes on 14 May, 1264, became the masters of the Kingdom. St. Thomas was then elevated from being Chancellor of Oxford to being Chancellor of England, in which high post his justice, prudence, temperance, fortitude, and incorruptible integrity made him acceptable even to the defeated King. But he did not hold the Great Seal long. Evesham followed swiftly on Lewes, which meant the return of the *status quo* and disgrace for Earl Simon's supporters. Thomas retired to Paris and forgot politics in theology. Three years later he was back in Oxford, which for a second time elected him its Chancellor. It is significant that no action of any kind was taken against him by the triumphant royalists who were far from being paragons of magnanimity. At this time he began a sort of apostolate of his various benefices, renovating the churches and preaching with great love and zeal to the humble parishioners, not a man of whom was half as humble as himself. On the poor and the sick he lavished his wealth like water. Though extremely ascetic himself, he liked people to make merry on suitable occasions and organized literal "bean-feasts" for his numerous spiritual sons and daughters on the Church holidays which were so frequent in the mediaeval

---

as King, reckoned him among the most trusted of his advisers. Once, the King sent for him very early in the morning to discuss some urgent business. But it was the hour of his Mass, and to all the pleading and pressing of the royal messengers his only answer was: "The King of Heaven comes first, and you can tell your Master that I said so, if you want to." Edward was big enough to accept the admonition in good part (*Acta Sanctorum,* Octobris t. i, p. 605).

calendar. Each, we are told, received at his expense enough corn, peas and beans "to satisfy a horse after its daily toil".[1]

In contrast to those charitable activities, our hero, who was not a fine lawyer for nothing, engaged in much litigation with various aggressive prelates who trespassed on the rights of his parishes. But the biggest lawsuit of his life, a regular Tichborne case, was directed against himself. Though the details are not very clear, it seems to have been largely a matter of English versus Foreigner, a common source of trouble during the reign of Henry III. A former Burgundian bishop of Hereford had presented one of his countrymen, Pierre de Langon, with a stall in Hereford Cathedral and the living of Little Wenlock in that diocese. The next bishop, an Englishman, ejected the foreigner on some unknown pretext and gave both benefices to our Thomas, evidently hoping thus to secure his succession in the see. But Langon was as bonny a fighter as Thomas himself and at once commenced a suit against him in the Roman courts. Meantime, in 1275, the bishop died and Thomas was unanimously chosen by the Hereford Chapter in his place, on which occasion, instead of restoring Langon, he presented the vacant benefices to two other Englishmen. Langon continued his suit in Rome. "It lingered on through more than sixteen tedious years, and passed through many hands. Auditors and proctors and Popes disappeared, but still the cause of 'Langon versus Cantilupe and others' survived. Innocent V, John XXI, Nicholas III, Martin IV were no more. Then came Honorius IV in whose time Cantilupe himself went to his rest. At length when Nicholas IV filled the Papal chair, the prosecution came forth with redoubled vigour, and, forasmuch as, in the language of the lawyers, 'no process could or ought to be taken against the dead,' it was directed against the executors of Cantilupe's will, Richard de Swinfield and

---

[1] *Acta Sanctorum,* Octobris t. i, p. 550. It may sound like "austerity" fare, however liberal in quantity, but it was what the commoners of England liked in those days, and what St. Thomas himself lived on year in and year out.

William de Montfort." [1] Judgment went against them on every count and they were mulcted in heavy damages, which, however, the victorious and generous Langon remitted, being content with restoration to his long-lost dignities.

As Bishop, St. Thomas's chief contention was with Gilbert de Clare, the powerful Earl of Gloucester, against whose encroachments he carried on a magnificent fight in the English courts for five whole years, even going the length of engaging a champion, at 6s. 8d. a day, to withstand Gloucester in the lists, had the matter warranted an appeal to judicial combat. He won this case, and to the present day there remains as the memorial of his victory the enormous fosse or trench which the infuriated Earl caused to be dug along the Malvern Hills between his property and that of the Bishop. One of the many other trespassers whom the Bishop worsted in the courts, a certain Baron Corbet, said to him at the conclusion of the case: "Either you are full of the devil, my Lord, or else you are a very close familiar of God." [2] Remembering the camel in the Gospels, we would be entitled to think of St. Thomas as one of the Bactrian species, with at least two pronounced humps, his litigiousness and his pluralism, yet he passed through the needle's eye as sweetly as an angel might dance on its point, which is somehow very encouraging.

He was so much a familiar of God that one who served his Mass hundreds of times said he never knew him to get through without abundance of tears. Another who shared his room when he was bishop testified that he used to spend half the

---

[1] Webb, *A Roll of the Household Expenses of Richard de Swinfield, Bishop of Hereford,* vol. i, pp. clxxviii–clxxxii. The case cost St. Thomas a mint of money and untold anxiety, but believing that there was a principle at stake, he never contemplated giving in.

[2] *Acta Sanctorum,* Octobris t. i, p. 565. Their extortion and usury caused the Saint to be very hostile to the Jews, and he was probably in part responsible for their expulsion from England by Edward I, though that event did not take place until eight years after his death. Edward, as is well known, treated the exiles humanely and allowed them to take all their property abroad.

night sitting on his bed preparing his sermons by the dim light of an oil lamp, or else on his knees, leaning against the bed in prayer.

Of his private austerities, especially in the matter of food, the stories are endless. He had a particular liking for the lampreys of the Severn and would frequently order dishes of them to be prepared for him, but his servants, or "Brothers", as he invariably called them, observed that he never partook of more than one mouthful, after which the fine dish, almost intact, was sent out to some needy family on his list. He played the same trick on his appetite in the matter of game, of which he had abundance on his estates and was very fond. Once, when his chancellor, Robert of Gloucester, an excellent trencherman, was dining with the Bishop, he ventured to expostulate with him on his excessive abstinence, saying: "You eat and drink too little, my Lord; you won't be able to last out." Getting no answer, the bold Robert repeated his remark, whereupon his Lordship retorted with some heat: "You, Sir, eat and drink what you like, but hold your tongue and mind your own business." The same Robert is our informant that the Bishop usually took only one meal a day, consisting of a scanty portion of vegetables or stew. For his supper, when he indulged in it, he allowed himself one slice of bread dipped in beer. Sometimes he would drink a single glass of wine but out of a glass "no bigger than a salt-celler". He admitted in strictest confidence to his relative and executor, William de Montfort, Dean of St. Paul's,[1] that for thirty-two years he had never once risen from table less hungry than when he sat down. "Yet, William," he continued, "I am strong enough to take you on in single combat." About his hair-shirt, an inheritance from Uncle Walter which he wore day and night, we are given much information. The man who used to wash and, be it said, de-louse it for him expressed his belief that it was the most fearsome of such objects to be found in all Christendom.

[1] This is the William who made himself famous by dying of fright at the prospect of having to preach before King Edward I.

When through constant use it lost some of its hardness and roughness, it was regularly sent to a secret address in Oxford to be reconditioned. After the Saint's death, the marks of this instrument of torture were plainly to be seen on his poor emaciated body.

An even more formidable instrument of torment in the Saint's history has now to be considered. After the elevation of his dear friend Kilwardby to the cardinalate in 1278, the Pope nominated John Peckham, O.F.M., eminent pupil of St. Bonaventure at Paris, to the see of Canterbury. Peckham was a fascinating character, a man consumed with zeal, almost as much a lover of poverty as the Poverello himself,[1] bound-lessly charitable to the poor, and personally austere as a Desert Father. At the same time he showed himself a pompous, fussy, tactless person, a kind of small-scale Boniface VIII, possessed of an altogether exaggerated and uncanonical opinion of his rights as metropolitan. The famous Franciscan annalist, Luke Wadding, admitted that he had quarrelled with "practically every bishop in England and with all of them together". Thomas of Hereford was in the field as leader of the aggrieved suffragans from the very beginning, but his personal duel with Peckham did not begin until a little later. The first explosion occurred over a marriage case tried in the Hereford court, from which the losing party appealed, over the head of his Bishop, to the court of Canterbury and was upheld. St. Thomas's official thereupon excommunicated the successful appellant for his irregular action, and was himself promptly excommunicated by Peckham's official. In fact, the air became thick with excommunications, which was one of the crying abuses of that age. In December, 1281, "Friar John, by divine per-mission humble minister of the Church of Canterbury and

---

[1] Kilwardby helped him to practise it by taking with him to Rome for mysterious reasons a good deal of the property of Canterbury! Historians have a grievance against him because he also bore away the episcopal registers, which Peckham tried in vain to recover. They have never come back.

Primate of all England," addressed to his "Venerable Brother of Hereford" a letter peremptorily ordering him to publish every Sunday and feast-day in his Cathedral of Hereford and all other churches of that diocese the sentence of major excommunication pronounced on his official, Robert of Gloucester, until notified that the said Robert had sought and been granted absolution. The letter, which, as from one bishop to another, is distinctly offensive, ended with a threat: "See to it that you carry this our order into execution if you wish to avoid canonical penalties."

St. Thomas replied very calmly and courteously, pointing out that the case had gone to Rome, and consequently, *pendente lite,* was removed from both their jurisdictions. But shortly afterwards another cause of contention supervened, this time over a will which the Archbishop claimed the right to administer, though the legal executor, the Vicar of Ross, was St. Thomas's subject. More excommunications then flowed out from Canterbury, until finally St. Thomas, though he, too, anticipating the worst, had appealed to the Pope and notified the Court of Arches of that fact, found himself under sentence and his chapel under an interdict. Peckham's letters to his proctors in Rome and to the Bishop of London, who steadily refused to promulgate the excommunication of Hereford, reveal the full bitterness of that strange man's soul. At the present time, we are often told by preachers and others what scum we are, but with all our iniquities we can claim moral superiority in some respects over the highest ecclesiastics, including the Popes themselves, of the thirteenth century. We do not, as a rule, offer or accept bribes in our courts of justice, and it is as clear as daylight, for their letters remain to prove it, that both Peckham and St. Thomas resorted to such measures, on the revealing plea that otherwise they could not hope to have their cases expedited at the centre of Christendom.[1] Indeed,

---

[1] Martin, *Registrum Epistolarum Fratris Johannis Peckham,* vol. i, pp. 269–73, 278–9, 299–300, 315–16, 321–2; vol. ii, 393–4; Webb, *A Roll of the Household Expenses of Richard de Swinfield,* vol. ii, p. xcvii (St.

bribery, or what amounted to it, seems to have been generally regarded in those genial times as a legitimate method of obtaining one's ends, just as forgery, or what closely resembled it, was thought to be no great harm at an earlier stage of Church history. Say the pessimists and *laudatores temporis acti* what they like, we *have* progressed in some directions.

In the summer of 1282, St. Thomas betook himself to Orvieto, where the French Pope, Martin IV, resided, and, in spite of all that Peckham could do and did to blacken his name, was affectionately received by the Holy Father. Before his case could be investigated he fell gravely ill at Montefiascone from some form of intestinal obstruction that had tormented him for years. He died on 25 August and his bones, separated by some means from the flesh, were brought back to England, where Peckham for a time endeavoured to deny them Christian burial. But Heaven soon intervened between the dead Bishop and Canterbury by making his sepulchre at Hereford glorious. A few years later, when the number and the magnitude of the miracles could no longer be denied, the poor Primate, grown old and infirm, humbly sent a priest to pray for him at the shrine, and caused himself to be "measured to" the Saint whom he had so grievously wronged.[1] Finally, it is

------

Thomas's letter to his proctors in Rome, sending them £100 as gratuities for various cardinals and other curial officials). The Bollandist analysis of the whole case is magnificently done (*Acta Sanctorum,* Octobris t. i, 568–77).

[1] This measuring was a very popular mediaeval custom, especially in England, and consisted in having a candle or candles of the same height as the suppliant lighted at the shrine of the saint from whom some favour was hoped. The Bollandist devotes more than a hundred pages to the miracles of St. Thomas, many of which, if we can believe in human evidence at all, are impossible to impugn. A good many of them were cures of poor people's animals, including pigs, which is just what might have been expected from this great lover of common men. The skull of the Saint is now venerated at Downside Abbey, whither it was removed at the close of the nineteenth century from a Benedictine monastery in Germany. The only other relic of the Saint known to exist is the left tibia or shin-bone, ten inches long and in almost perfect preservation,

pleasant to record that among the many celebrated men who petitioned the Holy See for the Bishop's canonization was his former arch-enemy, Gilbert de Clare, Earl of Gloucester.

---

which by an intricate chain of circumstances, came into the custody of the English Jesuits and is at present a chief treasure of the sacristy of Stonyhurst College.

ST. HUGH OF AVALON

Carthusian and Bishop of Lincoln

THE grandmother of King Henry II, conqueror of Ireland and murderer, by incitement, of Becket, was the daughter of a pelterer or furrier of Falaise and lived by her stitches. Thereby hangs a very good tale. Not many of the courtiers or common people of England knew the story of Arlette and her needle, for it was a thing as unmentionable as paper-hanging in Germany after 1933. But St. Hugh of Lincoln knew it, as he did most other things. Hugh had fallen into deep disgrace at court because of his stand against the royal tyranny, and Henry determined to teach him a lesson that he would not easily forget. Having peremptorily summoned the offender to his presence, he seated himself on a grassy slope near Woodstock Castle, surrounded by his chief vassals, whom he strictly forbade to rise or utter a word when the Bishop approached. Hugh greeted the King and his picnic party pleasantly, but they maintained a stony silence and did not even glance in his direction. There was thunder in the air and blue murder on the King's face. Undiscomfited by this extraordinary reception, the Saint gently squeezed into the closed circle and sat down on the grass immediately beside the raging King. Silence then resumed her reign, but after a short while Henry, realizing that a Carthusian could beat him at that game any day, called for a needle and began ostentatiously to stitch a loose bandage on an injured finger of his left hand. Hugh watched him amusedly for a time and then suddenly exclaimed: "How like you are now to your kinsfolk of Falaise!"—*Quam similis es modo cognatis tuis de Falesia.* In the circumstances and considering the volcanic tempers of the Plantagenets, it was one of the most daring sallies that ever issued from human lips. It was also one of the most successful, for Henry, to his everlasting credit, instead of whipping out his sword and killing Hugh where he sat, exploded with laughter, and even rolled on the ground in a very ecstasy of mirth. The astounded courtiers tittered nervously in accompaniment, not seeing the joke until the King himself explained it to them between gusts of laughter. "Do you understand," he asked, "the outrageous thing which this barbarian here, this mocker, has said to me?" and proceeded to tell of Arlette and her skin-stitching.[1]

King Henry's reference to Hugh as a barbarian was a genial tilt at his foreign birth, which took place in the year 1140 at the Château d'Avalon, fronting the Alps in Burgundy, not far from the recently founded Grande Chartreuse. His family, long ennobled, was related to the Bayards, whose castle ad-

[1] *Magna Vita S. Hugonis Episcopi Lincolniensis,* ed. Dimock, Rolls Series, London, 1864, pp. 126–8. This biography of St. Hugh by his chaplain and intimate friend, a Benedictine of Eynsham named Adam, is, in the opinion of the late Father Herbert Thurston, "a Life which for fulness of detail and reliability of statement has hardly a parallel in mediaeval literature". The Anglican Vicar who edited the *Magna Vita* deprecated saint-worship but nevertheless felt constrained to write: "I say it with no fear of saying too much, that in the whole range of English worthies few men indeed deserve a higher and holier niche than Bishop Hugh of Lincoln." As against that, it may interest the reader to know that the *Encyclopædia Britannica,* which has found room for notices of Mary Pickford and Douglas Fairbanks, devotes not a single line to the man who planned and partly built the first and most magnificent of England's Gothic glories, Lincoln Cathedral. So much for our modern scale of values. Besides the *Magna Vita,* there has come down and been published in the Rolls Series a shorter account of Hugh by that most fascinating of mediaeval writers, Giraldus Cambrensis, Gerald the Welshman, who lived for some years at Lincoln during the Saint's episcopate. Gerald did not like monks and, besides, considered that he had a personal grievance against St. Hugh, as he had against pretty well every bishop and authority he encountered in his tempestuous life, so the warm admiration which he expresses for the Saint is the more significant. A man who was loved by Giraldus Cambrensis and a swan must certainly have been a lovable man. Incidentally, Gerald, who was something of a naturalist and a keen observer of birds, is our chief authority for the story of the famous swan. He says that he often witnessed its antics while it acted as self-constituted bodyguard of St. Hugh. Far the best life of the Saint in English is that translated from the French of a Carthusian monk and edited for the "Quarterly Series" by Father Thurston in 1898. It contains a good deal of devout padding taken over from the French, but Thurston's copious additional notes render it extremely valuable. The pity is that he was precluded from attempting a completely new English biography.

joined that of Avalon and whose famous chevalier, *sans peur et sans reproche,* would afterwards display as a soldier the very qualities of courage, gaiety, piety and chivalry which made St. Hugh the most fearless and faultless bishop England has ever known. It is very wonderful that he grow into such a rounded, charming character, "full of talk and joyousness and fun," as Giraldus Cambrensis testified,[1] for his strict and somewhat puritanical parents allowed him hardly any normal childhood. "I never tasted the joys of this world, I never learned any amusements," he told the canons of Lincoln afterwards (*Magna Vita,* p. 9), and perhaps it was the remembrance of his own frosty springtime that made him so passionately fond of little children in his mature years. It is a fact that he was the greatest baby-lover among bishops in the history of the Church. He would play with the little things by the hour, and none of his episcopal duties did he enjoy more than giving them the Holy Ghost, which was commonly done in those days when a child was six months old.[2]

When Hugh was only eight years old he received the tonsure and donned the habit of a monk at the neighbouring Priory of Villard-Benoit. He did not have much say in the matter, for his mother died, and her husband, the Lord of Avalon, who was a knight of the Galahad type, always, even in battle, dreaming of the Grail, decided to retire from the world and to take the greatest treasure he possessed, his little son, into the cloister with him. Off they went hand in hand, a new Abraham and Isaac, to give themselves to God. It is not for

---

[1] *Giraldi Cambrensis Opera,* Rolls Series, vol. vii, pp. 68 and 106.

[2] A few of the many words of the Saint's chaplain and biographer on this point are worth giving in the original: "Talibus (sc. infantibus) ubi eos reperisset, spirituali quadam suavitate dulcius adjocabatur; a talibus, vix adhuc balbutientibus, miri cujusdam leporis semiverbia eliciebat. Imprimebat subinde frontibus, vel quibusque sensibus eorum, vivificum sanctae crucis signum, fausta eis imprecans, eosque iterata saepius benedictione communiens. Illi quoque mira ei vicissim celeritate familiariter alludere gaudebant. . . ."(*Magna Vita,* pp. 142–3).

us to criticize that high gesture, but we may fairly question whether the discipline to which the nursery-novice was subjected had much to do with the will of God for little boys. There were other boys at the Priory, gentlemen's sons receiving an education suited to their birth, and with them Hugh shared all the solemnities and austerities of school life, but none of the fun. When they went to play, he, poor little budding monk, was kept firmly indoors, his small nose glued to some monastic grindstone. It is plain to read between the lines of the story as recounted by his devout biographers that he frequently kicked over the traces and let his natural high spirits have a fling, after which escapades the humourless though kindly old religious in charge of him would say with tender reproach: "Hugonete, Hugonete, jocari non est tuum"— Little Hugh, Little Hugh, the fun is not for you! But the boy was endowed by God with splendid resilience and became a sweet human saint in spite of Villard-Benoit's efforts to turn him into a statue.

After taking his vows at the age of fifteen, Hugh was given charge of his old father, then broken with infirmities and near to his vision of the Grail, and waited on him hand and foot with untiring love to the end of his days. It must have been a touching sight to observe the bowed veteran of many wars tottering, supported by his son's sturdy shoulders, to some monastic duty, or being put to bed and tucked up by him at night, or, too feeble to lift an arm, receiving his food spoonful by spoonful from the gentle hands that would afterwards be laid in benediction on crowds of little children (*Magna Vita,* pp. 16–17). Ordained deacon at nineteen, Hugh was made responsible for a small parish dependent on the Priory. His administration revealed another facet of his many-sided character, namely, that he could be a terror to unrepentant evil-doers, and deliver them over publicly to the Devil for the destruction of the flesh that the spirit might be saved. This was the Hugh who later on knew how to put the fear of God into three very unsaintly and tyrannical English kings.[1] The turning point in his diaconal existence came when he visited the Grande Chartreuse for the first time and promptly lost his heart to that amazing institution. Here would he make his everlasting rest, but the seventh successor of St. Bruno received his application very coldly, in accordance with Carthusian technique. "Why, my dear fellow," said he, "our hair-shirt alone would tear the skin off your back and leave you standing in your bare bones. Our rule would make short work of a delicate lad like you" (*Magna Vita,* p. 25). The bluff was wasted on Hugh, who had an appetite for hardships and did not at all consider himself a delicate lad. A far more serious obstacle to his design emerged from the love and veneration with which his fellow-religious of Villard-Benoit regarded him. In the end, he was compelled to steal away secretly to the Wilderness which had seemed to him and became to him a Paradise.

Then followed seventeen years of Carthusian solitude, the world forgetting, by the world forgot, a time with little history except such as was known only to God.[2] Hugh endured long and heavy interior conflicts before winning for his shield,

---

[1] But the way had been well prepared for him by the heroism of St. Thomas Becket, on whom he seems, in many respects, to have modelled his conduct.

[2] Carthusian solitude is not absolute but kindly and discreet. Every Sunday and on the numerous "chapter feasts" the monks dine together in the refectory and have recreation after None. They are even told the news. They meet regularly three times in the twenty-four hours, for the chanting of Matins and Lauds at night, for the Conventual Mass in the morning, and for Vespers in the evening. Except on Sundays and chapter feasts, the Little Hours of the Divine Office are recited privately by each monk in his four-roomed "cell" or cottage, which is furnished with a set-in stall and misericord, so that he may follow the rubrics exactly as though in choir. Compline is always said in private. His cell is the monk's main world where, apart from Sundays and feasts, he has his *maigre* meal and collation in solitary state, and where he chiefly sanctifies his soul by prayer, penance, study, carpentry and amateur gardening. It is the grandest and most fruitful and creative life lived by men on this earth. It is also the most profoundly apostolic life.

as he so completely did, the lovely device: *Viae ejus viae jucundae, et omnes semitae ejus, pax*. During those hidden years he attained pre-eminence among his brethren as a nurse of the sick, and once had the privilege of "mothering", as only he knew how, the grand old Cistercian Archbishop, St. Peter of Tarentaise. From 1173 to 1180 he was Procurator of the vast monastery and proved himself, as contemplatives have so often done, an excellent man of affairs. The lay-brothers, among whom were some fascinating characters, born in the purple, came under his jurisdiction, and he had complete charge of the never-failing guests. It was those guests, ranging from princes and prelates to beggarmen, who brought his Carthusian peace to ruin by spreading abroad his fame in France. But his most constant visitors at this time were the brown, bushy-tailed denizens of the woods *"qui vulgari vocabulo Scurelli dicuntur"*. Giraldus Cambrensis reports that they overran his cell daily at dinner time, boldly poked their noses into his dishes or fed from his hand, and altogether made themselves completely at home. He was hardly ever without a retinue of squirrels, for the wild little creatures somehow divined his innate kindness and friendliness. But when the Prior learned what was happening he put a stop to it, "lest the man of God should take too much delight in the squirrels' company and be hindered in devotion." [1] It was a common sight also, we learn from another, nearly contemporary, source, to find Hugh in his garden festooned with little birds.

Meantime in England King Henry II had absent-mindedly established the first of the country's charterhouses at Witham, in the Forest of Selwood near Frome, Somerset, as part of his penance for the murder of St. Thomas Becket. He came near to murdering the Carthusians, too, by his negligence, and only roused himself when, tried beyond endurance, the few monks seemed likely to pack up their bundles and depart. That would not have been good for his prestige, so he sought advice across the Channel, learned the fame of St. Hugh, and captured him,

[1] *Giraldi Cambrensis Opera*, vol. vii, p. 92.

the best prize he ever took, for England.[1] Hugh's English life began in 1180, the year St. Edmund was born at Abingdon, and he opened it with a characteristic action. Finding that the tenants on the land given to the monks had been, or were to be, evicted without compensation, he informed the King that he could not accept the property until the last penny rightly due to those displaced persons had been paid—*usque ad obolum novissimum.* With a grimace, Henry paid, recognizing the spirit of Becket in the man before him. But Hugh was far from satisfied. Justice had been done but charity was still out in the cold. "Come now, Sire," said he, "look what a rich man I, a poor foreigner, have made you, acquiring for you ownership of all those houses on your own land." Henry, who was good-humoured and already under the Avalon spell, laughed and said: "I don't know that I fancy your methods of making me rich. Your riches have almost beggared me. And what am I to do with a collection of peasant hovels and sheep-pens?" This was the retort that Hugh had been angling for. "You could give them to me," he said sweetly, "who have not a place to lay my head." The King gasped with astonishment. "What an extraordinary man you are!" he exclaimed. "Do you imagine that I haven't the means to build you a proper monastery? But tell me, what would you propose to do with those shacks?" The Prior turned that last question adroitly, and, having been granted the dwellings, waited only until the

---

[1] The County of Maurienne, a bijou Alpine principality of immense strategic importance as it straddled the main routes to Italy, had come into English history a few years earlier when Henry contemplated an alliance between the daughter of the reigning Count and his son John. The lady died, but a friendship had been established and it was an eminent person of Maurienne who directed King Henry's attention to St. Hugh. "Get him as Prior of the monastery," said he, "and not only Witham will flourish but the whole Church in England. No one will look upon him as a foreigner but as a brother or intimate friend, for he is one who embraces all mankind in the folds of his great heart" (*Magna Vita,* pp. 54–5). Freeman, the historian of the Norman Conquest, described Hugh as "a foreign bishop who became in heart one of the truest of Englishmen".

sound of the King's hunting-horn died away in Selwood
Forest to restore them to their former owners that they might
use the materials to build themselves new homes elsewhere
(*Magna Vita,* pp. 69–70).

Hugh, for all his quite air and gentleness, was a dynamo of
energy, one of the master-builders of the Middle Ages, and
soon had his charterhouse springing from the Somerset soil.
But unpaid bills nearly drove him distracted, and he was at
length obliged to protest in person to the King, taking with
him by the wish of his community, who feared that his meekness might not have the desired results, a fiery old baronial
lay-brother named Gerard of Nevers. This Hector of the
cloister who had beaten his sword into a ploughshare was
barely in the King's presence when he started to denounce
him in unmeasured terms, to the horror of Hugh. "Lord King,"
he cried, "do you think you are doing us a favour by doling
us out a bit of bread of which we have no need? We don't
require your charity, and it will be far better for us to return
to our barren rocks in the Alps than to have to haggle with
a man who thinks that every penny distributed for the
salvation of his soul is so much waste. Keep your money
until you have to leave it to some spendthrift heir. Neither
Christ nor any good Christian will deign to touch it." Hugh
avowed that he was never able to recall the scene without a
fresh shudder. It is a valuable scene historically, for it reveals
a Henry II much less black and brutal than some eminent
modern historians, notably Bishop Stubbs, have chosen to
regard him. Throughout the tirade he never said a word, but
when Gerard had exhausted his camp-fire rhetoric turned
quietly to his blushing companion and asked: "What are your
intentions, good Sir? Will you also abandon me and my
Kingdom?" Hugh replied very gently: "No, my Lord, for
I do not think so meanly of you. Rather have I sympathy
for you in your many cares. You are very busy now, but in
God's good time and with His help you will complete the
holy work which you have begun." At those words the King

sprang up, threw his arms round Hugh, and cried: "By my soul's salvation I shall never part with you as long as I live. You are the spiritual director for me." And there and then the King paid all the bills of Witham.[1] So much confidence did Henry come to repose in Hugh that the bemused courtiers invented and spread abroad an ingenious theory to explain it. The Prior must be one of His Majesty's numerous illegitimate sons! (*Magna Vita,* p. 76). Once, in a great storm at sea, the King was heard to pray aloud: "O God, by the merits and intercession of the Prior of Witham, Thy true servant, have mercy upon us in these straits to which our sins have reduced us." And the sea, we are told, at once grew still.

In his new charterhouse Hugh led a life so divine that even when fast asleep he seemed to be praying, for he could be heard whispering softly, sweetly, innumerable times, Amen, Amen, Amen, thus, as it were, fulfilling the beautiful aspiration of a Carthusian hymn, *Te cordis alta somnient!*—may the depths of our hearts dream only of Thee. He was a great lover of books and regarded them as his chief treasures in tranquil times, his weapons in the spiritual warfare, his best food when he was hungry, and his surest medicine when he was sick (*Magna Vita,* p. 92). King Henry, knowing of this addiction, presented him with parchment and leather for the making of new books, and also promised him a complete copy of the Bible. On inquiry, the King found that the monks of St. Swithin's, Winchester, had just finished writing and illuminating a magnificent new Bible for their own refectory, and induced them to sell it to him, much against their inclination. This he presented to Hugh, and it became the delight of his heart until one day he accidentally discovered its

---

[1] *Magna Vita,* pp. 71–5. The speeches put into the mouths of various persons in the Life are obviously not verbatim reports but paraphrases based on St. Hugh's reminiscences. He was as frank and simple as a child, and rather liked to talk about his past, sometimes to encourage other people, sometimes to amend them, as when he told an unpunctual canon of Lincoln that in seventeen years he had never kept anybody waiting at the Grande Chartreuse.

provenance. It was returned that same day to St. Swithin's. At Witham as at the Grande Chartreuse Hugh made friends with the birds and had one especial pet which haunted his cell and took up its station on his table while he dined. Only in the mating season did it discontinue its visits, but afterwards, "as if to compensate him for its long absence, returned with all its young family and presented them to him."[1] When, four years later, the bird died, it was not *"absque viri sancti et benigni molestia grandi"*.

In the year 1186 King Henry issued the mediaeval equivalent of a *congé d'élire* to the Dean and Chapter of Lincoln, which diocese through His Majesty's own manipulations had been bereft of a pastor for all but eighteen months of eighteen years. Without consulting St. Hugh in any way, the King and the Archbishop of Canterbury, a Cistercian, pretty well forced him on the canons, and he was elected, though not in an enthusiastic fashion. None of the parties reckoned with Hugh himself. When a deputation from the chapter, many of them noblemen, waited on him at Witham, they were informed politely that he considered the election null and void. Let them return home and try again, uninfluenced by the Constitutions of Clarendon. Profoundly influenced by the Prior of Witham, they elected him a second time with unanimous enthusiasm. But again he balked, and it was not until they had been to France and secured a formal command from the General of the Carthusians that he bowed his head to the yoke. A splendid cavalcade arrived to escort him to London, but he joined it so meanly accoutred that he might have been a peasant jogging

---

[1] *Giraldi Cambrensis Opera,* vol. vii, p. 93. Gerald says that it was a little bird and called a *burneta,* but neither his most learned editor, James Dimock, nor Dimock's successor, the great E. A. Freeman, were able to identify it. Judging by the name, it seems to have been a brown bird. At any rate, here is an unsolved problem for naturalists who also happen to be mediaevalists, but they should be warned that Du Cange will not help. Father Thurston fell to the temptation of calling the bird a barnacle goose, but, besides the difficulty that those Arctic visitors are purely coastal birds, who ever heard of a goose being described as an *avicula?*

to market at Frome rather than a great prelate on his way to Westminster Abbey.[1]

Nothing much can be said here about his fourteen years as Bishop, 1186–1200, except that he more than repaired the dilapidations of eighteen years and made Lincoln the model diocese of England and of Christendom. No labour was ever too much for his selflessness, no danger too great for his courage. It often happened to him to get up before dawn and to spend the entire day, without sup or bite, consecrating churches and administering confirmation. He and his horse would tire the sun with their journeyings into the remotest corners of the vast diocese, embracing nine counties, and no matter how late the hour or bad the weather he would always gladly dismount to confirm a ploughman's child or to bless and comfort the sick. The care of the sick was a passion with him, and for the sickest of the sick, the lepers, who were numerous in England then, he showed the same marked partiality as his Divine Master. Nothing he loved better than to gather up to thirteen of those poor outcasts about him in his palace that he might wash and kiss their feet, feed them, and give them abundant alms. He liked to go and live with the lepers in their lazarhouses. "God forgive me," says his chaplain, "but the sight of them used to fill me with horror, yet would the holy man embrace them one by one, and the more hideously disfigured they were the longer and tenderer would be his kiss" (*Magna Vita*, p. 163). He cherished a special devotion to St. Martin of Tours who also had been a father to lepers. Knowing this, his Chancellor, an eminent theologian named William de Monte whom he greatly loved, said to him teasingly one day at Newark: "My Lord, Martin cleansed a leper with a kiss." Hugh, who was no great admirer of miracles as such,[2] at once retorted: "True, he healed the leper

---

[1] He returned to Witham to live a completely Carthusian life for a month each year until his death.

[2] "Nihil minus quam miraculorum prodigia mirari aut aemulari videretur ... cum illi sola esset sanctorum sanctitas pro miraculo" (*Magna*

in his body with a kiss, but the leper with a kiss heals me in
my soul." [1]

If St. Hugh loved the lepers, he detested the keepers and
verderers of the royal forests, who were the chief oppressors
of the poor in Angevin England. The forests, vast tracts of
waste-land, moors, heaths and open commons, as well as
woods properly so-called, belonged. immediately to the King
and fell outside the scope of the common law of the realm.
"Among the scourges of England," writes St. Hugh's chaplain,
"the first place goes to the tyranny of the foresters which
ravages and depopulates whole countrysides. Violence is the
law of those men and rapine their glory." Mutilation and even
death were ordinary penalties for poaching or other offences
against the sanctity of the fox, the wild boar, the badger, the
otter, the red and fallow deer, the hare, and all game birds.[2]
The foresters constituted a sort of mediaeval Gestapo, feared
by the greatest in the land, but no sooner was St. Hugh installed
at Lincoln than he declared open war on them and solemnly
excommunicated their head, in defiance of the Constitutions of
Clarendon.[3] King Henry raged, but himself feared the Saint
too much to do anything about it. Hugh was a strong man and
no mistake. Another powerful person whom he had excom-

Vita, p. 97). Once, in France, St. Hugh, whose devotion to the Blessed
Sacrament was famous, received an urgent invitation to come and see a
miraculous bleeding Host. But he refused to go, saying: "There is no
need for us to see with our bodily eyes that which we see clearly with
the eyes of faith every day in Mass." If the ancient, mediaeval and, sometimes, modern hagiographers had been of the same mind, how much
more attractive and helpful might not our Second Nocturns be!

[1] *Giraldi Cambrensis Opera,* vol. vii, pp. 107–8. Gerald learned the
story from William de Monte himself, to study under whom he had
come to Lincoln.

[2] It is significant that in the *Vision of the Monk of Eynsham,* an
English *Divina Commedia* taken down in 1196 by none other than
Adam, St. Hugh's biographer, King Henry II is grievously tormented
in Purgatory "because he would be avenged on men that slew his
venery".

[3] In theory the King had repealed the Constitutions, but woe betide
anyone, except St. Hugh, who violated them in practice.

municated for injustice appealed to the new Archbishop of
Canterbury, Hubert Walter, then virtual ruler of England, and
was by him released from the censure, whereupon he returned
insolently to thrust the form of absolution into the Saint's hands.
Having read it, Hugh said quietly: "Even should the Lord
Archbishop think fit to absolve you a hundred times, I shall
re-excommunicate you a hundred and one times, so long as you
persist in your evil courses" (*Magna Vita,* p. 180).

In 1197, Archbishop Walter demanded a subsidy from the
baronage of England, including the principal bishops, in aid
of King Richard the First's wars in France. St. Hugh disapproved of those wars as being mere predatory adventures
and refused the grant, which threw Lion-Heart into such a
rage that he ordered all his goods to be confiscated. But no
man dared proceed against the Bishop of Lincoln, for, as his
chaplain tells, "his anathema was feared like death". Indeed,
it was Hugh who took the offensive. Crossing to France, he
found the King in his new "Saucy Castle" at Roches d'Andeli
engaged hearing Mass. Walking boldly up to the Monarch's
throne, he made his obeisance, but Richard glared at him
fiercely and then turned his head away. Nothing abashed,
Hugh said to this Terror of the Infidel: "Lord King, give
me a kiss." Receiving no answer, he seized the King's mantle
and shook it vigorously, saying: "I have come a long journey
to find you, and I have a right to a kiss." Richard, with his
face still averted, sulkily denied that he had any such right,
whereupon Hugh gave him an even more thorough shaking
and said in his ear: "Come now, kiss me." At that, Lion-
Heart, beaten as his father had been, grinned sheepishly and
kissed him.[1] Another instance among many of the Saint's

[1] Bishop Stubbs regarded St. Hugh's refusal of a money-grant to the
King as "a landmark of constitutional history". This has been contested,
but who will deny that the incident at Château Gaillard is hardly to be
matched for daring and charm in the whole story of England? "Sicut leo
absque terrore in omni terrore fuit," says his chaplain, and he proved it
by walking with his eyes open into danger again and again, as when he
hastened at the risk of his life to King Richard's funeral at Fontevrault.

fearlessness is provided by his defence of the Jews, who suffered dire persecution at this time owing to their inveterate habit of accumulating immense fortunes.[1] We are shown him at Lincoln, alone in the midst of an armed and infuriated mob, quelling the Jew-baiters by the sheer power of his personality, or at Northampton, tearing down with his own hands, in the teeth of determined resistance, the votive offerings placed by the townspeople over the tomb of a so-called victim of the Jews, who in fact was a common thief, murdered by one of his partners in crime.

St. Hugh died at "the Bishop of Lincoln's Inn," High Holborn, London, 16 November, 1200, lying on the bare ground with ashes spread in the form of a cross beneath him. As the end approached he was heard to whisper again and again, "O merciful Saviour, give me rest, give me rest." He was a very tired Saint. During his illness, the doctors persuaded the Archbishop of Canterbury to order him to eat some meat. It shows the type of man he was that he at once obeyed and for the first time in forty years broke his cherished Carthusian abstinence. By his own avowal he had a peppery temper (*sum revera pipere asperior*) and he is reported on occasion to have cuffed some of his clerics whom he found being harsh to little children. He was addicted to making puns, and in general his manner is best described by the adjectives "hilaris et jocundus". His favourite burlesque oath was *per sanctam nucem*. "By the holy nut," he used to say to bereaved people, "it would be a terrible thing if we never could die." His remains were carried to their resting place in the great Cathedral which he had planned and partly completed, working himself as a common labourer with hod and chisel, on the shoulders of two kings, William the Lion of Scotland and John Lackland of England. It was fitting that it should be so, for not even Tobias of old had shown more charity to the dead than did St. Hugh of Lincoln. His homily to his priests on the subject (*Magna Vita,*

[1] Aaron of Lincoln was the wealthiest man in England and held even the great and proud Abbey of St. Albans in mortgage.

p. 226) is one of the most perfect gems of Mediaeval Latin literature. Sometimes he officiated at as many as five Requiems and funerals a day, often of the poorest people, and Heaven help the priest who failed to notify him of any death in his parish! Taking him all in all, Hugh surely merited the tribute paid to him by John Ruskin in his autobiography, *Praeterita*: "The most beautiful sacerdotal figure known to me in history".

DECEMBER 29   ST. THOMAS OF CANTERBURY

THE only apology possible for including in this little series of English and Irish Saints the most famous and familiar of them all is that the December Martyrology provides no alternative except St. Birinus, the stout-hearted stranger from Rome who so unobtrusively converted the West Saxons and then faded back into the beautiful obscurity of his origin. Not even the Venerable Bede, with his special advantages, was able to make much of Birinus. The trouble with St. Thomas Becket is exactly the opposite, a huge *embarras* of biographical riches. Like a cat, he had nine "lives" circulating within a decade of his martyrdom, not to mention an Icelandic saga based on a tenth one.[1] This surely constitutes a world's record in posthumous publicity, and seems clearly to prove one precious fact, namely, that, whatever his faults and mistakes, St. Thomas was immensely loved.

After his martyrdom in 1170 and his canonization a little more than two years later, "his cult spread all over Europe with lightning speed and the consequences of this were very soon to be seen in all the arts: indeed, the Middle Ages supply no quite comparable case before his time, and after him the nearest analogy is only afforded in the next century by St. Francis of Assisi, whose international effect upon the

[1] All were published in the Rolls Series during the decade 1875–85, by authority of the Crown and Parliament of England, a fact that must have made Henry VIII turn over several times in his Windsor tomb. The Lives, all in Latin, and the Saint's letters occupy seven volumes under the general title, *Materials for the History of Thomas Becket, Archbishop of Canterbury.* The saga, Icelandic text with an attractive English translation, fills two more, entitled *Thomas Saga Erkibyskups.* Of modern lives in English the most notable are those by W. H. Hutton (2nd ed., Cambridge, 1926), John Morris, S.J. (2nd ed., London, 1885), and Robert Speaight (London, 1938). Dean Stanley's *Historical Memorials of Canterbury,* first published in 1855, is very valuable though often inaccurate. Henry Irving considered Tennyson's *Becket* to be "a very noble play", and it is certainly remarkably faithful to the original sources, except for the intrusions of the Fair Rosamund. Everybody is familiar with *Murder in the Cathedral.*

155

arts was, however, of much slower growth." [1] Thomas of London, as he liked to call himself with a touch of cockney pride, was to be found represented among the Byzantine mosaics of Monreale Cathedral, Sicily, within twelve years of his martyrdom, and within another thirty years among the frescoes of San Martino ai Monti, Rome, as also at Spoleto, in the glorious sculptures and stained glass of Sens and Chartres, in a whole series of wall-paintings in the Church of Santa Maria at Tarrasa, near Barcelona, and on a baptismal font in the wilds of Sweden. The most interesting case of early foreign veneration for the Saint is to be found in the great basilica of Notre-Dame de Fourvière, Lyons. There is no proof that Thomas ever set foot in Lyons, but the fact remains that when Olivier de Chavanne built the original nave, beginning in 1168, he had it dedicated to the English Martyr immediately upon his canonization in 1173. Nothing of this work now remains except the apse, which still keeps St. Thomas's name and has a little altar with a painting of him above it, a spot dear to English visitors and redolent of heroic memories. In England, of course, his image was ubiquitous and his shrine for three hundred years drew pilgrims of every land and condition, from the Wife of Bath to the Emperor of Germany, to Canterbury, "the holy blissful martyr for to seek," [2] until Henry VIII, in his Proclamation of 16 November, 1538, declared war on him as a rebel and imposter: "The kinges maiestie, by the aduyse of his counsayle, hath thought expedyent to declare to his louynge subiectes, that notwithstandynge the canonization [of

[1] Tancred Borenius, *St. Thomas Becket in Art,* London, 1932, p. 9. No book affords better proof of the extraordinary impression made by St. Thomas on the mind of Western Christendom, and this not only on account of his famous miracles, which were the result rather than the cause of his wonderful popularity.

[2] One twelfth-century biographer maintained that the Pilgrimages to Canterbury already surpassed in numbers and brilliance those to Rome, Compostela, and even the Holy Sepulchre (*Materials,* iv, 141). We have our doubts.

Becket], there appereth nothynge in his lyfe and exteriour conuersation whereby he shuld be callyd a sayncte, but rather estemed to haue ben a rebell and traytour to his prynce. Therefore his grace strayghtly chargeth and commandeth that from hense forthe the sayde Thomas Becket shall not be estemed, named, reputed, nor called a sayncte, and that his ymages and pictures, through the hole realme, shall be putte downe and auoyded out of all churches, chapelles, and other places, and that from hense forthe the dayes vsed to be festiuall in his name shall not be obserued, nor the seruice, office, antiphones, collettes, and prayers in his name redde, but rased and put out of all the bokes...vpon peyn of his maiesties indignation, & imprisonment at his gracis plesure. GOD SAVE THE KYNGE."

The man thus vainly "de-canonized" by England's strange new private Pope was born in Cheapside of bourgeois Norman parents on the feast of the Apostle St. Thomas, A.D. 1118, and lived only to be fifty-two. But what a round world of experience he crowded into that half-century, the experience of scholar, courtier, sportsman, diplomat, justice, soldier, great ecclesiastic, and saint. At the end of it all he might have said as truly as the poor French poet did boastfully, "J'ai plus de souvenirs que si j'avais mille ans." Of his childhood we learn from his philosopher friend, the gentle and wise John of Salisbury, that his devout mother Matilda taught him "sweetly to invoke the Blessed Virgin as the guide of his ways and the patron of his life, putting in her, after Christ, all his confidence" (*Materials,* ii, 303. Also *Thomas Saga,* i, 19). From time to time, too, his mother used to weigh him against a quantity of food, clothing and money, which was then immediately distributed to the poor (*Materials,* iv, 7). So the Aga Khan was not the first to devise that charming ceremony! The best of the biographers, William Fitzstephen, who tells us proudly that he functioned as perpetual sub-deacon at St. Thomas's Mass, was such an inveterate Londoner that, absorbed in describing the greatness and attractiveness of their native City, he entirely omitted to supply any details of his hero's doings as a boy.[1]

Thomas went first to a London school as a day-boy, next to the Priory of Merton in Surrey as a boarder, and finally, to round off his education, spent some years at the famous schools of Paris, then slowly evolving into the first and greatest of universities. Returning at twenty-two, he found himself obliged to earn his living, and became clerk to a City merchant bearing the delightful name of Huitdeniers or Eightpence. Eightpence must have been a tolerant employer and very fond of him, for he seems to have spent most of his time hawking and hunting. Falconry was the passion of his life, and nearly cost him that same life on one occasion in an endeavour to save his imperilled hawk. It is amusingly significant that several of the miracles attributed to him after his martyrdom had to do with the ailments of hawks, or their restoration to life, or recovery when lost.[2] But while thoroughly enjoying his youth, Thomas was ambitious and went abroad again at the first opportunity to study law at Bologna and Auxerre. We can fairly agree with Henry VIII about him at this period, that there appeared "nothynge in his lyfe and exteriour conuersation whereby he shuld be callyd a sayncte". Rather was he a dazzlingly successful young man of the world, though untouched by its grosser vices. John of Salisbury, who dearly loved him, admits that in youth and early manhood he was "supra modum captator aurae popularis", a courter of the popular breeze, while Herbert of Bosham, his brave, intolerably prolix champion against all

[1] He devotes eleven pages to the glories of London but only eleven lines, including two from Horace, to the boyhood of Thomas. The amenities of London, and especially its summer and winter sports, particularly engaged him, for, says he, and what a good maxim it is for all town planners, "non expedit utilem tantum et seriam urbem esse, nisi dulcis etiam sit et jocunda" (*Materials,* iii, 8). That sentiment was heartily shared by the future Primate of England.

[2] One distressed sportsman is reported to have cried to the Saint: "Get me back my lost bird, Martyr Thomas, you who flew hawks yourself and suffered such sorrow as is mine!" (*Materials,* i, 502. Also, pp. 388–90, 466–7, 528). Needless to say, he got back his bird.

comers, tells us reluctantly that he continually progressed in favour with men, "sed apud Dominum non adeo". A delightful clubbable fellow, "slim of growth and blithe of countenance was he, winning and lovable in all conversation, frank of speech, but slightly stuttering in his utterance" (*Thomas Saga,* i, 29; *Materials,* ii, 302). Like his own London he was "dulcis et jocundus", and he had the most beautiful manners. The real wonder is, not that he failed to be a saint, but that he did not go entirely to the devil.

When he was about twenty-four Thomas was taken into the household of Theobald, Archbishop of Canterbury, and by his gifts of mind, prudence, and charm of character soon won his way to the heart of this new master. Before many years had passed he was the Archbishop's most trusted adviser. "Theobald was a simple man, somewhat quick of temper, and not as wary of word, if his mind was stirred, as the rule of meekness utmost demandeth. But against either failing the Blessed Thomas setteth his good will and wisdom, in such a manner that if the bishop happened to wax wroth, Thomas giveth forth answers all the meeker, thus appeasing the heart of his spiritual father. So also, on the other hand, if the speech of the archbishop happened to fail him in aught, Thomas hastened to succour him, and clothed it in clerkdom in such wise that at once the discourse appeared like a text with a fair commentary." [1] Many times the two journeyed to Rome to-gether or to councils in France, and the excellent diplomacy of Thomas secured Papal support for the chief desire of Theobald's heart, that Henry of Anjou should succeed to the throne rather than Eustace, the son of turbulent King Stephen. But Eustace considerably helped the negotiations by dying a year before his father. Not until he was thirty-six did Thomas receive deacon's

[1] *Thomas Saga Erkibyskups,* i, 37. This is the testimony of Robert of Cricklade, Prior of St. Frideswide's, Oxford, and contemporary of St. Thomas, whom he believed, after the Martyrdom, to have cured him twice of serious diseases (*Materials,* ii, 96–101). He was a frequent pilgrim to the shrine at Canterbury and there gathered at first hand the materials for his biography.

orders and then only that he might be made archdeacon of Canterbury, the finest jewel in his crown of many benefices. Just at that moment, A.D. 1154, Henry II arrived, aged twenty-one, and in a trice made Thomas Lord High Chancellor of England.

Novus itaque erigitur super Aegyptum Joseph! [1] "Nearly all the affairs of the King and of the government have fallen under his power and will, as have cities and townships, trade-ports and castles, gold and treasures, and all royal armories. And although he was like unto folk of pride in his worldly good hap, yet was he right unlike those who love this life overmuch, for he never held in lesser worth a good man because of his poverty, nor honoured an evil one any more because of his riches" (*Thomas Saga,* i, 49). The chief virtue which he displayed as Chancellor, at least to the world, was that favourite one of the pagan moralists, magnificence. Sent over the water to negotiate a royal marriage, he determined to show the French that England could make it, and so went squired by two hundred knights splendidly caparisoned. In his train followed eight great waggons of presents, each drawn by five horses, and a regular circus of hawks and hounds, monkeys and mastiffs. Two more waggons were laden with beer in iron-bound casks, "donandam Francis, id genus liquidi mirantibus".[2] The French gasped with admiration, but not so much the next time (1159), when Thomas in full armour came against them at the head of seven hundred knights, the flower of the English Army, laid siege to their towns and, cleric though he was, engaged in hand-to-hand encounters.

But that is not the whole story of his Chancellorship. On one occasion a person of no consequence sought audience with him in London, very early in the morning. "Now, the way

[1] So Edward Grim, the gallant biographer of the Saint who attempted to ward off the blow aimed at him by William de Tracy and nearly had his own arm severed as a consequence of his devotion (*Materials,* ii, 363).

[2] *Materials,* auctore Fitzstephen, iii, 30-1. In pre-Reformation England Thomas was patron saint of the Worshipful Company of Brewers.

taketh such turn that he must needs go by a certain church, and in the twilight he soon seeth lying before the door of the temple a man prostrate in prayer even unto earth. And whenas he stands bethinking him of this sight, there comes upon him, as oft-times may happen, some sneeze or a kind of coughing. And forthwith starts he who lay kneeling on the ground, and rises straightway up, then lifteth his hands up to God and thus ends his prayer. The newcomer was right eager to know who of the townspeople might follow such laudable ways, and therefore he taketh an eye-mark against the lifting day-brow, both of his growth and of the manner of attire he wore, that he might the rather know him if he should happen to see him afterwards. Nor did that matter long wait a true proof, for no sooner hath he leave to see Chancellor Thomas than he well perceiveth that the very growth and raiment which he had noted before belongeth to no man but to him alone. This person testified to his kinsman, Robert, when he came home what virtue and godly fear he had found in the blessed Thomas, straightway against the thinking of most people." [1] No incident in the Saint's career is better authenticated than that, and it makes rather unnecessary the elaborate theorizing and psychologizing indulged in by scholars to account for the remarkable change which came over him when he was appointed Archbishop of Canterbury. [2]

That fateful event took place in the year 1162, almost entirely

[1] *Thomas Saga Erkibyskups*, i, 53. The Robert referred to was Robert of Cricklade, author of the lost Latin life of St. Thomas on which the Saga is chiefly based. Thomas is known from the vestments he wore to have been exceedingly tall, and so easily identifiable.

[2] As, for instance, the late Professor Z. N. Brooke's, "that he was one of those men who, exalting to the full the role they have to play, picture themselves as the perfect representatives of their office, visualizing a type and making themselves the living impersonation of it; actors playing a part, but unconscious actors" (*The English Church and the Papacy*, Cambridge, 1931, p. 193. Professor Brooke is not at his best when writing about the character of St. Thomas, and it is very difficult to see how he can reconcile his play-actor, unconscious and sincere though he be, with the figure kneeling in the London street at break of day).

by King Henry's contrivance. The honeymoon of himself and his Chancellor had lasted, apparently without a cloud on it, for eight golden years. They truly loved each other; they were publicly believed, as John of Salisbury testified, to "have but one heart and one soul"; at times they romped together like a pair of schoolboys; and yet Henry, with all his cleverness, saw only a very little way into the deep heart of Thomas. Externally, he seemed to be the most fortunate man in England, for it was always his way to show a smiling front to the world, but he told his friends Theobald and John with tears in his eyes— *sub lacrymarum testimonio*—that his courtly grandeur made him weary of existence and long for the peace beyond death (*Materials,* ii, 305). When the King, then with him in France, first broached the subject of his succession to Theobald, recently dead, Thomas caught up a fold of the gay robe in which he was dressed and, displaying it, said: "What a religious man, what a saint, you would place in that holy See and over so famous a monastery! Were such a thing to happen in the designs of God, I am very sure that you would speedily change your tune, and the great love now existing between us would be turned to black hatred" (*Materials,* iii, 181). And so it befell, as all the world knows, and as a little wisp of an essay like this need not render itself ridiculous by trying to rehearse. Henry gambled on the connivance of Thomas with his totalitarian plans for the Church in England. He lost his gamble and Thomas lost his life, that is the gist of the tremendous conflict and tragedy which startled and affected the whole of Christendom. Let us resolutely leave it and steal behind the scenes to observe England's Hildebrand *en famille.*

"It well behoveth that we should hear how meekly he dealeth with the limbs of our Lord Jesus Christ, the poor folk of alms. Every night, when matins have been sung, thirteen poor people are called in and shown into a certain lone chamber, where a table is set forth and laid. Into this chamber goeth the Archbishop himself and laying aside his robes kneeleth adown and washeth the feet of those sitting there, with such fulness of godly compassion that the tears from his eyes flow together with the water wherein he washeth. Thus meekly kneeling adown he entreateth these almsfolk to pray on his behalf for the mercy of God. After this he serveth them at tables both with meat and drink, and beyond this giveth four shining pennies [1] to each, kneeling down at the same time. A second time, towards day-dawn, another batch of poor folk is led in...A third gathering is ordained towards the third hour of the day, wherein there be one hundred poor people, all of whom receive bread and drink enow. Now, these alms-givings are so great that no Archbishop of Canterbury had ever gone further therein than half the way that Thomas goeth, and yet it shall be full right to think that they be not all told of here; for to all who asked for them alms were as certain as if they lay in their hand, no matter whether the Archbishop was at home, or abroad in his diocese...Hot as was his love to his Lord and Redeemer, the love to his neighbor was ever blended together with it in his heart, being common to all, and yet most chiefly so to the wretched, the wounded and the sick." [2]

If St. Thomas played a part it was certainly a noble one. He described himself as "an ambitious and vain-glorious man", and every day of his seven years as archbishop he did heavy secret penance for his sins. When his clerks undressed his mangled body for burial, they found next to his skin something none of them had ever suspected, a complete suit, shirt and drawers, of the roughest hair-cloth (*Materials,* iv, 134). Self-dramatizers, however sincere, do not usually go in for such garments. The Saint was up daily before any of his household and began his morning with the study and meditation of the Scriptures. He said or sung his Mass briskly, in accordance with a Sarum rubric, but during it "his holy countenance was never dry from tears" (*Saga,* i, 103; *Materials,* iv, 286–7).

[1] Literally, coins, Icel. *penninga.*
[2] *Thomas Saga Erkibyskups,* i, 99–101. The same testimony is borne by all the Latin lives.

Then all the world and his wife had access to him, for he was the most approachable great man in England, and nothing that he could do to right a wrong or comfort a sorrow was ever thought too much trouble. Pleasant to relate, he took a siesta in the afternoon, though goodness knows, with those underclothes he wore, it cannot have been very refreshing, for, dare we breathe it of this "extremely civilized man"? [1] they were alive with what St. Teresa and her nuns used to call "bad people". For a little while he continued to array himself outwardly in the magnificent style to which he was accustomed, until one day a bold monk reproved him for the ostentation, whereupon he burst into tears and ever after wore a plain black soutane, trimmed with lamb's wool (*Materials,* iv, 21). *In veste pretiosa spiritu pauper, in facie laeta corde contritus,* that was the way with him, as it was with another martyred and canonized ex-chancellor of England. He habitually carried a linen stole about his neck so that he might be ready at every and any moment to administer the Sacrament of Confirmation.

The first big rift in the relations between the Archbishop and the King occurred at the palace of Woodstock in 1163, when Henry demanded that a certain tax, voluntarily paid to the sheriffs of the counties to secure their protection, should in future go directly to his treasury. It was graft on the grand scale, but only Thomas of all the nobles and bishops present had the courage to oppose it. "By God's eyes it shall be paid," exclaimed the King in a rage. "By the same eyes by which you have sworn," answered Thomas, "not a penny shall be paid from my lands as long as I live" (*Materials, ii,* 24). Perhaps he might have made his stand, "the first case of any opposition to the King's will in the matter of taxation recorded in our national history," [2] with a little more moderation, but it was his failing to have a quick temper and not to know how to mince words. The more serious quarrel over the Constitu-

[1] The very true description is Robert Speaight's, *Thomas Becket,* p. 60.
[2] Stubbs, *Constitutional History of England,* vol. i (1873), p. 463.

tions of Clarendon followed in 1164 and led up to the dramatic scenes at Northampton and to St. Thomas's famous ride through the night and the rain to Sandwich for his perilous escape in a small rowing-boat to the Continent. Not for six years would he see England again, a time of the heaviest suffering and persecution, for the King, in the most up-to-date Moscow manner, confiscated the goods of all his friends, relations and domestics, and banished them out of the realm. As a final touch, he exacted from each exile an oath that he would present himself to the Archbishop penniless and forlorn, in order that the sight might break his resolution, and then, to complete the modern analogy, threatened the Cistercians of Pontigny with the confiscation of all their houses in his dominions if they continued to harbour the fugitive. But Thomas never wavered; rather did he give blow for blow, excommunicating the craven bishops who sided with the King. It is too easy to criticize his truculence at eight hundred years' distance, so we shall spare ourselves the labour, and cite instead a few lines from one of his letters to the bishops of England:[1] "Thomas, by God's grace, humble servant of the church of Canterbury, sendeth all his venerable brethren the greeting that they do what as yet they do not. The Lord Jesus Christ died for us, obedient to His Father even unto the Cross. How can your order keep so great a love before your eyes, if ye fear less God than man, and love your body more than the Creator? We have listened in silence if any of you would remember his ordination and defend the freedom of the Church; but now it is manifest from your letter, which grieveth our soul, that ye stand ready rather to put her to shame than to hold her up. Now, if you could but wipe away from your eyes the blindness which for a long time hath been your great bane, it would behove you to consider what end these affairs must have. Ye desire that I should call to

---

[1] The version is that of Eirikir Magnusson, the admirable translator of the *Thomas Saga*. The original Latin is to be found in Migne, *P.L.*, 190, 536 seq., as well as in *Materials*, v.

mind how humble a cot-carl's son I came to the King's court, and I own that my kin is not of a royal line, as is that of some of you. To this we have to answer that it seemeth to us preferable to become the pride of a small stock than the disgrace of a great one.[1] Now if ye obey and follow my counsel for a holy change and repentance, ye will do well, but if ye hold to what you have begun, let God Judge between ourself and you. *Valete.*"

By the good offices of the King of France a peace of sorts was patched up between Henry and Thomas at Fréteval in Normandy on 10 July, 1170. The Archbishop's journey home from Sandwich to Canterbury was a triumphal progress, but he knew that he was going to his death.[2] He was back barely three weeks when King Henry, roused to ungovernable rage by the complaints of three of Thomas's episcopal enemies, let fall at Bur, near Bayeux, the fatal words which sent four of his knights speeding across the Channel to commit the Murder in the Cathedral. And that will be enough here about this exciting and inscrutable great man of God, so humble and haughty, so gentle and inflexible, so human and super-human, who died for a question of priestly privilege that also happened to underlie the liberties of England and of the World.[3]

[1] St. Thomas's actual words are even more incisive: "Malo tamen is esse in quo facit sibi genus animi nobilitas quam in quo nobilitas generis degeneret."

[2] St. Godric, the Durham hermit, who had a deep veneration for the Archbishop, sent him a message in March 1170, prophesying both his reconciliation with the King and his death shortly afterwards (Reginald, *Libellus de Vita et Miraculis S. Godrici,* Surtees Society, 1845, pp. 293, 297).

[3] As part of his rationalistic higher criticism of the New Testament, Dr. Edwin Abbott issued two volumes on the death and miracles of St. Thomas Becket in 1898, with the intent of showing up the discrepancies of the various writers. Whatever his purpose, he produced an interesting and valuable work, out of which St. Thomas comes with flying colours. Dr. Abbott dedicated the volumes to him in the following words: "To the memory of Thomas, once Archbishop of Canterbury, now venerated by some as saint and martyr, by others admired as a hero, by some few vilified as a narrow ecclesiastic, but deserving to be studied by all,

whether friends, critics or enemies, as a conspicuous proof that the spirit may then be manifested in its full power when defeat and corruption have triumphed over the flesh." As to the contention of the critics that it was the circumstances of the Saint's death, and not the spirit of the man, which caused him to be identified with justice and holiness, Dr. Abbott writes: "The miracles by themselves go far to prove that those who see in Thomas Becket nothing more than a hot-tempered ecclesiastic, jealous for the exclusive privileges of his order, are virtually drawing an indictment not only against a nation but also against the very laws of human nature. And, so far as I have studied the records of his life, it seems more consistent with them also to believe that not till his consecration as Archbishop did the former Chancellor realize the abominable badness of the forces that were at work among the secular rulers, and the pitiable condition of the lower classes.... Gradually, but with all sincerity, he may have grown into the conviction that he was called to contend for his 'order', and that in fighting this battle he was championing the cause of the Universal Church, the spiritual Commonweal of mankind. For this in his last moments he professed his readiness to die; and dying for this, unarmed against arms, with faith in invisible against visible forces ... he seems fairly entitled to the name of Martyr" (vol. i, pp. 6–7).

VENERABLE MARIE OF THE INCARNATION

THIS lady's right to inclusion in a book of English and Irish saints is distinctly adventitious, for she was French, as Abbé Bremond boasted, to the tips of her fingers, and has not yet even been beatified. But thirteen is the right number for a book such as this, and Marie of the Incarnation has a claim to complete the baker's dozen by being a sort of spiritual conquest of the British Empire. When Wolfe stormed the Heights of Abraham, he captured the relics and the glory of Marie for England.

One of the sublimest and most finely balanced contemplatives the Church has ever known, she was born on 28 October, 1599, at Tours, a town which claims, to the indignation of its rival, Arles, that it produces the most beautiful girls in France. Her father was a baker, which gives us her social status, and she herself took a little innocent pride in what she described as her "talent pour le negoce". A dream is all that distinguishes her maidenhood from the springtime of other tradesmen's daughters, not that they are without any dreams, but hers was different, a vision of the night at the age of seven wherein our Lord appeared to her and asked, "Will you be Mine?" and she answered with a "Yes!" which reverberated in eternity. It was a simple affair, that first beckoning of the finger of God, but it marked the beginning of a complete dedication, without in any way harming the beautiful "humanness" which made her sanctity so attractive. At fourteen, she confided to her mother, a holy hard-working soul, her desire to be a nun. "Ma mère," she explains, "ne me croyait pas propre, parce qu'elle me voyait d'une humeur gaie et agréable, qu'elle estimait peut-être incompatible avec le vertu de la religion." The scruple of the good lady, a first snow-flake of the Jansenist blizzard, did not cure Marie of her high spirits, so a marriage was arranged for her in the practical French, Irish and Ancient Roman style which works so astonishingly well. Marie entered into it puzzled but thinking that her parents knew best, and learned to love and be extremely happy with her husband, Claude Martin. Alas, Claude, though certainly "un brave homme" was not so decidedly "un homme brave", with the result that by one of the many paradoxes of Marie's life she was at the same time extremely miserable with her mother-in-law. After two years Claude died, leaving her with a baby son bearing his own name, and a bankrupt business.

That hour of desolation was God's hour. On 24 March, 1620, the vigil of the feast of the Incarnation, Marie left her home early, bent on the business of this world. Single-handed and valiant-hearted, she had set to the task of straightening out her dead husband's affairs, and as she walked along repeated to herself over and over again in ceaseless litany, *In te Domine speravi, non confundar in aeternum.* Then, there in the street, under the misty morning sky of Touraine, with no more warning than our Lady had of Gabriel's coming, she underwent her first tremendous mystical experience. It took the form of a realization of her sins so piercing that she believed she must have died immediately of horror at their foulness, if God had not sustained her. This is how she describes the visitation: "De voir que personnellement l'on est coupable, et que, quand l'on eût été seule qui eût péché, le Fils de Dieu aurait fait ce qu'il a fait pour tous, c'est ce qui consomme et anéantit l'âme... Mon coeur se sentit ravi à soi-même, et tout changé en l'amour de celui qui lui avait fait cette insigne miséricorde, lequel lui fit souffrir... un regret de l'avoir offensé le plus grand qu'on se puisse imaginer; non, il ne se peut imaginer. Ce trait de l'amour fut si pénétrant et si inexorable pour ne rein relâcher de la douleur, que je me fusse jetée dans les flammes pour le satisfaire." [1]

[1] *Marie de l'Incarnation: Ecrits spirituels et historiques.* Edited by the Solesmes Benedictines, t. ii, pp. 182-3. The first four volumes of this magnificent work were published at Paris during the decade 1929–1939. Others are to follow. Abbé Bremond, who so often laments his lack of space, devotes half of the sixth volume of his *Histoire Littéraire du Sentiment Religieux en France* to Marie, finding her, as he avows, completely

It need hardly be said that Marie's "Relations" of her spiritual experiences were written, not spontaneously or for her own satisfaction, but in obedience to the express commands of two of her directors, the Jesuits Père Georges de la Haye and Père Jerome Lallemant. That first touch of God, with its simultaneous agony and bliss, marked what she called her "conversion", though she had been since childhood a model of devotion. Thereafter she was another being, "si puissamment changée que je ne me connaissais plus moi-même". But as yet she stood only on the first rung of her Jacob's ladder whose top disappears from our eyes in the infinite azure of God. She applied herself with such dexterity to affairs that soon her dead husband's credit was redeemed. Then her sister's husband, who was the Carter Paterson of Touraine, begged her to come and manage for him, and for three or four years she played the part of Martha to perfection in his swarming household, while never ceasing to be Mary in her soul. This Buisson and his wife, her sister, were, for all their horses and carts, graceless exploiters of her charity, but so far from resenting it she made a secret vow to obey their least wish. Her brilliant management as cook, nurse and housekeeper of the Buisson family and its tough retainers, the porters and vanmen, inspired her brother-in-law, astute fellow, to put the whole conduct of his affairs in her hands.

Then was witnessed, but only by the angels, an extraordinary thing, a doubling of attention that kept two worlds in focus and made of Marie's life in the bustling, noisy warehouse, with her ledgers around her, one long, unbroken ecstasy. "I found myself", she writes, "in the thick of the merchants' hubbub, and, nevertheless, my spirit was plunged in the Divine Majesty. I used to spend almost the whole day in a stable that served as a warehouse, and sometimes I would be in the wharf at midnight directing the loading or unloading

irresistible. A good book on her mysticism in general is Père Joseph Klein's *L'Itinéraire mystique de la Vén. Marie de l'Incarnation,* Paris, 1938.

of merchandise. My usual company consisted of porters, carters, and even fifty or sixty horses which it was my business to care for." One likes to think of those great, patient, shaggy-footed beasts being rubbed down and given their oats by one of the grandest mystics in history. In keeping her accounts, she writes that the process of dipping the pen in the ink was precious to her "parce que l'esprit et le cœur se servaient de ce moment pour former leur entretien". The hide-and-seek of the mystical life caused her inexpressible suffering, tolerable only because it seemed to tend to some great disclosure. In words that it would be a sin to try to translate she says: "Notre Seigneur semblait se plaire à me continuer la douceur de sa sainte familiarité; mais c'était dans un amour qui souffrait une langueur continuelle, quoique l'âme en cet état fût en Dieu ... Elle était dans la possession des biens qu'elle attendait par la jouissance de l'Époux celeste, qui semblait se plaire à la faire ainsi souffrir, mourir, et remourir. ... Quoiqu'il fût en moi, il semblait s'enfuir de moi, et se retirer dans sa lumière inaccessible. ... Je m'enfermais dans un lieu à l'écart où je me prosternais contre terre pour étouffer mes sanglots."

Her "tendance continuelle" during this topsy-turvy period when we see her by the fitful gleams of lanterns against a Rembrandtesque background of dark, swirling waters, dray-horses and bargees, led to ineffable communications of the Divine Trinity. Her penances, carefully concealed from all but her director, were terrible. She treated her poor body like a slave, tormenting it with a hair-shirt and spiked chains. For hours of the night she scourged herself till she was covered with blood and then lay on the bare floor for the little sleep "qu'il lui en faut pour ne pas mourir". As she said herself if men only knew how lovable God is they would jump out of their very skins to run after Him. Her austerities did but lend to her incessant charities a more exquisite tenderness. We catch glimpses of her sitting down to table, the only woman among twenty workmen, listening like a mother to their simple confidences. They flew to her in all their troubles and she flew to them when they fell ill. Sometimes, she says the house was like a hospital, and she was its only nurse and doctor. Of sick and sound she made the beds with her own hands, and, did any poor fellow suffer from a loathsome disease, he became her absolute baby.

Then, after many days and many dyings, her long inquietude, her "doux martyre", found its term in that mystic marriage with the Word Incarnate of which a profane pen dares scarcely to write the name: "En ce moment cette suradorable Personne s'empara de mon âme et, l'embrassant avec un amour inexplicable, l'unit à soi et la prit pour son épouse. Lorsque je dis qu'il l'embrassa, ce ne fut pas à façon des embrassements humains. Il n'y a rien de ce qui peut tomber sous le sens qui approche de cette divine opération, mais il me faut exprimer à notre façon terrestre. Ce fut par des touches divines et des pénétrations de lui en moi, et d'une façon admirable de retours réciproques de moi en lui, de sorte que n'étant plus moi, je demeurai lui par intimité d'amour et d'union. . . . Il faudrait que j'eusse la faculté des Séraphins et autres Esprits bienheureux pour pouvoir dire ce qui se passa en cette extase et ravissement d'amour."

The "tendance continuelle" which had hitherto been the ground-bass of all Marie's spiritual experiences now came to an end, but only to be replaced by a tension of human love the most excruciating that the heart can bear. She explains herself how it arose: "If there was one thing in the world that appealed to me it was the life of a nun. Sometimes I used to be afraid that this was a temptation, and I complained about it to God, saying, 'Alas! my Beloved, take away this thought from me, for I have a son for whom I must care.' This plaint was followed by an interior reproach that I was wanting in confidence, the divine bounty being rich enough for my son and for me." These "appels intérieurs" to the religious life, which really dated back to her childhood, became ever more frequent, clear and pressing, while the objections with which she endeavoured to counter them seemed inversely to lose all their force. But Marie had a horror of every form of illuminism and was the least temerarious person in the world. Later in her life at Quebec, when that outpost of France was threatened by the Iroquois, she said that once sure of the enemy's approach she would pack up and take her nuns home, even though she should have had a revelation from heaven that they would suffer no harm. "I would hold my views for suspect, and abandon them in order that my Sisters and I might follow the most obvious and safest course." It was the same in her mystical life. At the very times when God was showering His most extraordinary graces on her, she made desperate attempts to meditate in the ordinary way, to use vocal prayer, to quit her mountain path and follow the broad highway meant for us, God's pedestrians. She made herself seriously ill by such efforts to be ordinary, but relinquished them only at the express command of her director, who was himself no little of a saint. Every movement of her soul was made known to her director. "When God calls the soul," she wrote, "to this kind of interior life, correspondence is absolutely required, with the complete abandonment of oneself to Divine Providence, *supposée la conduite d'un directeur, duquel elle doit suivre les ordres à l'aveugle.* O my God, how I could wish, were it in my power, to cry the importance of this point at the top of my voice!"

But when the imperious voice in the soul and the no less decided voice of her director bid a mother abandon her son, what then? Marie loved her boy passionately, being the sort of person who could never do anything by halves, but, with a strange foreboding of the sacrifice that would one day be demanded of her, she had schooled herself from his babyhood not to be demonstrative in her affection. For instance, she kissed him rarely, and would not allow him, poor little Isaac of this "land of vision", to hug her or to stroke her face, thinking, poor mother, by such stratagems to make the eventual parting easier for them both. For once in a way she was mistaken.

Marie's predilection among nuns was for the Ursulines, "parce qu'elles étaient instituées pour aider les âmes, chose à laquelle j'avais de puissantes inclinations." Every time, she tells us, that she passed their convent in Tours on her way to the *tracas* of the merchants "mon esprit et mon cœur faisaient un subtil mouvement qui m'emportait en cette sainte maison." But her saintly and stern director, the Feuillant, Dom Raymond de Saint-Bernard, had other ideas for her. One with so marked a contemplative vocation must be destined for the nuns of his own Order, the terribly austere Feuillantines, so he made all preparations, ignoring her humble report from her Divine Spouse. Once again she thought that she must have misinterpreted the voice of God and submitted peaceably to the brusque and managerial voice of her director, only praying to her Divine Lover that in this perplexity He would choose for her Himself. It was then Dom Raymond's turn to have command from heaven, whereupon the excellent man surrendered his prize without a shot to the Ursulines.

But there was still Marie's son, Claude, to be reckoned with, a frail, moody, half-lost lad of eleven. The wealthy Buissons had grudgingly undertaken to give him a home, which was the least they could do for the child of their benefactress. But they did not make things easy for the little fellow, being utterly opposed to what they considered his mother's crazy determination. She had carefully concealed her project from the boy, hoping that if she slipped away unobserved he would soon reconcile himself, with a child's resilience, to his orphanhood. He relates the sequel himself. People seemed afraid of him, he said. If their eyes met his they looked away without saying a word. He saw pity on every face, and unable to stand or understand the gloom about him, fled from his new home with the intention of reaching Paris. In a torment of anxiety his mother sent friends to scour the countryside for him, but three dreadful days went by before he was discovered at Blois and brought home. "O Dieu," she wrote, "je n'eusse jamais cru que la douleur de la perte d'un enfant pût être si sensible à une mère."

Then began a drama of human love unmatched for pathos in the entire annals of sanctity. Marie was distracted with grief, torn in twain, not by wild horses, but by two eternities. Nearly forty years later the wound was still unhealed, and she writes from her heroic post in Canada to her son, then one of the brightest ornaments of the great Benedictine Congregation of St. Maur: "Know once again that in actually separating from you, I subjected myself to a living death. The Spirit of God was inexorable to the tender love which I felt for you, and gave me no rest until I had taken the step.... This Divine Spirit was pitiless to my feelings, saying to me in the depths of my heart: 'Hurry, hurry, it is time!' His voice urged unceasingly with a holy impetuosity which allowed me no repose. You came with me, and in parting from you it seemed as if my soul was being wrenched from my body, with intensest pain."

At the Convent gates, where she arrived in sad procession with sympathetic townspeople, this new Mother of the Maccabees could not find her voice, but with a supreme effort turned and *smiled* a good-bye to her weeping son. That was only Act I of a drama which, as Bremond well says, lasted her whole life long.[1]

In his new home, Claude was desperately unhappy, for the Carter Paterson people had no love to waste on the lonely little boy and they also felt a grudge against his mother who had shown so poor an appreciation of the importance of the

[1] In spite of his glowing and so thoroughly justified enthusiasm for Marie, Abbé Bremond tended to the opinion that she should not have abandoned her son. "Pour moi, préférant un devoir clair à un devoir obscur, il me semble que je lui aurais défendu d'abandonner son fils, mais, ce faisant, il me semble aussi que j'aurais senti peser sur moi l'antique menace: Maudit celui qui ramène les choses de Dieu à la mesure de l'homme; maudit, qui sacrifie les inspirations célestes aux troubles sommations de la chair" (*Histoire Littéraire*, t. vi, pp. 70–71). Justement!

Touraine transport service. At this time (1631) new buildings were being put up at the Ursuline Convent, so the gates remained open all day to allow the masons to pass to and fro. Claude seized this chance to roam the Convent grounds in search of his mother. Sometimes he waylaid her in the garden with the other novices. At other times, he ventured into the house itself, once, after a long exploration, making a dramatic appearance in the refectory as the community were about to sit down to dinner. He even wandered as far as the grille opening on the choir, and now and then took it into his head to leave his cap and coat hanging there as a reminder to his unfortunate mother. "The Sisters," he wrote afterwards, "might have addressed her as did Joseph's brethren their father, Jacob: 'See if this be not the coat of thy son.'" The other novices used to weep at sight of Claude or his coat, and to say to Marie that she was indeed cruel not to share their tears. "But, alas!" she explained to Claude the man, "they did not see the anguish in my heart for you."

It appears that Carter Paterson was a poet, which may be one reason why he had so readily resigned the conduct of his business into Marie's hands, exchanging, so to say, transport for transports. This bard now began to produce doleful elegies on the subject of his general manager's retirement, making Claude the mouthpiece of reproaches and expostulations so heartrending that, as Claude himself wrote later on, "one would have had to have been less than human not to be affected by them". These effusions were given to the boy for presentation to his mother.

Claude was popular with his schoolmates at the Jesuit College, who felt in their own awkward fashion a deep sympathy for his trouble. One day they gathered round him in a crowd, saying: "Come along, let's find your mother, let's make such a row that they'll give her back to you." Then, armed with sticks and stones, they rushed off to picket the Convent. Above the din they made, shouting, stamping, throwing stones,

Marie inside heard the poignant treble of her boy, crying: "Rendez-moi ma mère! Je veux avoir ma mère!" It was a cry that she would have heard, and was indeed to hear, at the ends of the earth. Never in her life, she said, was she so *combattue*. Even now, after these hundreds of years, we can appreciate the bitterness of her Gethsemane, as she pleaded heartbrokenly with God, "Hé! le voulez-vous, O mon Amour? Hé! dites, le voulez-vous?" Among other of the great graces accorded to her was a revelation of the devotion of the Sacred Heart, fifty years before our Lord appeared to St. Margaret Mary. Not a day passed, she said, that she did not sacrifice her boy anew to God, "sur le Cœur de son Bien-Aimé Fils". In that pierced Heart she found peace, while the storm of her own frustrated heart raged within her. Seventeen years later, she wrote to Claude from Canada: "You have reason to reproach me, and I, in my turn, shall reproach, if I may, Him Who came to bring upon earth a sword which causes there such strange divisions. There was no resisting the power of Divine Love, but that has not prevented me from thinking myself, an infinity of times, the most cruel of all mothers. I ask your forgiveness, my dear son, for being the cause of so much sorrow to you. But let us take comfort from the thought that life is short, and that we shall have a whole eternity of each other's company." At seventy, Marie was still haunted by the same problem of mother and son. She asks Claude, then a distinguished Benedictine [1] and the confidant of all her sublime secrets, whether he is not now content that she had left him long ago to the holy Providence of God. It would almost seem as if she wished to hear from his priestly lips before she died an *Ego te absolvo, Mater; Vade in pace.*

It was Bossuet, with his genius for a comprehensive phrase, who christened Marie of the Incarnation the St. Teresa of

---

[1] So distinguished that his biography was written at great length by the celebrated Maurist scholar, Dom Martène.

Canada. As a great adventuring soul, an explorer into God, Marie yields hardly at all to Teresa, and, though she had not the Spanish Saint's marvellous literary power and fecundity, she wrote many a page on the beatitude and martyrdom of the soul under the action of divine love worthy to rank with the finest in the classics of mysticism. But their beauty and sweetness are no more to be described than the tints of a sunset or the perfume of a rose. They have to be experienced, to be read and savoured in the lovely old French of which she was a natural master. Her style, as Bremond well says, did not take the veil when she became an Ursuline. It made no vow of poverty and kept to the end the tang of Touraine. But while the style may be the man, it is certainly not the mystic, which is a reason for giving here some other words of the same eminent and charming historian. Speaking of the mystics in general, he says: "Willy nilly, we bring them down to our own level. We place them in an intellectual, a sentimental, a literary setting which not only is not theirs, but which in some fashion is the negation of theirs. . . . In fact, the admiration which we profess for a Teresa and a Mary of the Incarnation is in inverse ratio to their real greatness. The higher they are raised up, the more they escape us. When they seem to us to touch the utmost summits of lyricism, they are only at the stammering stage of the first years. Where ours comes to an end their true sublimity has its beginning." [1] That daunting judgment is absolutely fair. In heaven we shall all be mystics, thanks to purgatory, but until then we inevitably tend to shy away from what is most divine in the saints and to grasp at the human ties and touches of nature which make them our kin. With the poets, we find easy symbols of the beauty of their holiness in flowers and starlight and music, but before God they are much more like flashes of lightning or the tremendous pageant of the sea. Having thus saluted conscience and again emphasized that the essential Marie of the Incarnation is in her two incomparable "Rela-

[1] *Histoire Littéraire du Sentiment Religieux,* t. vi, p. 46.

tions" of the mystical life,[1] we may dare to be more carefree in our approach to her.

Marie took the veil which her prose refused on Lady Day, the day of the Incarnation, 1631. She was thirty-two then, and an expert of two worlds. The most venerable of her fellow-novices was sixteen. Some would count the *tracas* of merchants, once her heaviest affliction, a featherweight cross compared with the *tracas* of girls of sixteen, but Marie found life in their excruciatingly intimate company almost too good to be true and used often to put her hand to her veil to make sure that she wasn't only dreaming her happiness. She had always loved stillness and solitude, and there she was, an Ursuline nun whose only solitude is in her bed when the noisy business of the day is over. God had directed her to that beloved convent, "la petite Bourdaisière", but she could not throw off a feeling that it was only a half-way house to some unknown bourne, to some "further shore" towards which the hands of her desire were unconsciously extended. "From my entrance among the Ursulines," she wrote in her Relation of 1654, "something in my heart told me that God in His goodness had put me in this holy house as in a place of refuge until He should dispose of me for His designs. I used always to put away this feeling for fear that it might be a trap of

[1] Besides these, Marie composed a parallel pair giving the shadows that were the counterpart of her great light, temptations of every kind, as to blasphemy, impurity, pride and even suicide, as well as violent antipathies, long periods of aridity, and what she calls "une insensibilité et stupidité ès choses spirituelles". It seemed to her that she had been deceived by the devil or by her own pride, and that all her high dealings with God were the product of a diseased imagination. These Relations her Jesuit directors burned when they had read them. Marie's life, let us say it again, passed on two planes which to our short thoughts appear so incompatible, and yet are as real as the plus and minus conceptions of mathematics. She lived simultaneously on a Sinai where God talked to her face to face as a man talks to his friend, and in a Valley of Hinnom where there seemed to be no God at all but only dark phantoms of sin and disillusion. This experience was common to all the great mystics, even after their "spiritual marriage", and arose from the impact of God on human finitude.

the devil, but it invariably returned. So I argued with myself no more about it and simply abandoned myself entirely to God." [1]

It was not until Christmas time, 1634, when four years had passed with their rubrics of sorrow and splendour, that God gave Marie a part interpretation of the persistent sense of expectancy which troubled her and which she could not appease. At that time, and for many months afterwards, she knew no more of Canada than most of us do now of Kamchatka. "Je n'avais jamais su", she wrote, "qu'il y eut un Canada au monde." Indeed, French people in general had only the vaguest notions about their new colony and rather tended to treat it in conversation as a sort of geographical cloudland. Of a man in straits or nursing some hare-brained scheme they would say: "He is thinking of going to Canada to marry the Queen of the Hurons." Off to that mysterious bourne went Marie in a Christmas dream. She found herself, she says, hand in hand with a secular lady, hurrying at a great pace through many obstacles to a distant goal which neither of them knew. At last they reached an exquisite place, lofty and lonely, under a vast expanse of sky, "and the silence that was there made part of its beauty". By the entrance stood its guardian, clothed in a white robe "as the Apostles are painted".[2] In an angle of the plateau on which the dream-travellers had emerged there was a tiny chapel, with a statue of our Lady and the Divine Child on its façade. "Elle était comme à l'âge qu'elle allaitait notre très adorable petit Jésus." Mother and Child seemed to look out sadly over an illimitable expanse of mountain and valley all shrouded in thick mists and shadows, a country "autant pitoyable qu'effroyable". Our Lady appeared to speak to

[1] *Ecrits spirituels et historiques*, t. ii, p. 309.
[2] Knowing nothing of Canada at the time of her dream in 1634, Marie was, of course, unaware that Champlain and the Récollet Fathers, the country's first missionaries, had chosen St. Joseph as the patron and protector of New France ten years earlier.

her little Son about this poor land and to have some design for Marie with regard to it. "Je soupirais après elle, mes bras étendus. Lors, avec une grace ravissante, elle se tourna vers moi et, souriant amoureusement, elle me baisa sans me dire mot."

How adorable it is, that reticence of God, that tact and delicacy with which He canvasses our freedom. He left Marie to discover almost by haphazard that her dream plateau was a geographical reality, the great rock of Quebec which sentinels the approaches to Canada. She writes: "J'avais eu toute ma vie un grand amour pour le salut des âmes, mais depuis ce que j'ai dit des baisers de la très sainte Vierge, je portais dans mon âme un feu qui me consommait pour cela. . . . Donc, à l'âge de trente-cinq ans j'entrai en l'état qui m'avait été comme montré et duquel j'étais comme dans l'attente. C'était une émanation de l'esprit apostolique, qui n'était autre que l'Esprit de Jésus-Christ, lequel s'empara de mon esprit pour qu'il n'eût plus de vie que dans le sien et par le sien, étant toute dans les intérêts de ce divin et suradorable Maître . . . à ce qu'il fût connu, aimé et adoré de toutes les nations qu'il avait rachetées de son Sang précieux." [1]

While her body remained within the Convent walls, training the novices and looking after the chapel and sacristy, her soul, she tells us, led by the Spirit of Jesus, roamed the "grandes vastitudes" of India, Japan, Africa, and the Americas, pleading with the Eternal Father "par une activité amoureuse plus vite que toute parole" for the extension in those unevangelized places of the Kingdom of His Divine Son. [2] So intense

---

[1] *Ecrits spirituels et historiques,* t. ii, p. 310.

[2] The Kingship of Christ is an ever-recurring motif in Marie's spiritual writings, parallel with an intense devotion to the Sacred Heart of Jesus. Just as the foundress of the Ursulines, St. Angela, anticipated the principal modern developments in the regulations governing the religious life of nuns, so did Venerable Marie of the Incarnation anticipate the most significant modern developments in the devotional life of the Church. Long and sensitive indeed are the spiritual antennae of the mystics.

was her abstraction, so consuming her desires, in the pursuit
of this mystical apostleship, that her poor body wasted away
to nothing and her anxious Superior felt obliged to command her to desist. Might and main she struggled to obey,
but, as the Superior soon saw, it was not in her power to desist. There was a singing in her sails not of the four winds of
this world.

At that critical moment she learned casually the clue to her
long puzzlement, *le mot de l'énigme,* from her good director
the Jesuit Père Dinet. God, he said, having heard the story
of her dream, seemed to be calling her to Canada. And the
way thus cleared by human intervention, God Himself spoke
without ambiguity: "C'est le Canada que je t'ai fait voir; il
faut que tu y ailles faire une maison à Jésus et à Marie." [1] It
was as strange a command as the Protector of Canada had
once received when told to take the Child and His Mother
and fly into Egypt, and Marie could see no light at all as to
how she might carry it out, "eu égard à ma profession re-
ligieuse et de recluse dans un monastère." [2] She blamed herself for the difficulty, and in a passion of tears before God
bargained with Him to suffer gladly "toutes les peines imagin-
ables pour être dans l'état de pureté requise... à ce que mon
bien-aimé Epoux, qu'il avait constitué Roi des nations, en fût
paisible possesseur par leur conversion." In answer, God bade
her ask Him by the Heart of Jesus, His Divine Son, and from
that moment she experienced so close a union with the Sacred
Heart that her very breathing became, as it were, attuned to
the pulsations of Eternal Love. Her own heart now, day and
night, at meals and even in her dreams, was always in Canada,

[1] Marie, with true Teresian daring, revised the form of the command
in her prayers to God about it, begging Him to put it in her power to
found the house for Jesus and Mary, *et qu'il n'en séparât point le grand
saint Joseph.*
[2] It may be as well to point out that in Marie's day it was an unheard
and undreamt of thing in the Church for a nun to be a missionary or to
stir abroad at all. Nuns were enclosed in the strictest legality of the term,
and it seemed there could never be again St. Walburgas and St. Liobas.

"ma demeure et mon pays", and she was kept from dying by the excess of her homesickness only because God in His mercy flooded her straining soul with "une paix savoureuse et féconde".

Meantime, the Superior of the Jesuit missions in Canada, humorous and heroic Paul Le Jeune, had written his famous "Relation" of 1634, in the course of which he declared that a principal means to make the Faith welcome to the Red Indians would be the establishment at Quebec of a seminary for native girls, "under the direction of some brave mistress, some Amazon of the great God" whom zeal for the divine glory might lure over the seas. Father Paul was somewhat embarrassed by the results of his cunning appeal, with its stress on the dangers and hardship of the enterprise, for half the young nuns of France wanted to be away on the next ship sailing. It was a glorious spirit, but even missionaries cannot live on fresh air, and Le Jeune felt compelled to throw a little cold water, or, better, a few handfuls of Canadian snow, on the enthusiasm. "I must give this advice to all these good Sisters," he wrote, "that men can extricate themselves much more easily from difficulties; but as for nuns, they must have a good house, some cleared land, and a good income upon which to live and relieve the poverty of the wives and daughters of the Savages. Otherwise, they would be a burden to our French and could accomplish little for these peoples." Wise Father Paul, but at least the late General Manager of Touraine Transport Limited did not need his warning, for in business matters she was worth ten of him.

One of the outstanding heroes of the Canadian epic, Père Poncet de la Rivière, dispatched a copy of Le Jeune's Relation to Marie, with a holy picture of missionary import which, he said, he sent her as an invitation "to go and serve God in New France". She marvelled at this because neither to Poncet nor anyone else on earth except her director had she ever breathed a word about what was passing in her soul. At this point, her former director, the saintly but somewhat fierce

Dom Raymond de Saint-Bernard, again came into her life. He, too, had read Le Jeune's soul-stirring Relation and decided without hesitation, to Marie's amazement and delight, that Canada was the place for him. He thought he was keeping his plan a great secret, but he made such a fuss and pulled so many strings to bring it about that soon everybody knew. To say that his brother-Feuillants were shocked would be to put it mildly. They were thrown into a state of utter confusion, and at Tours had the rashness to accuse Marie of being an accessory after the fact, a plain abettor of Dom Raymond's crazy resolution. The two good monks sent to expostulate with her met their match. After days and days of hot argument and even downright abuse on their part, she ended the controversy by calmly informing them that they would both presently change their minds and find themselves longing to go to Canada, without, however, being able to satisfy their desire. "Ils se moquèrent tous deux de moi." But he laughs best who laughs last. A few days later Marie had a letter from Dom Raymond at Paris to the following effect: "I think Father So-and-so will have turned over a new leaf three days ago. I have had a very extraordinary vision about him, in which he seemed to be haled before the Sovereign Judge to receive punishment for his rebellion against the divine will. You were his accuser. Then the poor criminal all trembling with fright and half-dead, threw himself on his knees before the Judge, crying, 'Mercy!' and saying, like another St. Paul, *Domine, quid me vis facere?* On being commanded to rise, he turned towards me and said gently, 'Why did you do that to me?' I replied, pointing you out to him, that it was your work and that he must lay the blame at your door. I do not know whether he will be converted.... Keep me posted as to what happens." What happened was that the unfortunate monk became suddenly obsessed with a wild, insatiable longing for Canada which allowed him neither to sleep nor eat nor enjoy a moment's peace. All weary and worn, he appeared at the grille of the Ursuline Convent and said to Marie reproachfully:

"Qu'est-ce que vous avez fait pour moi? Je ne puis vivre. Priez Dieu qu'il lui plaise me faire miséricorde; de ma vie, je ne contrarierai la vocation de la Mission de Canada, non, je ne dirai plus rien contre une si sainte vocation." [1]

Marie's correspondence with Dom Raymond on the subject of her and his Canadian aspirations drew from Abbé Bremond some of his most joyous pages. He was a critic by no means easy to please, and he had a hawk's eye for anything the least banal, artificial or cock-a-hoop in the people whose characters he so brilliantly analysed. But Marie swept him completely off his feet, and filled him with a love and reverence that just managed to stop short this side of idolatry. Fearful lest his readers might miss in their haste some delicate nuance of irony, so gentle and so devastating, some exquisite touch of femininity, some sally of mischievous humour always in ambush for Reverend Father Sobersides when he walked abroad with his bell, book, and candle, Bremond italicized these charmingly human

---

[1] The other monk repented even more expeditiously and thoroughly. Marie's prayers had indeed rare power with God. Through them her son Claude, whom the Jesuit Provincial rejected because of an apparent lack of character and brains, became so eminent for holiness, learning and practical ability among the celebrated Benedictines of St. Maur that he was actually elected Superior-General of the entire Congregation. To his own great content he was, however, prevented from accepting the office by the veto of the King of France whose predatory designs on Benedictine abbeys he had successfully opposed. To him is due the great Maurist edition of St. Augustine and other Fathers of the Church. For seventeen years on end he was Prior of various famous abbeys, and for sixteen years assistant to the Superior-General. He died in the odour of sanctity, "dans tout ce qu'il a de grand et de saint, qui inspire la sympathie, l'image de Marie de l'Incarnation". As Bossuet truly said, Marie was even more his mother according to the spirit than according to the flesh. More remarkable still in some ways, but too long to tell here, is the extraordinary story of her pretty, pampered, pleasure-loving niece who, to escape a persistent and extremely influential Don Juan, pronounced sacrilegious vows as an Ursuline, with not the slightest intention of remaining a nun a day longer than was necessary to cool off her pursuer's ardours, and then, through Marie's prayers and dreadful penances for her, became, by a change almost as dramatic as the conversion of St. Paul, one of the most perfect and beautiful characters in her Order's menology.

ebullitions in the letters of his heroine. Dom Raymond admired her enormously, but took up a very high and mighty attitude with regard to the Canadian project. He was the sort of man who believes that women must be kept in their place, be made to realize their weakness and unimportance. Converting Red Indians was a man's job, so who was this nun to be hankering after it and actually wanting to join him, Dom Raymond, Prior of the Abbey of St. Bernard, Paris, on the great enterprise which he meditated? Certainly she must be snubbed and made to bite the dust.

Accordingly, the good, innocent monk informed his penitent that she was entirely unworthy to be chosen for such a mission of heroes and that he had every intention of sailing without her. Thereupon, she quoted to him the reproachful words of St. Laurence to St. Xystus, and continued, as though they settled the matter: "I feel impelled to beg you to hurry on the affair both for yourself and for us. It is not, of course, that we have the impertinence to think ourselves capable of affording you solace in your labours, but that we want to stimulate our courage by your example. We regard ourselves only as mere midges, but we feel that we have enough heart to fly with the eagles of the King of Saints. If our strength is insufficient to follow them, then they will carry us on their wings, just as ordinary eagles carry the little birds." Yes, replied Dom Raymond, you quote to me St. Laurence's words to St. Xystus, but I would have you know, Ma Mère, that nevertheless St. Xystus went off without St. Laurence. True enough, rejoined Marie, "but reflect, mon révérend Père, that St. Xystus went ahead of St. Laurence only by three days, after which it was easy for the son to follow his father." Beaten on that point, the dear old monk entrenched himself behind the Gospels and thence hurled St. Peter at Marie's head, with dire warnings as to the consequences of presumption. Her answer was that she had been waiting for him to mobilize St. Peter and wondering greatly that he should till then have overlooked so obvious an ally. "Mme du Deffand n'aurait pas mieux dit," adds Brem-

ond. Marie continued, more seriously: "I admit to you that
my distrust of myself often makes me apprehensive of what
you say.... I strive to enter into the dispositions which you
propose to me and abandon myself into the hands of one who
can give me the solidity of his spirit while checking the impetuosity of mine.... But tell me, Reverend Father, would
you wish me to conceal from you what passes in my soul? Is
it not my way to be completely candid in my dealings with
you?... The rebuff you gave me some time ago made me
consider whether I should not be more reserved in declaring
to you the state of my soul, but I saw that God may possibly
wish me to finish my days as I began them under the direction
of so good a Father. Mortify me, then, as much as ever you
like, I shall not cease to reveal to you the feelings which God
gives me nor to submit them to your judgement.... Oh, do
hurry up, my Reverend Father, for if you are not careful our
hearts will have burnt away altogether before we are in Canada.
Do not condemn us if we seem to be impetuous, as you say,
without reason. We are not without reason, as you know very
well, and you cannot condemn us for being so importunate
without at the same time condemning Him who taught me
that only the violent bear away the Kingdom of Heaven."

The next act in this little comedy of temperaments reveals
Marie in an independent mood, making her own arrangements
with the Jesuits. She was still the Marie of the warehouse,
and in her shrewd way she soon saw that Dom Raymond, for
all his grand notions, was no business man, that he would
never get nearer to Canada than a Paris shipping-office. Meantime, Father Le Jeune's infectious "Relation" had spread its
Canadian germs in the blue blood of a wealthy widowed lady,
Madeleine de la Peltrie, who resolved to devote her ample fortune to the foundation of that "seminary" for Red Indian girls
on which the Jesuits had set their hearts. Hearing of Ursuline
Marie's holy ambition from Père Poncet, Madeleine descended
on Tours like a whirlwind, won the Archbishop's ready con-
sent and then presented herself with her great friend, the

saintly M. Jean de Bernières,[1] at the Convent doors. All the nuns were drawn up to receive them, for by this time Marie's secret had been revealed, and there was tremendous enthusiasm in the community for the Canadian mission. No sooner did she set eyes upon the visitor, "who seemed to bring the joy of Paradise into the house," than Marie recognized "by the candour and sweetness of her face" the Lady of her dream. Three days were then spent in deciding who should be Marie's companion on this first venture of nuns into heathendom. She herself asked for Mother St. Joseph, but the Superior strongly demurred as Mother St. Joseph was not yet twenty-three. However, Marie knew what she was about. "Madame et Monsieur et moi persistions à la demander" and, of course, they got her. Then her parents, great aristocrats of Anjou, made trouble, "mais Notre-Seigneur, qui en avait fait le choix, en fut le maître. Elle me fut donnée pour compagne." Finally, Marie's sister, Veuve Carter Paterson, arrived on the scene with a solicitor to stop the nonsense. "Elle fit enfin l'imaginable," says Marie, "mais notre bon Dieu dissipa le tout." [2]

Enter again Dom Raymond, who, knowing nothing of Marie's *démarches* with the Jesuits, continued to deluge her with stern exhortations to patience and humility. Then one morning in October, 1636, he received a letter which made him open his eyes very wide and possibly also bite his tongue, for in it Marie very sweetly invited *him* to come with *her* to Canada at once! It was a pretty turning of the tables. "Well,

[1] He was also her reputed husband. Her father had made re-marriage a condition of keeping his wealth, so M. de Bernières, who was as keen on the Canadian project as she, obliged by posing as her new husband until the old gentleman died.

[2] One thing the sister did was to withdraw in legal form the allowance she was making to Marie's son, Claude, and another was to send Claude himself to intercept his mother on the way from Tours to Paris, but Marie made an easy conquest of him this time. The sister also moved heaven and earth to get an injunction against Marie's departure from the Archbishop of Tours.

then, let us be off in the Name of God, my dear Father, to taste the delights of Paradise in the crosses which are to be found fine and big in New France.... I shall pull at you so far if you won't come that I shall tear away a piece of your habit." But there were still three years between her and her Paradise, and Dom Raymond made the fullest use of them to teach her her nothingness. Once, after storming at her as though she were a criminal, he pretended that he wished to have nothing more to do with such a wretched creature. She answered: "Your way of acting towards me would seem to mean a final 'good-bye', and I would have thought it such had not my dear Mother Ursula assured me to the contrary. If it ever comes to that between us, you will be no better off, because I shall find you wherever I find Jesus Christ, and in revenge for your refusal to speak to me I shall talk to Him about you. Are you going to be silent till we go to see you, or till we have the happiness of seeing you here? The second is the easier course, so come as soon as ever you can and make arrangements to stay a long time. There is not a soul in the house who has not something to say to you. As for me, I shall require at least eight days of you all to myself."

A final scene with Dom Raymond, and one, in Bremond's words, of "la plus exquise gentillesse". She had gone over to the Jesuits, but he must not be allowed to think that that made any difference. The Jesuits would be, so to say, merely his proxies to carry on his own cherished work of putting her where she belonged, "We have received news", she told him, "from the earthly Paradise of the Hurons and Canada. Reverend Father Le Jeune has written to our Mother and to me.... Not a word did he say to me about Canada but made me a big letter as humiliating as his first one. Is not that a good Father? Why, he is another Dom Raymond to me! I am infinitely obliged to him because I see by that that he wishes me well and that if I were near him he would treat me as you

like to do." [1] Is it surprising now that Abbé Bremond worshipped this woman of women, "souple et volontaire, rieuse et
grave, infiniment riche et diverse"? Shall we ever know the
full truth of her? he wonders, and goes on to say that, thanks
to the bouquet of letters to Dom Raymond, we know at least
two things for certain, that this high mystic was a true woman
and that she wrote "à ravir". [2]

But we are keeping her from her Paradise of the Hurons
much too long, [3] though, in fact, she is herself to blame for
that, being such seductive company. The trouble with her is
not what to put in but what to leave out. On almost every
page of her many pages there is some pearl of feeling or expression, something rich or strange, which it hurts to renounce,
as, for instance, her vision of the vast building whose every
stone was not a stone but a man or woman crucified, or her
touchingly human shrinking from what was shown to her as
her lot in Canada, "des croix sans fins ... un abandon intérieur
de la part de Dieu et des créatures ... la solitude affreuse
d'esprit," or her humble confession, when at last the moment
had come for her to risk her life for God: "Je voyais que ce
n'était rien que ma vie; mais le néant que j'étais ne pouvait
pas davantage, joint mon cœur et mes amours." [4]

[1] Le Jeune became one of her closest friends and warmest admirers.
A born humanist and humorist, as well as a saint, he was one to appreciate her qualities.

[2] Here is another good critic's opinion: "L'on peut se demander com-
ment cette épistolière de génie n'a pas le rang qui lui est dû dans la
littérature."

[3] Claude was a very long-winded writer. Describing once how, having
heard that some little Red Indian girls were sad because they could not
have nice dresses like the little daughters of the French settlers, his
mother procured a quantity of silk and made ten dresses for the native
children with her own hands, the good monk embarks on all sorts of
high and holy explanations of her act. "Mon Dieu qu'il est lourd!"
comments Abbé Bremond. "Pendant qu'il pérore, sa vive mère aurait
eu le temps de tailler dix autres robes."

[4] These three examples occur in the small compass of six pages (*Ecrits*,
ii, pp. 348–353) and are immeasurably more effective in their context.

Before leaving Paris for her ship Marie had audience with the Queen of France and other famous ladies, but by no contrivance could she catch a glimpse of Monseigneur the Archbishop. The fact was that she had set her heart on having a certain nun from the Ursuline Convent in Paris and Monseigneur was equally determined that she should *not* have this particular nun, so he went to earth as the only safe way of dealing with the situation. There followed a regular hue and cry of the Court ladies after His Grace, and even the Queen took part, sending a gentleman in search of him with orders that the nun was to be delivered up. "Mais il se tint en lieu si secret," writes Marie reproachfully, "qu'il ne fut pas possible de le rencontrer. Enfin, il nous fallut partir sans cette bonne Mère." [1] When she said good-bye to Claude, never to see him again in this world, she felt "as if every bone in her body was being wrenched from its socket". Then followed the terrible three months' voyage to Quebec, in itself a capital story of hardship and great perils smilingly borne. A fortnight from Dieppe, she wrote back by a passing ship to reassure those at home: "We are already so accustomed to the sea that we might have been brought up on it." But we know from another source that there was no Mass or Communion for the nuns during that time, owing to the fierceness of a gale which made it impossible even for the hardened Jesuit missionaries aboard to keep on their feet. Even Captain Bontemps himself, a tough old salt, was heard to exclaim on another occasion when an iceberg shaved the ship: "Nous sommes garantis, mais c'est un miracle!" There were many such miracles on that memorable crossing.

The first Ursuline house in Quebec consisted of two rooms, the larger sixteen feet square, through the bark walls of which the stars shone in on the nuns and the frolicsome winds took a pleasure in blowing out their candle. These two rooms shel-

[1] One feels tempted to say, "Bravo, Monseigneur!" for he was the only man who ever worsted Marie in a battle of wits.

tered eighteen people the first year, the three nuns,[1] a few French girls, and a motley collection of greasy, grimy, abominably smelly Red Indian children. The dirty habits of these woodlanders made even Marie marvel. They used to make a sort of waste-paper basket of her cooking-pot, and sometimes the nuns would find such things as old shoes simmering with their bit of pork, "ce qui portant ne nous donnait pas trop de dégoût". Nothing that they could do, and they had infinite resources of annoyance or mischief, would have disgusted her, because she loved with consuming love every verminous hair of their heads. She becomes lyrical when she speaks of them. They are much more wonderful than the children at home in France, they remind her of the early Christians, to hear them saying their prayers is like being in heaven listening to the angels. Ah, love, love, what an alchemist you are! These waifs and strays of the human family had to be fed, clothed, sheltered and educated. To teach them one must know their language, so our nuns went to school with expert Father Le Jeune. Marie is forty-one, not a good age for picking up Iroquois and Algonquin,[2] as indeed she confesses: "There are many thorns in learning a language so contrary to ours. But the desire to be able to speak helps greatly. I am longing to let my heart issue through my tongue in order to tell my dear neophytes what it feels of the love of God, and of Jesus our good Master." So proficient did she become under the tutelage of love (and, of course, also of Father Le Jeune) that in 1661 she composed a catechism in Huron, three cate-

---

[1] Marie had secured a second Ursuline companion from the Convent in Dieppe.

[2] The fearful difficulties of the Indian languages entirely baffled some of the Jesuit missionaries. St. Noël Chabanel, for instance, never learned to speak them, though he was a gifted man and tried with all his might. Le Jeune, in his Relations, waxes indignant with the crazy syntax of Algonquin: "The verb, *nisiicatchin,* means 'I am cold'; the noun, *nissitai,* means 'my feet', but *nitatagouasisin* is the proper word to say, 'my feet are cold'. What ruins the memory is that such a word has neither relation, nor alliance nor any affinity in its sound, with the other two, whence it often happens that I make them laugh in talking" (Relation of 1634).

chisms and a prayer book in Algonquin, and a large dictionary of the same language. These she followed up in 1668 with "un gros livre algonquin d'histoire sacrée et le choses saintes," as well as with an Iroquois catechism and dictionary.

Three years the nuns toiled in their two rooms, with never a moment's respite or privacy, before the convent built for them by Mme de la Peltrie was ready. Marie was so proud of that convent: "Cest la plus belle et la plus grande qui soit en Canada, pour la façon d'y bâtir," she declared. Eight years later it was burned to the ground. That was the least of her crosses. Again and again smallpox carried off her little Indian "seminarists", who were to her as the apple of her eye. The Iroquois constantly menaced the missions, and in one vivid scene, we catch sight of her, again the Marie of the wharf at midnight, handing muskets and powder to her convent garrison. In bad times, or when the ships from France failed to arrive, she had to watch her nuns and her children slowly starving. But these were trifling things, the mere small change of Calvary, compared with the big bills of her debt to God, "la solitude affreuse d'esprit", which she had contracted in the heyday of her mystical experience.

And she never lost heart, never even lost her invincible gaiety. To the convent parlour came everybody weary, dejected or in any sort of trouble. A little talk with Ma Mère soon put them right, whether colonial governors, or captains of the garrison, or fur-trappers, or Indian braves. In one year alone she succoured temporally or spiritually as many as eight hundred Indians. Through that parlour, too, passed all the heroes of the Canadian epic. One day it would be St. Isaac Jogues, another St. John de Brébeuf, another St. Gabriel Lalemant, "le plus saint homme que j'aie connu que je suis au monde," she wrote. In a letter to her son Claude, who received the longest and most beautiful of her letters,[1] she tells him that her dear friend,

[1] She used to write two copies of them and send them by different ships, so as to make doubly sure of her boy getting his post. But she was indefatigable in writing to other correspondents also, and would regularly

Père Bressani, is returning home and will pay him a visit. "You will see a living martyr," she says. "Without letting on, look at his hands. You will observe that they are mutilated and almost without a single finger whole. This year he received three arrow wounds in his head which were meant to give him his crown and put an end to his labours. As a result of them, one of his eyes is almost completely useless." Her love for Claude seemed only to grow tenderer with the years. Once, a young friend of hers called to say good-bye before returning to France. In the letter which she gave him for Claude there is this exquisite touch of her mother's heart: "I lifted my veil in his presence, so that he would be able to tell you he had seen me as well as talked to me." Another time she writes: "You ask me whether we shall ever see one another again in this world. I know not, but God is so good that, if it is to the glory of His Name and for the welfare of your soul and mine, He will bring it about. Let us leave it to Him. I could long for it as much as you do, but I do not want to wish for any-thing except in Him. . . . I see you every day in Him, and when I am at Matins in the evening, I think to myself that you are at them too, because we remain in choir up to half-past eight, and, you having the sun five hours earlier than we, it seems that the pair of us meet to chant the praises of God."

One is inevitably reminded of Marie de Sévigné, for whose honour a thousand pens, including this leaky one, would leap from their clips. But adorable though she was, she is not in the same class as our Marie, who, equally gay, equally interested in the tragi-comedy of life around her, equally the foe of the solemn and lachrymose,[1] counted the whole world well lost

---

dispatch two hundred letters in her own hand by the fleet sailing home. These letters were written late at night, as she had too much else to do during the day. Sometimes she used to be so tired that she fell asleep half way through a letter.

[1] Claude, himself addicted to gravity, wrote of his mother: "I. ne se pouvait voir une personne plus commode et plus accortel. Son abord était doux et son visage un peu riant."

for the privilege of breaking her royal heart to save a few poor Red Indians. She died at her post on 30 April, 1672, in her seventy-third year. Just two hundred years later Pope Pius IX received a letter from Canada: "We, the chiefs and braves of the Huron nation, on our knees before Your Holiness present to you a precious perfume, the perfume of the virtues of Reverend Mother Mary of the Incarnation.... She it was who called us from the depths of our forests to teach us to know and adore the true Master of life. Through her we learned to be meek.... Our mothers have kissed the imprint of her feet. With her hand she marked on our hearts the sign of the Faith and the Faith remained graven on our hearts.... Many a moon has passed since that first dawning of the true light upon us. Our nation, then great, is now threatened with complete extinction, but, Holy Father, we beg you to receive with the last wish and the last breath of the Huron Tribe the testimony of its profound gratitude to Reverend Mother Mary of the Incarnation."

INDEX

Adam of Eynsham, 141*n*, 151*n*
Adamnan, St., 94, 95
Aelred, St., 1-13, 33*n*, 60, 66*n*
Aelric, 64-5
Agilbert, Bp. of Dorchester, 21-3
Aidan, St., 17, 19, 37, 92-105
Aldhelm, St., 56-7, 71-2
Anschar, St., 34
Anselm, St., 8, 42-54
Augustine, St., Ap. of England, 58-9

Bamburgh, 17, 37, 102
Bari, Council of, 53
Bec, 48-51
Bede, St., 15-18, 19, 21*n*, 24*n*, 26, 29,
    30, 35, 36-7, 57-8, 70, 92, 98*n*, 99,
    155
Benians, E. A., 82-3
Berengarius of Tours, 48*n*
Bernard of Clairvaux, 5
Bernard of Menthon, 47*n*
Birinus, St., 20*n*, 21, 70, 155
Bocking, Ralph, 42-3
Boniface, St., 56*n*, 68-78
Boswell, St., 39
Bremond, Abbé, 168, 169*n*, 175*n*, 178,
    185, 190
Bridgett, T. E., 82*n*, 87*n*, 89

Cadwallon, King of North Wales,
    16, 17, 96-7
Caedmon, 21
Cantilupe, Barons of, 125-6
Cantilupe, Walter, Bp. of Worcester,
    126, 130-1, 135
Caprave, John, 31-2
Cedd, St., 18, 22
Chad, St., 18, 99
Charles Martel, 73
Colman, St., 14-28
Columba, St., 15, 17, 24, 93-4, 95
Columbanus, St., 20*n*
Constitutions of Clarendon, 149, 151,
    164-5
Corby, Bl. Ralph, 106-24
Corby, Gerard, 107-12
Cronan of Roscrea, 94
Cummian, St., 20*n*
Cuthert, Abp. of Canterbury, 78

Cuthbert, St., 19, 29-41, 63, 105

Daniel, Bp. of Winchester, 70, 72, 74
Daniel, Walter, 6, 13*n*
David, King of Scotland, 2, 3, 4, 12
Dinoot, Abbot of Bangor, 98*n*
Dionysius Exiguus, 20
Duckett, Fr. John, 116-24
Dunstan, St., 55-6

Eadmer, 45*n*, 49, 50, 51-4 (*passim*)
Eata, St., 19, 26, 39, 99
Edburga, St., 77
Eddi, 22, 26
Edward I, King of England, 125,
    131, 132*n*
Edwin, King of Northumbria, 15, 16
Egbert, Abp. of York, 68
Espec, Walter, 5, 12

Farne, 40, 63
Finan, St., 18, 19, 102
Fisher, St. John, 79-91
Fitzgerald, Lord Thomas, 108-9
Fulda, 76

Gage, Fr. George, 122
Gervase, Abbot of Louth Park, 6
Gilbert de Clare, Earl of Gloucester,
    134, 139
Giraldus Cambrensis, 141*n*, 142, 145,
    149*n*
Godric, St., 38, 55-67, 166*n*
Grande Chartreuse, 144-5
Gregory the Great, Pope St., 58, 101
Gregory II, Pope St., 70*n*, 74
Gregory of Utrecht, St., 75
Gundulf, 44, 47

Hamsterley, 115
Heathfield, Battle of, 16
Henry I, King of England, 1, 53
Henry II, King of England, 140-1,
    145, 147, 148, 160, 162-3, 164-7
Henry III, King of England, 129, 131
Henry VIII, King of England, 79-80,
    156-7
Henry, Prince of Scotland, 2
Herbert of Bosham, 54*n*, 158